Go Away, I'n

John Saunders

Dedication

I would primarily like to dedicate this book to all those who buy it and help me live well in my old age! To all those who read it and think that they could fake their death and rip off an insurance company. To all those who think that they could do better than those who are mentioned in my book and who were caught out. To all those who read the last two sentences and will hopefully provide me with interesting future trips overseas to bring them back to life.

But my main dedication is to those who appear in my book, either having been prosecuted in a court of law or those whose names I have changed to protect the guilty. My gratitude for giving me the opportunity to visit 83 countries investigating false life and health insurance claims.

John Saunders

Acknowledgement

I would like to thank my wife, Jennifer and my two lovely daughters, Natalie and Claire, for putting up with my long absences from home while travelling abroad investigating insurance claims. Hopefully, you will all agree that it was worthwhile when you think of the presents I regularly brought back from Africa. Maybe you did, though, run out of space in which to place all those wooden elephants!

Andrew and Pat Young employed me in January 1988, and I would like to thank them for their guidance, for providing a wonderful opportunity, and their help up until they retired, having sold the business to GE Reinsurance and leaving me in charge. Unfortunately, Andrew is no longer with us.

Barbara McWalter had been a wonderful secretary for many years and helped me understand the complexities of Microsoft. Peter Savage and Mike Gates, both retired police investigators, worked alongside me for several years and provided valuable assistance. Both were involved in some of the cases mentioned in this book.

My thanks to the re-insurance industry, who always supported me and introduced me to new clients.

Ge Reinsurance, now part of Swiss Re: proved to be an excellent employer and the management there were always very supportive. I would especially like to mention Bob Ratcliffe at GE. He was involved when Andrew and Pat sold Linden Management Services Ltd to GE Reinsurance. Eventually, he was in overall charge of claims. Bob was unique in that he could take a large file containing numerous facts about a complex claim. Within 30 minutes, he would have all the main facts at his fingertips and would be able to suggest a relevant solution. I was surprised when Swiss Re: took over GE Reinsurance that Bob did not become responsible for claims Worldwide. I could not think of a more qualified candidate. Thanks, Bob, for your assistance (and for arranging those excellent golf days).

My gratitude to all the life offices for which I have worked. As I have not mentioned the names of insurers involved in the various cases I investigated, then I do not think it correct to mention them here.

Since 1988 I have worked with many people abroad. They have acted as translators and guides and have occasionally handled small claims on my behalf. I would like to make a particular mention of Michael Kofi Boateng (Boat). He was the first person to work with me back in 1988 in Ghana. We became friends, and he worked with me until his death in March 2020. Covid-19 prevented me from attending his funeral. Boat does get a special mention in my book.

Edward Mekwuye in Lagos has worked with me for several years, and prior to him, his father, Erasmus, ably assisted me until his death. There are far too many associates to mention here, but I will mention a few who I have known for many years. My thanks to Chaki, Mike Barker, Harrison, Fakhrul, Maria, Waiel, Hesham, Khalid, Balbir, Zuber, Sanjay, Balbir plus John (now deceased) and Steve in Zimbabwe. My thanks to you all and my apologies if I have missed you off my list.

Most of the photographs in the book were taken by me personally. Over the years, contacts have occasionally sent me humorous photos. If you recognise a photo that you sent me, then please accept my gratitude.

About The Author

John Saunders has 33 years' experience investigating life and health insurance claims ranging from thousands to millions of pounds. These mostly involved fake deaths, disappearances (especially at sea), murders, and self-mutilation. They have taken John to 83 countries, and in his book, he has described some of the most prominent, unusual, macabre and amusing claims. This shows the extremes people are willing to go to in order to make money.

You will see that he has survived landmines, floods, being mugged, corrupt police officers, a drunken army officer holding a gun to his head, riots, attacks from violent mobs, rats in his bed, and being dragged from the steps of an aircraft by a corrupt air force officer, to mention just a few of his escapades!

He is probably the only person to hold a licence to carry a toilet in a car in River State in Nigeria. Not a voluntary purchase, but with a gun pointing in his direction!

He has appeared in several British television programmes in respect of notorious fraud cases.

Visas For Many Countries

Prologue

"Go away, I'm dead", said the lady.

A "dead man" found hiding under wife's bed said, "It's a fair cop guv."

A claimant's doctor told me that I was putting her under pressure over her husband's alleged death. If she committed suicide, he would hold me responsible. This was some years ago, and the husband is still alive but in a British prison.

A man, along with a corrupt police officer, identified a corpse as his friend, and he was cremated. The perfect crime, well, almost. I proved he was never born, so how could he die?

A family was killed in a tragic car accident in Nigeria. It was headline news in one national newspaper, the day before the accident!

What is the weight of a small urn containing human ashes? Not 20 kilos as in one case.

A man had clearly lost a hand. But the accident he described meant it was the wrong hand.

"Stop thief", shouted a man as I left a mortuary in Lagos carrying a body.

When the villagers in Kinshasa stormed our car, we left hurriedly with 2 police officers clinging to the roof.

I paid a licence fee in Nigeria for carrying a mobile toilet in my hire car. The man did have a gun pointed at my head.

A lady travelling back to London sat next to her father on the plane. She had his death certificate in her handbag!

"My husband was buried at sea," the lady told me, "dropped overboard in the Mediterranean." So, on your next holiday to a Greek island be careful when swimming!!

Mike claimed his friend died in Palestine. Nonsense. A while later, Mike changed his name and claimed that another friend died in Palestine. Nonsense. Mike is running out of friends!

While we were in the process of obtaining an exhumation order to open a grave and prove that it did not contain the body of the insured, the claimant dug it up early one morning and transported it to another country for a cremation.

A man claimed for the loss of part of 2 fingers when attacked by robbers in Nigeria. The policy covered the loss of a whole finger, not part of a one. A year later, he went back to Nigeria, was again attacked by armed robbers in the same location and lost the remainder of those 2 fingers!!!!

Over the years, I have refuted claims totalling in excess of £200 million. So read on, and you will come across many unusual cases where people have faked their deaths or serious illnesses or lost limbs.

Having spent 33 years travelling to 83 countries investigating insurance claims, I thought it time to put pen to paper and share some of my unusual experiences. Most of the claims involved people faking their deaths. There were claims where the insured person was murdered by their partner, who was the beneficiary of the insurance policy. A suicide was often covered up to suggest an accidental death. Cases of false disappearances at sea also feature in my book. Interestingly, some of the *dead* people never existed.

Some people obtained fraudulent documents to indicate that they had suffered a serious illness. Others actually self-mutilated in order to claim.

I looked at cases where people aged over 100 were alleged to be still living and claiming a pension from their ex-employer in the UK. They had retired back to the country from which they originated. But they were really dead, hence no longer entitled to receive the pension.

There were several cases where fraudsters stole documents from the post, often the international post arriving in Nigeria, where the name of a financial institution appeared on the envelope. They then took on the identity of the person named in the letter and attempted to cash in their investments.

There are cases where a person approached an insurer and sought their agreement to utilise their licence to sell a new style of a policy covering accident and disability. Within weeks 90% of policyholders claimed!

In many places, I have changed the names to protect the guilty!

Note: The cases I describe are often from memory. My memory is not perfect, but the events are true to the best of my knowledge and recollection. I have changed people's identity unless they were convicted in court or, as in many cases, a false identity was used so that person never existed.

I have shown various newspaper headings for successful prosecutions. As I do not have the original copy, I am often unable to recall the name of that newspaper but my thanks to the press for covering such cases.

Chapter 1: Introduction

I joined HM Customs & Excise aged 18 and first worked in the port of Southampton, mostly boarding ships and clearing passengers arriving on the liners and ferries. In those days, 1967, most junior officers were sent to work for a time at Heathrow Airport. Many officers dreaded this move and counted the days until they could return to a port. On the contrary, I thoroughly enjoyed working at Heathrow, asked to stay and remained there for over ten years.

I enjoyed the challenges laid down by the travelling public. Often when met by, "Don't you know who I am?" I asked for the person's passport. Opening it at the page containing their name and photograph, I would show it to the passenger and remind them of their forgotten identity! When I suspected that a passenger was perhaps being economical with the truth, I enjoyed the challenge in front of me. 'No, Madam," I might say, "Hatton Garden jewellery is not hallmarked 18k but 18ct", or "that Nikon camera was not bought in London as it has not been released here yet!" During my time at Heathrow, I met some well-known individuals, including stars of the screen and stage, politicians, titled people, footballers and so on, many of whom paid fines for smuggling rather than appear before a magistrate, but this is not the time nor the place to divulge such secrets. If only!

I enjoyed investigation work, and looking back, my first successful investigation took place when I was 17 years old and at school in Bournemouth. One day I sneaked away from school early; I think it is safe to admit that 55 years later, and went on my motorcycle with my good friend John to the centre of Bournemouth. We had heard that there were weekend jobs available at a supermarket called Pricerites (I think that is what it was called then). Those of you who know Bournemouth will realise that Richmond Hill is a very steep incline into the town centre. Halfway down the hill, by the offices of the Evening Echo, a car pulled out in front of me. I was thrown towards the front of my motorcycle, and my legs somehow wedged behind the handlebars. John smashed into my rear, and we ended up in pain, me with a damaged, un-rideable bike. The young man driving the car apologized, and stated that he was fully to blame. There was no need, he insisted on trying to find any witnesses as he was admitting liability and he was a solicitor. We exchanged telephone numbers and addresses, and I then pushed my bike nearly 5 miles home while in pain.

I reported the incident to my father, who rang the solicitor. He immediately handed the phone to his father. It transpired that he was a well-known local businessman. He claimed that I was fully responsible for the accident and that I would be hearing from their solicitor. I think this was the first time in my life that I became angry and incensed with a feeling of injustice. I was determined to defeat this person! The truth had to prevail.

The next day I insisted that John accompanied me back to the scene of this accident, now known to me as the scene of the crime. I told John that we would each take one side of the street, visit all of the offices and ask if anyone had witnessed the accident. After about 30 minutes visiting multiple offices in the Evening Echo building, in one office a man asked how I was. He said he had been leaning out of the window the previous day and saw an idiot drive straight into a motorcycle. He recognised me and hence asked how I was? I had found my witness!

The police took statements, and the car driver appeared at the magistrate's court and pleaded not guilty of careless driving. Knowing that one of the magistrates might be a governor of our school, I suggested to John that we wore our school ties to the court. Luckily our Governor was on the bench, and the driver was rightfully convicted. My motorcycle was duly repaired, I acquired a new school uniform, having torn mine in the accident and received a small sum of money. I cannot describe the feeling of satisfaction having witnessed justice prevail.

Between 1988 and around 2015, I had a fairly constant number of claims to deal with and regularly travelled abroad. However, there has since been a decrease in the number of suspect deaths overseas. There are various reasons for this, such as tighter control on the financial advisers arranging life cover and improved underwriting. I often speak with people who are, say 3rd generation immigrants; their grandfather originally arrived in the UK from abroad. They might occasionally visit family in perhaps India or Nigeria but are very British and have told me that, under no circumstances could they live in those countries. However, persons from such places who come to the UK to study or work for a set period seem to think that investing in a life insurance policy is a good investment when they have to eventually return home and "die".

That is not to say that people born in the UK, with only their family in the UK, have not tried to fake their deaths. There have been lots of television programmes about Russell Causley from Bournemouth (that place again) who "died" at sea. At the time I was doing that investigation, I had another scam involving a disappearance at sea: I proved that fraud in Bournemouth. To think that for years people thought it was full of old people in bath chairs! And I come from there.

I have proved numerous claims to be false in many countries. I have often met the "dead" person. Comments such as "go away, I'm dead" have been made to me on multiple occasions. If only I could have filmed them. I have been in situations where I felt threatened but have somehow managed to live to tell the story. Walking across a minefield in Angola where someone had been blown to smithereens was perhaps not one of my most sensible moments. Being attacked by a mob outside Kinshasa was somewhat frightening. Meeting a mugger in Mozambique who was wearing designer clothes and speaking good English was a surprise.

I have come across many corrupt doctors and medical officials. They always have the same excuse for having issued documents. They were tricked, is often the party line. Once when I asked a doctor in Nigeria why he had issued a death certificate when he never saw the body, he responded, "Because I was offered a lot of money". That is always the reason but rarely has a doctor actually admitted this to me.

Over the years, such frauds have been committed by persons from all walks of life, such as religious leaders, civil servants, military personnel, doctors, nurses, lawyers, accountants, diplomats and so on.

These are real cases!

A doctor from London was rushed to hospital from a plane at Heathrow after collapsing upon arrival. He had

A man has now died twice in Somalia but again was reincarnated in England!

So, read on if you want more details of what people try and do in order to make money.

Chapter 3: Travelling In Nigeria

I have travelled to many places where there are few facilities, such as those we take for granted in the UK. I have stayed in places that have "hotel" written on a sign outside. The only reason for calling such an establishment "hotel" is that this is what is mentioned at the top of the bill. Years ago, I often spent ten days travelling across Nigeria at a time when nearly all hotels were government-owned. Only by drinking copious quantities of alcohol could one conceal the true image of one's room. Once in a hotel near Owerri, I had the Kings Suite, not realising that "King" was the name of one of the rats that lived there. It was a huge room, and an interior designer from Lagos, at least that is what he called himself after smoking some horrible smelling substance, had decided to decorate it using 30 different colours. The huge bed had a vast, colourful headboard, mostly made from animal skins. I awoke in the night hearing a strange noise. I then realised that the animals used for the headboard were not all actually dead. I saw six eyes at the bottom of the bed looking at me. Rats!! The next morning before checking out, I complained, only to be told that I was not allowed pets in my room. Honest. Would I make this up?

The clerk at check-out needed batteries for his calculator, so I had to await the arrival of the manager before paying my bill. In fact, I needed a refund because those days in Nigeria, they trusted no one. If the room was, say, 1,000 Naira a night, you paid 2,000 Naira upfront. Staff had to check the room before you left to ensure you had not stolen the 30-year-old black and white TV or a plastic coat hanger. I once tried to pick up a cheap metal ashtray, but it was screwed to the table! I digress; I was waiting for the calculator to work. The clerk could not calculate 10 times 120 Naira without his calculator. I kept telling him the total was 1200 Naira. Upon the arrival of the batteries, he agreed it was 1200 Naira and remarked that I must have had a good education. Who was I to disagree?

I was in that area a few weeks later, staying at another glorious state-controlled hotel. In many third world countries, particularly Nigeria, I had a simple breakfast and then, when travelling, only ate bananas and drank water all day. Upon arriving at a hotel in the evening, I'd take a tablet for diarrhoea before eating. Being caught short in parts of Africa and Asia is not something I would wish on my worst enemy. Anyway, I went with my Nigerian associate to the dining room and ordered chicken. My associate ordered a local dish. I think it was bushmeat on toast and his meal arrived fairly promptly.

After 30 minutes, my chicken was still absent, so I queried this. Ten minutes later, the waiter (he said he was a waiter and was wearing a food-stained white uniform to prove this) returned to say they had no chicken. I ordered liver as this is normally excellent in West Africa, at least when compared with bush meat. Another 20 minutes passed. *"Where is my liver,"* I asked? After 5 minutes, he returned, *"We have no liver"*. *"Can you find out what you do have?"* He came back to say they had eggs. At last, I thought I was getting somewhere. *"Can I have an omelette?"* His response was, *"I will see if we have any omelettes"*. *"Bring me another beer",* I shouted!

Nigeria is famed for what ex-pats call *"the women of the night"*. The number of times you get a knock on the door after retiring from the hotel bar and are faced by a lady offering a massage! It is obvious that a member of the staff telephones contacts with the room number of a foreigner. I was once in a dreadful place in Calabar. There must have been over 100 rooms, and my associate and I seemed to be the only people staying there. I was awoken by a knock on the door to find two young girls there. I slammed the door and tried to go back to sleep. I then awoke again in shock to realise that I had stretched out and touched live wires hanging from the wall plug. To be fair, hotels in Nigeria have improved over the past few years as private individuals and large hotel chains have invested money there. However, staying at a good international hotel in Lagos did often exceed the cost of a London hotel.

21

I do have fond memories of my visits to Kano in the north and Enugu in the east of Nigeria. In Kano, I stayed at a small, Italian owned hotel and, after work, would sit in the beautiful rose garden with a cold beer. In Enugu, there is a smart hotel by a lake, and I often arrived there Friday afternoon, stayed overnight before returning to Lagos on Saturday. The hotel had a French chef and dinner there was a splendid occasion.

When I first started travelling to Nigeria, the insurance company there that assisted me with the various formalities and introduced me to Erasmus Mekwuye. He had investigated claims on behalf of that Nigerian insurer. Erasmus worked with me for many years. He had been a Commissioner of Police. He was hardworking, honest and would never give up until fraud was proved. One day I arrived at his house in Lagos and saw a notice on the wall about his death. I was stunned. I spoke with his family, and his son, Edward, asked to work with me. I thought that he was perhaps too inexperienced at the time, but we kept in touch. I knew another retired police officer who had an investigation company. We worked together for a while, but due to his health, he was using a young, very inexperienced employee to handle claims.

Eventually, I contacted Edward, and as of today, he has worked for me for many years. We have travelled across

Nigeria together and enjoyed some fantastic experiences. I appear perhaps too critical of Nigeria in this book, but I do have a certain love of the place. In rural areas especially, I have met some wonderful God-fearing people. In the mainly Muslim north, I have received very generous welcomes and hospitality. I have always been critical of the fact that, if it were not for Government corruption, Nigeria would be a wealthy country and not have to suffer such hardships as are still present. It saddens me to see the state of some government hospitals, schools, the lack of law and order, police corruption, and the infrastructure in general and see the opulence enjoyed by a few in high authority. I have noticed a slight improvement and pray that things will soon improve for the public at large. I once interviewed a high-ranking policeman who was wearing a real gold Rolex watch.

Travelling in Nigeria, particularly in the wet season, can be very difficult, as you can see below.

My KING Bed

Chapter 4: Such A Variety Of Claims

It is not always a question of whether the person is really dead. I have investigated many cases where someone has died, but their true medical history was concealed when applying for the policy. Insurers are unlikely to insure a person who has a serious illness and often increase the premiums if someone has hypertension or diabetes, for example. Also, a person might lie about living in the UK in order to get life cover to which they would not be entitled if non-resident. In a large number of cases, we have found that the true cause of death on a medical death certificate from overseas is concealed. The mention of cancer, liver failure, AIDS, HIV might cause the insurance company to go into some detail about that person's true medical history. Hence, the cause of death might be shown as RTA (road traffic accident) or sudden heart attack.

In some countries, particularly parts of India and Pakistan, it is possible to take a dead person to a hospital where a doctor will issue a certificate stating that the person died from a heart attack. Sometimes they do not even see a body. No post-mortem is performed, and the body is buried or cremated without delay. Often, I query how a healthy, fairly young individual dies from a sudden heart attack in India or Pakistan but not in other countries. I believe that there have been many murders concealed in such a way. I have had some success proving murder, but it is extremely difficult. Local police are often not interested in pursuing allegations of crime, or they are bribed by relatives. In Pakistan, the partner of a victim of a crime or a relative can stand up in court stating that he or she asks God to forgive the accused, and the case is dropped. Of course, always a sum of money is agreed in advance and then paid. I recall a case in India where a young, allegedly healthy male was taken to a clinic with foam bubbling out of his mouth and nose. I felt certain he was poisoned, but the doctor stated he died from a sudden heart attack.

Before undertaking any investigation abroad in respect of a claim made in the UK, I always interview the family/claimant and undertake various enquiries in the UK. If I need to go abroad, then I will always have a fairly accurate idea of the real situation. On occasions, we have had a claim that seemed perhaps genuine, but as we were going to the country where the death occurred, it was perhaps cost-effective to check some of the facts. For example, was the cause of death accurately recorded, was it really an accident? If when abroad I find that the person did die, but in suspicious circumstances, then knowing something about that person's life in the UK assists the investigation. There have been cases where the insured had been subjected to domestic violence in the UK and then died suspiciously abroad. In such a case, I will look at the possibility of murder. Also, on many occasions, I have proved an overseas death as being false without venturing outside of the UK. You would think that if a person was trying to steal a large sum of money, he or she would at least fly abroad to properly start the proceedings rolling.

One of the cheapest types of insurance is accidental death cover. Without going into statistics, the chances of dying in an accident are small compared with natural death. You would be amazed at the number of older persons, for example, of Pakistani origin who have only accidental death policies and die in a car accident while on holiday in Pakistan. The doctor certifying death omits to mention that the car was about 50 metres away when the man had a heart attack!

I recall one case involving Nigeria. A man living there had a bank account in the UK at his daughter's address in London. It appears he lived once in the UK. A mailshot arrived in his name at the London address offering an accidental death plan for a cover of £10,000. The cost was about £4 a month. The policy was taken out, and lo and behold, a few months later, the man died in a car accident in Nigeria. I sent the papers to my man in Lagos, Edward. It would not be cost-effective to travel there just for that one small claim. There was a police report – the officer insisted it was genuine. There was a post-mortem report. There was a record supporting this at the hospital, and the doctor confirmed it was genuine. Edward went to the house of the alleged deceased. This is what he saw posted on the wall outside.

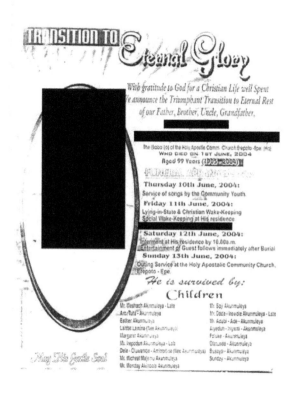

The man was **aged 99** when he was said to have "crashed his vehicle on the motorway in Nigeria". He was said to be the driver. Enquiries showed he had been bedridden for a long time and was dying of old age when his daughter in the UK took out the policy. She must have known at the time that she would be able to obtain fake documents from Nigeria when he died.

I have also investigated many claims in respect of critical illness and disability. Critical illness policies have proved popular in the past 20 years. This is when you ensure against having illnesses such as cancer, heart attack, stroke, liver failure, MS, to name just a few.

There have been cases where a person is diagnosed abroad with a serious illness. They then travel to the UK and take out a policy that pays out in the event that such an illness is diagnosed. According to the application, they are in good health, but a few months later …. Payments in respect of such illnesses, cancer, MS, liver disease, heart disease and so on can be significant. I have had cases where a sick person moves in the UK to another health area, registers with another GP, is shown to be in good health, takes out a policy and … some months later becomes very ill. People have also changed their names in order to conceal their true medical history. I have investigated countless claims where a person allegedly had a heart attack abroad, but I was able to prove this to be false. Hopefully, you will later read some stories about such claims that you will find interesting.

I have also investigated numerous travel claims, mostly involving sickness abroad. Having travelled to so many countries has resulted in me having associates abroad who work alongside me when I travel. I rely on them mostly for local knowledge and interpreting. Many of the countries I visit are English speaking, but often it is an "English" that is somewhat alien to me. Travel claims tend to be lower in value, so it is not cost-effective to travel abroad to investigate these. Therefore, my local associates carry out the enquiry. It is astonishing that persons who go on holiday to countries from which they originate are regularly taken ill, hospitalised there and eventually submit claims for inflated charges that are often far higher than would be charged in the UK. This is blatantly a method used to illegally fund one's holiday until caught! Numerous people have claimed malaria, having travelled to an area where there is no malaria. People regularly obtain false medical certificates in order to extend their leave and holiday abroad.

Sometimes people allegedly lose valuable items while abroad and submit an insurance claim. You would be amazed at the number of travellers with relatively low-income employment who are robbed of their Rolex watch, iPad, expensive jewellery etc. In over 30 years of travel, I have never lost a suitcase. There have been occasions when it arrived the next day, but everything was intact. I have dealt with claimants who have reported lost baggage on 15 plus occasions. I recall two individuals who worked for the world's favourite airline. Upon return to London, one of them would take two suitcases through Customs. Once through, his partner would report that his suitcase had not arrived. I recall a case in which a man claimed 35 designer shirts that he had left behind in a hotel and which disappeared. He was only away for the weekend and told me that he did sweat a lot!

Another scam used by residents in the UK but mostly by USA residents involves accidents where a person breaks their nose. They end up with a beautiful nose compared to the earlier version. This is a method for claiming plastic surgery from the travel insurer. You would be surprised to learn that Tehran is regarded by many as one of the best cosmetic surgery places in the world. Teeth also feature. Being treated for a bad tooth in Eastern Europe and ending up with a bridge and implants is pushing things a bit too far! But it happens.

I once had a man who claimed on 15 policies. While travelling in Nigeria, armed thieves allegedly cut off two of his fingers with a machete. We interviewed the doctor who had treated him in Nigeria, and he was genuine. However, he did say that when the claimant visited him, the cut did appear fairly clean and straight. Perhaps done carefully with a knife and not a violent blow with a machete. Only two of the policies might have covered such an incident. Why he should claim on his house, car, breakdown and boiler policies was rather unusual. Having interviewed the man, I realised he was perhaps not of sound mind!

He was informed that the two policies covered the loss of the entire finger, not half of it. A year later, he went back to Nigeria and, yes, you have guessed correctly. In the same location, he was again attacked by armed robbers with a machete and lost the rest of those two fingers! I will not reveal his name but if you shake hands with a Nigerian male, missing two fingers and who quotes the Bible to you …

I have carried out investigations to establish if pensioners were still alive. Many people came from abroad to work in England in the late 1950s, 60's and so on. They worked for UK companies and often retired with a pension and returned to the country from which they originated. Companies realised that they were paying pensions to people often aged over 100. Were they really still alive? Enquiries in countries such as Jamaica, Pakistan, India, Nigeria and Ghana revealed that about 5% of such pensioners were actually dead. Family members continued to claim the pensions.

I also carried out work for insurers and financial institutions in respect of insurance commission and identity frauds. Some years ago, a man, let's call him John Smith, would be engaged in selling life insurance policies by company ABC. Normally he would be employed on a commission-only basis. Often this would be an upfront payment of around 12 month's premium payment for each customer introduced. So, if your premium was, say, £20 a month, he would receive around £240 upfront commission.

Of course, should the customer cease paying, then the agent would have to repay the commission. This, under normal circumstances, would be repaid from future commissions. Except that John Smith would disappear, leaving behind a large debt. Enquiries would show that he had used a false identity, address etc. John Smith would then become Bill Brown and work for insurer XYZ. He would sign up the same clients, give them funds to pay 2 or 3 premiums by direct debit and then cease payments. His actions would be repeated, and he would sometimes steal from 6 or 7 insurers. One case involved organised crime in the area of Southall, and several million pounds were involved. Some people claimed they signed insurance applications with a gun held above their head.

Identity thefts involved people stealing documents relating to investments, regularly from the post, taking on the owner's identity and attempting to steal their investments. I had several cases where this failed, so the fraudsters then obtained documents to show that the policyholder was dead. They took on the identity of the next of kin and tried to cash in.

Perhaps it is now time to move on and mention some of the places and enquiries carried out. In many stories, I have changed the names to protect the guilty.

Chapter 5: Travelling Between Nigeria And Ghana

My first two overseas trips were to Ghana. That sentence might give you the impression that I was starting with Ghana. True, but mentioning the wonders of Nigeria will assist the reader in perhaps understanding why I hold Ghana in such high esteem. So, you might have to wait for a later chapter. I have now travelled to Ghana around 45 times, and it is one of my favourite countries. This probably stems from the fact that I have regularly travelled there after working in Nigeria for several days. Upon arrival in Accra from Lagos, I tend to relax, walk along the street, be greeted by pleasant Ghanaians and do not fear for my life. By this time, I have often thanked God that I have survived Nigeria!

Nigeria has a reputation for scams, violence, robberies, shootings, hijackings, petrol shortages, and clearly, the place deserves such a reputation. Traffic is a nightmare, and there a traffic jam is called a "go slow". Quite sensible, really, because we call it the rush hour, but we rush nowhere. Until about 2015, no traffic lights actually worked there. Drivers seem to believe that they will be classified as simpletons and cowards if they did not try to get to the front of every queue. If there are three lanes of traffic turning left, then rush to the front and form the 4th lane. Sod the oncoming drivers, they can wait. The result is that everything comes to a standstill, resulting in a competition to see who has the loudest horn. In many Arab countries, they drive the same way. I once spent 40 minutes in a car at a junction in Tehran when everyone tried to cross at the same time, and no one would give way.

Although it has improved recently, arriving at Lagos Airport was an experience not to be recommended. Departing from the airport was not much better. Some years ago, the main flight to Ghana was on Nigerian Airways. I recall my days at Heathrow when airlines in Terminal 3 feared being close to the Nigerian Airways desk when it was checking in each evening. Armed police were regularly present. Flights to Lagos were always full, and similarly, flights from Lagos to Accra were full. Yet the airline eventually went bust. Why? Corruption. Passengers at Heathrow with fully paid tickets were regularly offloaded in favour of people who had perhaps paid a bribe to staff (bribe is known as dash in Nigeria) or who were related to a staff member.

I recall flying one day from Lagos to Accra on dreaded Nigerian Airways. The gate was called, and everyone rushed there. The aircraft was not due to arrive for another hour. I met up with an American who had been there to preach the word, or so he claimed. I asked him to give me $10. I then spoke to the man in charge at the gate. I gave him the $10 and suggested that if he could board us first, then I would provide an additional $10. Eventually, the flight arrived, the jetty was moved toward the aircraft's door, and everyone at the departure gate rushed to get on the aircraft, apart from me and my newfound buddy, let's call him Bud. Eventually, the masses were moved back to allow the passengers to disembark from the aircraft.

When it was time to board, the man in charge allowed us to get on first after receiving the other $10 from me. I sat in the front seat and suggested that my friend Bud did likewise. Bud suggested this was unwise as passengers would probably step on our toes whilst boarding as there was no bulkhead at the front. This was the least of our problems, I explained. Eventually, all the passengers had boarded, but some were standing. A delay occurred until armed police arrived and removed six passengers. It transpired that they had no tickets, and this was the third time in 2 days that the police had removed them from an aircraft. Security? Only for those who refused to pay dash!

So, the plane took off and was clearly overweight as it just managed to leave the ground before running onto the grass at the end of the runway. I explained to Bud that any moment he would appreciate why we sat at the front. Banging and shouting erupted throughout the aircraft. Passengers had been allowed to board with unlimited hand baggage. Most had bags and parcels stored on their laps. As the plane climbed, these items went above the heads of their owners and hit the person in the seat behind. Bud seemed pleased to have met me. Next, the stewardess gave me a thin, plastic cup and commenced pouring coffee in it, but it melted into a small ball of plastic. Luckily my manhood remained intact as I had held it some distance from me, the cup that is. Thank goodness it was only a 45-minute flight, so no time for passengers to light a stove and cook a meal.

There were no landing cards on board for Ghana Immigration; someone forgot to load them. Upon arrival in Accra, there was a desperate rush towards immigration. Bud suggested we would be at the back of the queue. I told him we would end up at the front, but he clearly doubted my word. Numerous shouts came in our direction, asking to borrow a pen in order to complete a landing card. I explained to Bud that we were probably the only passengers with pens, so we would be first through immigration. We were, and my new friend was again impressed, but this did not last long. This trip was before we had mobile phones. Contacting Ghana involved using a landline, but most phones there never worked. I had arrived a day early and could not contact my associate, Boat (short for Boateng). My hotel reservation was not until the next day, and the hotel was full, so I decided to spend a night at one of the new international hotels that had just been built. Bud was in a similar position and also booked that hotel. I told him that rather than being ripped off by the taxi touts at the terminal, we should walk to the car park and select a taxi. We did so, but 5 minutes after leaving the airport, one of the rear wheels fell off! Bud was no longer so impressed with his newfound friend.

Chapter 6: My First Enquiries In Ghana

Around 1994, I was travelling to West Africa at least four times a year. Whenever I got back to my office, there would be a new, suspect claim from there awaiting my attention. There was another big difference between Nigeria and Ghana. Let's start with Nigeria, a false claim for Adetunle, for example. In support of a false claim, I would have a medical report from a doctor, let's say Dr Akintunde (4 vowels in a Nigerian name were sufficient to put it in the "suspect" file). I would approach Dr Akintunde, who would confirm that he had written the report, and he would try and convince me that he had certified the death. I would have a police report from Inspector Akinsola. Again, he would insist that he investigated the death. My investigation showed it was a fraud, and Adetunle was not dead.

Now, look at a similar scenario in Ghana. Let's call the dead man Owusu. At the hospital, I would ask to see, for example, Dr Mensah, whose name was on the death certificate. There would be no such doctor there. Similarly, at the police station, I would ask for Chief Inspector Tetteh. The officer in charge would tell me that there was no such officer there and the report was a fake. I could never comprehend why officials in Nigeria used their correct names on fake documents and insisted that the event had really occurred. In Ghana, officials hardly ever used real names, and most documents were forged and often not created by a real doctor or police officer.

I have probably been over 40 times to Ghana and dealt with 80 plus false claims. However, rarely if ever, did I fear for my safety there. I have travelled all over Ghana and regularly sat in mud huts, taking written statements. In villages, there is always a chief. He is respected, and the locals obey his rule. If someone from that village has allegedly died, then I will be confident that I will obtain the truth from the chief and his ruling committee. The same does also apply to rural Nigeria.

However, there is a certain procedure to follow. In Ghana, each village will have a "stool-keeper", the nearest translation would be secretary. Often, he speaks good English, can read and write and has been educated. It is necessary to sit around in a group and address the chief via the stool-keeper. One is expected to offer a bottle of locally brewed Schnapps to the chief. He will pray to the gods (not sure which ones, though) and then take the first drink. As his guest, I have to take the second drink. Not a good idea to go to a village too early in the day.

I went to such a village on my first ever visit to Ghana, but maybe I should start by explaining how I ended up working for 32 years with Michael Boateng, known as Boat. While starting to write this book (March 2020), I received a telephone call from Boat's son in Ghana. Boat had just died, probably a heart attack, but the family was awaiting a post-mortem. This eventually showed that it was a heart attack. A lovely, honourable, God-fearing man and I feel I have been lucky to have worked with such a great friend for so long. He had stayed at my house, and I took him to my local pub and rugby club, where friends were over-generous with pints of beer! In recent years he sometimes struggled financially, and as he has been such a reliable worker for so long, I financially assisted his two son's studies. I would like to dedicate everything that I write on a positive note about Ghana to my late friend Boat. Due to Covid 19, myself plus his family members in London were unable to travel for his funeral.

My first trip to Ghana was in 1988. I arrived and stayed at the Continental Hotel near the airport (now the excellent Golden Tulip Hotel). What a dreadful place, but this was in the days before international hotel groups moved to Ghana. It was also before Ghanaians returned there from abroad with funds to build small hotels. I arrived early evening and went to the bar. The place was full of cockroaches, but even they were outnumbered by the young ladies of ill repute.

Later I tried later to sleep but awoke with a strange noise made by cockroaches climbing up the wall of my hotel room. I tried to kill them, but more of their mates kept arriving and appeared intent on keeping me awake. The following morning, I went for breakfast. I soon lost my appetite when the man on the next table, while reading a paper, failed to notice two large cockroaches have a race across his eggs!

I knew no one in Ghana, but someone had given me the telephone number of a person in the Ghana Reinsurance company. I experienced a problem using the landline (that was the only form of communication in those days). There had been a storm in the night, and it was still raining heavily. The hotel operator said the storm had caused a problem and kept telling me to be patient. It was 2 hours later that I established the phone line at the hotel had not been working for several weeks! Since then, whenever anyone in Africa tells me to wait and be patient, I ignore them. By patient, they normally mean that if you sit there for the rest of the day, the person you want might arrive. On the other hand, he or she might not! When West Africans say they are coming, they go away. Over the years, I must have been told in excess of 600 times to take a seat and wait. But no one actually knows if the person I need to see will arrive that day. So much time is wasted by officials in Africa waiting around. If a police officer, doctor or civil servant is meant to start work at 9 am, then there appears to be no apparatus in place to ensure that he or she ever actually attends.

As the telephones at the hotel were not working, I decided to take a taxi to the offices of the reinsurance company. I hailed a taxi, a 20-year-old Peugeot that was way past its sell-by date. I think, like most vehicles, in that part of Africa, it was made of parts from 12 old cars. We drove through a flood, and suddenly the rear floor mat arose, and I was soaked in dirty rainwater. There was a large hole in the floor. After a few visits to West Africa, I became accustomed to such occurrences.

I met the man at the reinsurance company and asked if he knew someone who could assist me. He had a friend who was a dentist. A good start, I thought, if I had a sudden toothache. However, the dentist had a car, and he rented it out with a driver. Later I hired the car and driver, who was Boat, and we started work. I soon realised that Boat was far too intelligent to be just a driver. He told me he was an air traffic controller, but the Government had no money, and he had not been paid for three months. Hence, he was working as a driver. Thereafter, Boat has accompanied me on every one of my visits to Ghana. He stopped working as a driver for the dentist and worked in a multitude of business ventures as well as assisting me.

Our first enquiry involved a young man who had died in a fishing village along the coast of Accra. He was allegedly buried there. Locals pointed us in the direction of the cemetery, and this was a few graves in the bush; it was not properly controlled. Boat and I pushed back the large shrubs looking for graves. Suddenly Boat disappeared: he had found the cemetery. He had fallen into a recently dug grave, a premature burial. Had someone witnessed me pulling him out of the grave, then they would have thought they were witnessing a resurrection!

Anyway, we found the village on the coast and had to wait while the chief changed into his tribal costume. The stool-keeper told villagers to show us around the fishing boats. I inquired if I might later take a photo of the chief in his robes, and this was agreed. Villagers started placing stalls under a large tree, but I suggested they were moved as the tree was in partial shade, so not good for photography. Anyway, I spent a pleasant 30 minutes watching villagers mend their nets and carve boats out of trees. I was called back to see the chief. The tree had gone! The stool-keeper said it was in my way for a photograph, so they had chopped it down. I managed to conceal my horror and then drank Schnapps with the chief. He was able to confirm that the dead person never died there and was not known in the village.

Me with the villagers and stool-keeper

Later I will cover other interesting enquiries I made over the years in Ghana, but it is time to change continents.

Chapter 7: Dead Or Alive

WHAT HAVE ALL THESE PEOPLE GOT IN COMMON – APART FROM MEETING ME?

Abdel in Cairo

Almir in Yemen

Ali in Bahrain

Olu from Nigeria

Mavis from Kenya

Manu in Uganda

Mary in Zimbabwe

51

Corzon in the Philippines

THEY WERE ALL DEAD!!

Chapter 8: Buried At Sea

UK insurers asked me to make enquiries into the death at sea of Adolph Pecher.

He had taken out large life policies with four insurers totalling £1million in order to cover four mortgages on expensive properties in London. His death was allegedly in 1989 when £1 million was quite a large sum of money. Within months of taking out the policies, he reportedly died from a heart attack at sea while a passenger on a Panamanian registered ship, MV Ragat. The death was reported to the Panama Consulate in Cairo. The death certificate was printed by the Consulate on expensive, embossed paper with an original stamp.

REPUBLICA DE PANAMA

HABILITADO

ORIGINAL
PH-76 (90.0001

1a. Clase
Dos Balboas
(B/.2.00)

Consulado (General)

Bienio de 19.88. a 19.90.

Nº de Control: _D-01/89_

:n. Embajada. El Cairo. Egipto

PAGADO

A. C. Numeral 50

DEATH   CERTIFICATE

Hereby the Embassy of the Republic of Panama -Consular Bureau-
would like to reconfirm and certify the decease of Mr. Adolf PECHER, male,
born on 29 November 1925, who was the bearer of passport No.F-9591729,
issued on 17 February 1983 in the city of Munich, Federal Republic of Germany,
Mr. PECHER died on 7 July 1989 at 16:20 hours due to a heart attack. At
the time, Mr. PECHER was on board the vessel "Ragat" (with Panamanian flag)
whose Captain is Mr. Fouad Ahmed Kasouri- while navigating in international
waters in the Mediterranean Sea-North of Africa.
This Consular Bureau was notified of this issue on 13 July 1989.

Dr. E. MONTERREY/QUINTERO
Chargé d' Affaires Consulaires
du Panama au Caire, Egypte

The first question I asked myself was, *"Why would a Consulate in Cairo issue a death certificate for a German citizen who died at sea?"* Where did they put the body was also something puzzling me? Yes, the wife claimed that he was buried at sea. She must have been watching an old black and white movie depicting the days when a burial at sea occurred. Perhaps the Pirates of Penzance! But, not in 1989!

Pecher was said to be a banker and lawyer and lived in an expensive property with his wife near Harrods in Knightsbridge, London. I made various enquiries, and it soon became clear that a mortgage fraud had occurred as the four mortgaged properties had been overvalued. To obtain the mortgages and life cover, he had produced many documents from a company in Spain, stating that he acted as a consultant and was paid significant amounts of money. Mrs Pecher appeared to visit Harrods almost daily and spent large sums of money there on her newly acquired credit cards.

I found out that Pecher had a son and daughter in Munich, and I went there and interviewed them. They were in their 20s and well educated. Their main complaint was that their father had died without leaving them anything in his will. Pecher was divorced from their mother and lived in London with his new wife. I tried to explain that if he was not dead, then he would not want any of his estate to be given away. Therefore, only his current wife would be named in his will. Other enquiries in Munich suggested that Pecher and his wife had moved to London after complaints were made about their fraudulent activities there.

Mrs Pecher seemed to keep changing solicitors in London and was reluctant to be interviewed. Therefore, I decided to go and knock on her door at her townhouse in Knightsbridge. There I met a rather elegant lady who told me that Mrs Pecher had just travelled to Switzerland to return the children to finishing school. These were the "children" I met in Munich, and when I met them, they looked "finished" as far as I was concerned. The lady I met said she was the Countess of Almeria and then closed the door on me. Google was not so advanced in those days, but I could trace no such countess. Had I just met Mrs Pecher?

I went to Cairo and first spoke to a charming young lady at the Panamanian Consulate. She agreed she had issued the death certificate on the instruction of the Consul, who had received the telephone call from the ship's captain. I suggested that it was not the norm to issue such a document in those circumstances. She stated she was only following orders. The Consul would not see me.

It had been claimed that Pecher was on route from somewhere south of Egypt. If the ship was in the Mediterranean when he died, then the ship had to have passed through the Suez Canal. I made enquiries in Port Suez and Alexandria, but there was no record of such a vessel passing through the Canal. I will never forget driving through the Sahara Desert and suddenly seeing a ship on my right-hand side. It appeared to be floating in the air, but the

Suez Canal was above me. Official enquiries with the authorities in Panama suggested that the ship did not exist.

Mrs Pecher and her London solicitor were both adamant that he had died as claimed. I did eventually get to interview her with her solicitor. She was elegantly dressed in a long, mink coat, and it was my belief that her charms had negated the solicitor's professionalism and common sense.

Next, I went to Madrid. A company there had provided letters supporting Pecher's financial income. I met the owner of the business, an elderly man who spoke Spanish with an accent. He had a Spanish name, but I suspect he was of German origin and had fled to South America at the end of the Second World War. His office was adorned with photographs of various South American dictators, and he appeared in most of them shaking hands with them. Tanks and other military equipment appeared in several photographs. This man insisted that Pecher had represented his company, but he was somewhat vague as to the nature of his work. Stood by his office door were two rather large men; "gangsters" is the word I would use! I decided to leave, having given the name of a hotel where I was not staying. The two men followed me, so I took a taxi two blocks, walked into a building, out of a different exit and after 10 minutes, it was clear that I had lost them.

The case was eventually reported to the police in London, but it was difficult to proceed against Mrs Pecher on the evidence available. There was sufficient evidence, though, for the insurers to refute the claims. Mrs Pecher had changed solicitors several times, and I had warned all of her solicitors not to be taken in by her charms and perhaps take a deposit for their charges. I later received calls from 3 solicitors asking if I knew of her whereabouts as they had not been paid—bloody naïve fools.

One insurance company had actually paid out £200,000 upon receipt of the Panamanian death certificate. They were clearly very impressed by it. This was a company that would normally have sought our advice before settling such a claim. Anyway, as the pay-out related to a mortgage, the sum was retrieved.

A year or so later, the police received information that Pecher was living in Portugal. It seems he tried utilising his charms on a certain lady, causing resentment among various people. This rather annoyed an Irish organisation. The police went to Portugal and arrested Pecher, who had undergone a facelift. He was returned to London and sent to prison. I had always wondered how he had managed to get the death certificate. Papers found showed a large sum of money had been paid to a Panamanian official. It appeared there was also a connection with Noriega, who was deposed as

President of Panama when it was invaded by the USA in 1989. You will recall that I mentioned the photographs of various dictators I had observed on the wall of the office in Madrid. I think Noriega was in one of them!

Pecher had been a lawyer and a banker. I cannot believe that he and his wife really thought they would succeed with such an amateurish attempt at fraud. One insurer initially fell for it. Later you will see other examples whereby someone invents their CV and financial status, and an insurer readily accepts what they are told.

Chapter 9: Indonesia

Now I will move on to Indonesia. Being an ex-Dutch colony, few Indonesians live in the UK, so you might wonder how Indonesia could be a problem for UK insurers. A lot of them operate offshore from offices in the Isle of Man, Hong Kong and the UAE, for example. They sell life cover and investments in many countries. There was a period when there were several financial advisors introducing clients from Indonesia, and they were not entirely honest in their dealings. When a suspect claim was received, there were no enquiries to be made in the UK, but only in the country of the alleged death.

The first and the largest claim I investigated involved Sutjipto Salim. He took out a life policy with the cover of about $5 million in late 1993 with an international insurer. Numerous accounts and documents were produced to show that he was a wealthy businessman. He paid an annual insurance premium of $33,000 upfront.

Weeks before the second annual payment was due, he allegedly died in a car accident near Bandar Lampung in Indonesia. Although living in Jakarta in Java, he died in Sumatra, the island to the north of Java. Numerous documents were produced in support of this claim, including medical certificates, police reports, cremation certificates, a copy of his ID card, plus a report of his death on the front page of a national newspaper.

So off I went to Indonesia. I arrived in Jakarta and travelled across the city to the old, domestic airport and took the short flight to Lampung. I knew no one in that country and had been unable to make any hotel reservation. I arrived in a small shed that was the airport in those days, and there stood waiting for passengers, a young lady wearing a Holiday Inn badge. I booked a room via her and went off in the courtesy bus to a beautiful, small hotel. The lady spoke good English, and I asked if she could recommend an interpreter for me. She made a telephone call and said that her friend, Nancy, would meet me at the hotel later.

Nancy turned out to be a very educated lady who had studied in Australia. She was an engineer and married to an Australian. Her English was excellent. She agreed to work for me, and we started the following morning.

At the hospital, we met the doctor who certified the death, a very attractive young lady who was about 8 months pregnant. Her story about Salim being rushed to the hospital did not follow a logical sequence. Clearly, I had to be careful while interrogating her in her current state. Eventually, she did agree she had not actually seen the body. A local judge had informed her of the death, provided all the details and instructed her to prepare a death certificate. She agreed to give me a written statement.

Next, we went to see the police and met two officers who claimed to have dealt with the accident. I never believed them, mainly because the accident was allegedly not in their district. They drew me a plan depicting the position of the vehicles etc. Obviously, they were unaware that the claimant had already sent such information to the insurance company. The plan they drew was entirely different.

Then I went to the crematorium. The man whose name and signature appeared on the documents had recently died of cancer. There was an official record of the cremation, and without the presence of the author, it was not possible to prove the entry as being fraudulent.

Nancy knew of the judge who had instructed the doctor, and she suggested that I refrained from meeting with him for my own safety. All the rest of the enquiries were now in Jakarta, and I had a reservation to fly there the following morning. Nancy asked if she could continue to assist me. She was taking her car that night on the ferry to Java and back to her other home and business in Jakarta. I readily agreed.

The next day we saw the accountant in Jakarta who had provided accounts and tax records to show that Salim was a successful businessman. I did not believe the man, but there was no direct evidence to prove he was lying. Later that day, we located Salim's home on the outskirts of Jakarta. There we met a lady, she spoke no English, and she said she had worked for three weeks as a secretary to Mrs Salim. She had heard that Mr Salim had died in a car accident but claimed she had never met him. Currently, Mrs Salim, she said, was away from Jakarta and would be back in about three weeks. The lady was quite insistent that I went inside the house.

The reason soon became obvious. In the main room was a shrine containing lit candles, a large photo of Salim and an urn. The lady obviously wanted me to view these. I indicated to Nancy to get the lady to go into the kitchen for some water. When she left, I lifted the urn. What a shock; I almost dropped it, the heaviest urn I had ever held. It was sealed at the top, so I could not see inside. It had to contain concrete. I refrained from asking the lady if she had any idea of the weight of ashes from human remains. No doubt she would have told me that Salim had been a heavy man!

In Indonesia, there is normally a local man who is responsible for a small area of households. He keeps a list of all residents and takes payment for various tasks such as rubbish removal. I met this gentleman, explained the scenario, and he told me that the lady I had just met had lived there for years with her husband, an accountant. He turned out to be the man I had interviewed earlier who had shown me Salim's accounts. No one called Salim had ever lived there. It was obvious that the accountant had expected me to visit the address used for Salim, so had set up the shrine there.

The Secretary of Mr Salim

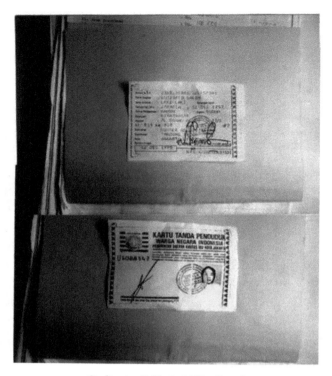

Salim's Official ID Card

Armed with written statements, I decided to interview the advisor who had introduced the business to the life office. I met him and asked him for a detailed, verbal report about how and where he met Salim. He tried to claim that he went to his house without an appointment and met him there. Of course, this could not be true as the accountant lived there, not Salim.

Present during this interview was the insurer's main financial advisor for the Far East. I suggested that someone had invested at least $33,000 to set up this fraud, the initial premium, a rather large outlay. There would also be various added costs such as bribing officials, obtaining an ID card, paying the accountant etc. The total commission payable to the advisors was around $31,500. I suggested that both of the advisors were involved in the fraud and had used their commission payment to help set it up. Naturally, they denied this, but the evidence indicated otherwise.

- - - - - - -

I went to Indonesia about eight times in the next few years. Nancy was an excellent interpreter and used her initiative to help me prove multiple frauds. Several claims were for persons who I suspected had failed to disclose their true medical history. They had actually died but would never have been insured had their medical history been correctly disclosed. Of course, in the UK, our GP (doctor) normally has our complete medical history, but in many countries, no such record exists. In Indonesia, some years ago, people of Chinese origin had to change their names to Indonesian names. I had several claims involving persons who turned out to be of Chinese origin. It was often obvious that the deceased had failed to be truthful when taking out the policy. Similarly, the claimant/next of kin was not being truthful when interviewed by me.

Nancy looked typically Indonesian but was actually half Chinese. Her mother was a Chinese interpreter. Whenever we interviewed persons of Chinese origin, Nancy never let on that she understood their language. I recall one interview where the man's death was perhaps indicative of alcohol abuse over a long time. The sons actually spoke to each other in Chinese, saying that they did not believe I knew their father was a drunk, and they hoped that Dr X had not spoken to me. Later Nancy informed me of this, and a visit to Dr X helped me dispose of that claim. We had countless similar situations involving policyholders of Chinese origin.

Several claims arose in respect of the business introduced by one advisor. It became clear that a gang was insuring sick people who were not expected to live for more than 2 or 3 years. Post-mortems were rarely carried out, so the exact nature of the death was sometimes a mystery. Cardiac failure was the norm. One young man who died turned out to be a street person, a tramp. He had been an alcoholic since the age of 16. There was a lady aged 61 who was the export director of a large Indonesian company, and she died from a sudden heart attack after two years. I proved that she had spent her entire adult life in a mental institution, apart from occasions when she escaped and ran down the road naked. Also, she was actually 75, but someone had obtained a false ID card with the lower age.

Another claim involved a death in India, and this related to Indonesia. A man called Khasim was insured by his employer in Jakarta, Ramesh, a travel agent, for $200.000 plus an additional $200,000 for accidental death. This was in March 2001, and Khasim was said to be a logistics expert working in travel. In July the same year, he died in a hit and run accident outside a restaurant on the coast of Chennai in India. Numerous documents were produced. At the time of his death, he was accompanied by Thiru, the business partner of Ramesh in Jakarta.

We made enquiries in Chennai. There was a record of the death at the hospital, records were held in the hospital's mortuary, and the chief pathologist insisted that this was a genuine death. The police agreed and had detailed records. Thiru was interviewed in India and provided detailed information about the accident. The body had been collected by Khasim's wife and driven about 500 km to their village in India. All of the villagers had attended the funeral, and there was a record at the mosque. A genuine death, one might assume.

However, villagers claimed that Khasim was an unemployed lorry driver. He started repairing rickshaws in the village and then left for Indonesia. So how did a man who repaired rickshaws get a visa to work in Jakarta as a logistics expert? Also, it seemed that apart from Khasim's wife and uncle, no other person in the village had seen his face prior to the burial.

I went to Jakarta and established that there were two insurance policies with local companies with a cover of $100,000 for accidental death. They had instructed a loss adjuster in India to make enquiries, and he reported that Khasim had died as claimed.

In Jakarta, I interviewed Ramesh and Thiru, who had by then returned to Jakarta. There were many discrepancies in their stories about how they employed and arranged a visa for a man who repaired rickshaws. I had met Ramesh previously and was aware that he was involved with the advisor who arranged the policy and other suspect characters there. I suggested that the circumstances suggested that they had insured Khasim in order to claim after murdering him in India. In those circumstances, I told them I had no option but to go to the police unless, of course, they told me the truth.

This ploy worked, and Ramesh said that some years ago he borrowed money from the Indian mafia in Chennai. He repaid them, but they wanted more money. Eventually, they told him to get a visa for Khasim, make out they were employing him in Indonesia, take out life insurance, and they would then fake his death. He was told that if he refused, they would kill his elderly father, who lived in Chennai. Where was Khasim? I asked. He had suffered several heart attacks, was currently in hospital in Chennai and expected to die any day. It was the hospital where his death was faked!

Poetic justice! There had been an unidentified corpse in the mortuary, and clearly, officials in India were bribed to identify the corpse as Khasim. Ramesh told me that his Indian mafia contacts had warned him that I would be travelling to Indonesia to interview him. I have no idea how they could have known this.

I will explain how a man who was in very poor health managed to pass the medical exam and obtain life cover in Indonesia. Khasim, plus nearly all the other insured persons who, although allegedly healthy, had suddenly died, were all examined by one doctor. I did meet her, a stunningly attractive Muslim lady who could have won Olympic gold for lying. She was having an affair with Ramesh, and this piece of information did help him eventually tell me the truth. The doctor worked in a medical centre in Jakarta. I will not mention its name as it is an excellent clinic and was not involved in any fraudulent activity.

When you went there for an insurance medical, you needed to show your ID card in every department so as to ensure that it was the correct person being examined. However, say I went there, said I was called John Smith and wanted an ECG, blood tests, HIV test and so on, then they would not challenge my identity. Assuming I was healthy, I would end up with documents in the name of John Smith detailing all of the tests.

Someone in good health had attended there using the name of the person wanting life insurance. They would have to be around the same age and know the date of birth of the person they were claiming to be. That person would then get various documents showing they had passed all of the medical tests. My corrupt doctor friend would then complete a full medical report using these documents, but she would never actually meet the client. And she was quite well paid for this by the insurance companies.

- - - - - - -

My interpreter, Nancy, moved to the USA. By this time, I was in touch with a large international company in Jakarta, and a lady there assisted me in getting a visa to visit the country. She told me that her friend spoke excellent English and was willing to assist me. The friend lived some distance from Jakarta, but it was inexpensive to fly there. So, I met Ranti, a young, well-educated lady who spoke excellent English. Ranti had never travelled abroad, and I was the first English speaking person she had met. She was excellent, but my work did take longer as Ranti had to pray five times a day.

After a successful investigation, I went out for dinner with Ranti and her friend, who had assisted with my visa. At the end of the meal, they took the uneaten food away in a "doggy" bag. The following day, Ranti remarked that it was obvious that I was surprised by this, but they took the food and gave it to the homeless people nearby. I was most impressed. That evening, I dined alone at the same restaurant and took the food away in a doggy bag. I instructed my taxi driver to find some homeless people. After 45 minutes, the meter was rising, so I gave up and threw the food away. We could not find any homeless people, but they did exist.

Chapter 10: Lebanon

I will move on to the Middle East and start with Beirut. I first travelled there in September 1991, just after the end of the war. Most of the old city was in ruins. You could see where buildings had been bombed and then machinegunned. The Syrians were in charge, and their tanks patrolled most areas. I travelled there with Andy Young, and it was one of only two occasions when we travelled together due to civil unrest. The other trip was later to Iran.

Some pictures of the old city of Beirut, destroyed by war.

Mohamed lived in west London with his English wife. He worked as a steward for British Airways and was insured for about £1.161 million. His wife notified two insurers that he had been killed in a car accident in Beirut in December 1990, having travelled there to visit his sick mother.

I liaised with British Airways as there was, in addition to the life policies, an employee death in service claim and a pension plan. When he was employed by the airline, they were unaware that he had just been released from prison after serving a sentence for drug smuggling. I believe, in those days, it was perhaps not possible to check someone's criminal background status. I actually remembered the case from my days in Customs. Mohamed travelled from Beirut to Heathrow and walked through Customs wearing an airline uniform (MEA, I think) carrying a case of cannabis. He was a normal passenger and had changed into the uniform before going through Customs. BA was also unaware of another misdemeanour that occurred on Ealing Common in London. Enough said about that, though!

I interviewed his wife, a very attractive lady who worked as a stewardess for private airlines. Andy Young also interviewed her on behalf of one of the other insurers by appointment, whereas I had turned up unannounced. Andy met her quite early in the day, but she was dressed to kill! Neither of us believed her, so enquiries were extended to Beirut.

Locals there were pleased to see us and kept offering us drinks, as they were delighted that foreigners were again visiting Beirut after the war. Mohamed had allegedly died in a car accident about ten months earlier. We visited the cemetery, Al Shouhad. I told the man in charge that I was investigating the death of Mohamed, who died in a car accident and who was allegedly buried in his cemetery. There was no record of the death in December 1990, but the man in charge there recalled the name. He searched the records and said that this person was buried there. He had died in a car accident in August 1991, six weeks ago. The man then examined various documents that recounted the story of how Mohamed crashed his Mercedes car and named the exact location, name of the hospital where he died and details of the police station where the matter was investigated. It transpired that he crashed driving a Mercedes. It was a Mercedes in the fake report. He died on the road mentioned in that report, was taken to the same hospital, and was investigated at the same police station. Fate, I wondered?

We decided to visit Mohamed's home address there. It was in South Beirut, still a dangerous place, particularly for Christians and our translator, George, was a Christian and extremely reluctant to travel to that area. In fact, all of the areas we visited were Muslim strongholds, and plenty of Western hostages were held there, including Terry Waite. We went to the home address. George tapped very gently on the door, claimed that no one was in and rushed off down the stairs. I knocked somewhat harder, and the door was opened by Mohamed's father. We were invited inside to meet the family, and they all insisted that Mohamed had died in December 1990. We explained that Mohamed had been granted compassionate leave by his employer to return to Beirut to see his sick mother. The mother was a little surprised and said she could not recall having been ill.

Mohamed's sister was present and was wearing a neck collar. She agreed she had been in a car accident but stated it had nothing to do with me. I suggested that enquiries with the police would obviously show that she was a passenger in her brother's car when he died six weeks earlier. I was bluffing, but it worked. She agreed this was correct, and the family admitted that Mohamed had died the previous month. He had told them earlier in the year that if anyone ever asked questions, they should insist that he had died in a car accident in December 1990.

The claimant in London was arrested by the police and charged with fraud. It transpired that while awaiting the life claims to be paid out, a travel insurance company paid out £15,000. We were actually working for the life side of that travel insurer! Mohamed's wife flew to Paris, met her husband and handed him the money. He used this to buy a Mercedes car in Holland and shipped it back to Beirut. He was driving that car when he crashed and died. Poetic justice, would that be the correct terminology, I wonder?

Anyway, at her trial, his wife said she was threatened by Mohamed's family, had a gun put to her head, so acted out of fear for her life. She was acquitted.

- - - - - - -

In 1996, I investigated another interesting claim in Beirut. A Lebanese man lived in London and took out a mortgage on a property he purchased, plus a life policy with the cover of £230,000. About three years later, he died in one of the best hospitals in Beirut. The medical death certificate showed that he died from cancer.

Examination of the original medical examination report obtained when the policy was taken out suggested that an HIV test should be considered. This was in the days when everyone suspected that HIV would present a serious problem to insurers. When asked to attend a test, the man produced one dated recently and done in a clinic in the UAE. He said this had been carried out in relation to obtaining a visa.

So, I went to Beirut and first made enquiries at the hospital. The staff were helpful, and many doctors and nurses agreed to check the name of the deceased against computer records. They did so, and each person said he had died there, and they all immediately turned off the computer and walked away. I could get no further information other than confirmation that he had died. Interestingly my associate pointed out that the doctor who certified death had recently been on Lebanese television talking about Aids.

I had an address in Beirut for the deceased and went there. A very upmarket property. A maid said that the family were out, and she took my card. I realised that the property belonged to a Government official, and he was related to the deceased. Later that day, I received a telephone call at my hotel from a family member suggesting it would be in my interest to leave the country. I did so.

However, instead of returning to London, I went to the UAE to examine the authenticity of the HIV test report produced when the policy was taken out. The doctor confirmed to me that he had carried out the test, and it was negative. However, the date on the test had been changed. It had not been done just before the policy was taken out but some months earlier. The doctor told me that he personally took the test result to the person in his hotel room. He was shocked to see that he was on the bed with three young, naked men, and there was an ashtray full of cigarette buts. He was aware that the man was a heavy smoker, and the doctor told him that he would need to undertake a further HIV test very soon due to his lifestyle.

Apart from changing the date of the HIV test result, when taking out the policy, he omitted to mention that he smoked about 60 cigarettes a day!

- - - - - - -

I have investigated plenty of claims in Lebanon for both the UK and international insurers. A lot of them were in relation to critical illness, and in most cases, I was able to prove that the insured person never told the truth about his or her medical history when taking out the policy. Several policies were taken by residents of Syria and Lebanon via international brokers in Damascus and Beirut. I recall one day being driven from Damascus across the border, through the Bekaa Valley and across the mountains to Beirut. An intriguing journey that I suppose one can no longer do safely.

- - - - - - -

There is another claim which was very different from the norm. I will refer to the man as Mohammad. His family had considerable business interests in Nigeria. Many years ago, Lebanese people travelled to West Africa, started a variety of businesses and remained there.

Mohammad spent various periods in Lagos, Beirut and at his large London home. He took out two life insurance policies for a cover of £240,000, a considerable sum of money in 1992. He attended a medical examination for one insurer and was deemed to be in good health. Within a few months, he allegedly died from a heart attack when visiting his father in Beirut. Several Lebanese documents were produced in relation to the death and burial in Beirut. In parts of the Arab world, residents have a registration card that shows what we would describe as the "family tree". When you are born, your details appear on your father's registration. When grown-up, you are provided with your own registration. Later your wife and children are added to this. Upon death, this is cancelled by the civil registrar.

81

Mohammad's documents appeared to have been cancelled correctly, and this is rare in cases of fake claims.

I wanted to interview his wife in London, but she claimed to be observing "Iddat" and would be in "purdah" (wearing a veil). This is a procedure often carried out by Muslim women after the death of their husbands and means they cannot speak to a male from outside the family. I did not believe this as my enquiries indicated it was a family who enjoyed alcohol, socialising and fashionable European clothing. I suspect that the wife was reluctant to see me, but why, I wondered?

I was about to travel to Nigeria, so I decided to undertake some enquiries while in Lagos. I located the family's house there, a rather up-market establishment. There I met the deceased's father and brother, and they explained in detail the death of Mohammad in Beirut. I did not believe them as it would be unusual for a healthy individual in Beirut to suddenly die, be buried without delay with for no post-mortem to be carried out.

I spoke to the guard outside the home, to other local people and to Lebanese businessmen locally. Everyone was aware of the death. However, while some said he died in Beirut, others thought he had died in London.

Upon return to the UK, I rang around the registry offices in London enquiring if the death of Mohammad had been registered there. I provided the date of the death. Westminster Registry confirmed that his death was registered there and that he had actually died in a London Hospital. Within hours of his death, permission was given for the body to be shipped to Beirut. I obtained a copy of the death certificate that showed his death to be Aids-related. I spoke to the doctor who certified the death and was assured that this person could not have attended the medical examination as he was far too ill. A stand-in, perhaps? Had his UK death certificate been provided to the insurance companies, they would have required a detailed report of his medical history in the UK. The result would have shown that he failed to disclose his illness when taking out the policies. By obtaining a death certificate from Beirut, the true cause of death was concealed. Had I gone to Beirut, realised that there was a genuine grave there then - - - would I have successfully located the truth? I will never know.

These claims were unusual, and I would not like to give any indication that Aids was ever prevalent in Lebanon. I enjoyed my numerous visits there and met some wonderful people. I also enjoyed some excellent meals along the coast and in restaurants in the mountains. How I would have enjoyed travelling there before the war when one could ski in the morning in the mountains, and then swim in the sea in the afternoon.

Chapter 11: Iran

I travelled to Iran many times. However, my associate there left the country, and I then had to utilise the services of an Iranian lawyer. He was reluctant to assist me in obtaining a visa to travel there. However, the political situation in Iran deteriorated to such an extent that it would probably have proved dangerous being a foreigner and making enquiries there.

My first trip there was in 1993, and Andy and I travelled together as there was much unrest in the country. The case involved an Iranian man living in the north of England with his English wife. He had allegedly died while swimming in the Caspian Sea in Babolsar. The wife produced a bundle of documents in Farsi (the Iranian language) in support of the death. However, she had a son attending a local school, and neither he nor the school had not been informed about his father's death. The wife's story did not tally with the information on the various documents.

In Iran and most countries in the Middle East, numerous official documents are prepared when a person dies. For example, if a doctor at a hospital certifies a death, then there will be official declarations and stamps on the certificate he issues. These will state that the doctor is registered with the Ministry of Health, that the hospital is registered, that the civil registry is authorised and so on. It will often end up with a stamp from the Ministry of Health, from the local Ministry of Foreign Affairs (if to be used overseas) and then perhaps the document will be stamped by the British Embassy. The forms were full of colourful, official stamps and signed by various ministries and the British Embassy. The death certificate in this instance consisted of several pages. I pointed out that the British Embassy was only certifying the authenticity of the stamp and signature of the man in the Ministry of Foreign Affairs. He, in turn, was only certifying the signature of the Ministry of Health official. There was no way the British Embassy could know that the person was really dead. The doctor completed a certificate about the cause of death, and every official thereafter assumed this was true. Had one checked with the various Ministries and the hospital, the death would have been certified as genuine.

We arrived in the early hours of the morning in Teheran. We went to change some money at the airport, and I suggested to Andy that we only changed £20. I saw the "official exchange rate" and calculated that the hotel we had booked would cost about £500 a night. This did not include food and well, as for alcohol! We met our associate, and his first remark was, "I hope you never changed any money?" The unofficial rate was something like eight times the official rate.

We had a medical report from a doctor in Babolsar, and this had been used to register the death and obtain numerous official documents in Teheran. Our first stop was the British Embassy. I had a map of Teheran, so I asked the taxi driver to take us to a certain place near the Embassy. I was concerned that a taxi pulling up outside the Embassy containing two Europeans could prove problematic. We then walked in the direction of the Embassy but stopped in our tracks when we saw a hostile crowd try to storm the building. Being aware of the anti-British and American sentiment at the time, I had ensured that my briefcase had Air France stickers.

We spent two days making enquiries in Teheran. Prayers were regularly broadcast from speakers in every street. The noise was horrendous, and I got through a record number of paracetamol tablets! I learnt that all demonstrations were organised by the revolutionary guard. Loudspeaker announcements were made about the people showing their disgust at the infidels at the British Embassy, so people would go and throw stones and chant outside the Embassy. It would then be announced that many true believers were showing their feelings and emotions against the tyrannical, British outside the Embassy. Within minutes there was a large, baying, stone-throwing mob outside the Embassy yelling about infidels and so on.

We visited several Iranian Government offices to try and see if the documents we had were genuine. We were passed from desk to desk, office to office, bureaucrat to bureaucrat. No one could make a decision, and we were only told that the forms we had were official documents. Therefore the man must be dead! We formed the impression that people were afraid of being seen giving assistance to foreigners. Several times we were told to put our request in writing, and I think I lost the will to live when eventually I was asked to write to the Ministry of Silly Walks, or something like that!

We interviewed various family members in Tehran, and they explained how the body was returned from Babolsar and buried in a village some miles away in an unmarked grave. Their stories just did not tally!

Andy decided that as it was safe in Tehran, he would leave me there and continue to Pakistan, where he had miscellaneous enquiries. He must have foreseen the journey I would have to Babolsar. At the airport, he was searched by a revolutionary guard who demanded a present. He suggested taking Andy's Omega watch to show gratitude to the wonderful revolution. Eventually, he noticed some tapes in Andy's bag, remarked how much he liked Western music – even Abba was preferable to the noise broadcast every day in the streets there – so he took a tape. Andy was in the process of learning Spanish and, had the guard been able to read English, might have noticed the label, "BBC teach yourself Spanish". So, if you visit Iran and meet a guard who speaks Spanish with a BBC accent …

Anyway, very early morning, I left on the 4 to 5-hour drive to Babolsar. It was winter, and deep snow laid around Tehran. We had to cross the mountains, and it was so cold that I wore two coats inside the car. Luckily the driver brought a shovel in the boot, and it came in handy a couple of times. We stopped at the top of the mountains for tea. Then we went downhill all the way to the Caspian Sea. In about 45 minutes, the temperature increased by around 25 C. I have a photograph taken of me in shirtsleeves picking an orange from a tree by the sea.

We had not been provided with any police report, and enquiries at the local police stations in Babolsar failed to locate any record of the death. We waited and, late that afternoon, eventually met the doctor who had certified the death. He had no records and only stated that someone brought a man to his small clinic and said he had drowned in the sea. His clothing was wet, and he appeared to have died from drowning, so the doctor issued a certificate using the name given to him. He had no idea of the name of the person who brought him to the clinic. The body was taken away, and the doctor said that was all he knew. Absolute nonsense because had there been such a body, it would have been sent to the Government mortuary, and the police would have been informed. While the local police agreed with me, they were reluctant to do anything, not because they were dishonest but probably out of fear of being seen helping a foreigner.

We then drove back late evening to Tehran, a frightening journey. Much of the road is a dual carriageway, and we drove on the right. Regularly cars came towards us on our side of the road with minimal, if any, lighting at all. If a driver entered the dual carriageway instead of driving until the next intersection to go in the opposite direction, they would just drive on the wrong side of the road for several miles. It was like driving upcountry in Nigeria, except the temperature was 40C lower!

The Road across the Mountains

What a Change in Temperature

Upon returning to Tehran, I again interviewed the relatives and their stories once more varied. There was sufficient evidence to refute the claim. About a year later, the insurer received a letter from the "dead man". He claimed that he had been held a political prisoner in Iran. Unbeknown to him, his family there had informed his wife in the UK that he was dead. She made a claim on his life policy, believing that he had died. She was shocked, he claimed, when he was released and made his way back to the UK. His wife, he insisted, had been tricked. I did think of asking the Iranian authorities if he had been held a political prisoner … but the thought soon left my mind! They are many interesting anomalies in his story. What did his relatives in Iran think would happen if he was released within a few weeks? He held a UK passport, so why was no report made to the British authorities about his incarceration? If only I could find someone to trick me into receiving several thousands of pounds!

Leaving Tehran after that investigation was a nightmare. The actions of the Revolutionary Guards were not so much security as daylight robbery. The main departure lounge was closed, and a planeload of passengers was kept standing in a small room. Eventually, we boarded the Swiss Air flight. Once it took off, a large number of female passengers removed scarves and veils and took on a completely different appearance. One poor lady was in tears. She said that the Guards had taken all of her jewellery, claiming that she never declared gold or diamonds when she arrived in Iran. Clearly, the Revolutionary Guards were a rule to themselves. Could you imagine a group of young thug-like soccer supporters dressed in leather jackets being given machine guns? If so, then you have an accurate picture of the people supporting the People's Republic of Iran's revolution at that time!

After the aircraft took off, we were offered drinks. *"A bloody large Scotch,"* I remarked to the steward. The man next to me said, *"give me a huge Scotch, please"*. The man next to him said, *"Give me the f------ bottle!"* In fairness, subsequent journeys to Tehran were very civilised and hassle-free.

- - - - - - -

Between March and June 1992, two Iranians took out two life insurance policies with a cover of £700,000. They were involved in property developments in Lancashire in northern England and required the cover to back loans from the bank in the UK. Allegedly on 2nd November 1992, one of them, Mr Ghulam, died in Iran and his partner, let's call him Zavi put in a claim. It transpired that Ghulam was a resident of Iran and visited the UK on business trips. However, the insurers were aware of this when issuing the policies but should not really have offered cover to an overseas resident. Ghulam had allegedly been knocked over by a car and killed in the city of Shiraz in Iran. Until the Islamic revolution, Iran had a tradition of winemaking that stretched back centuries. It centred on the ancient city of Shiraz. Hence the origin of the Shiraz grape.

I interviewed Mr Zavi in England and suspected that the claim was not genuine. It took ages to obtain a visa for Iran, and by the time I travelled there, a lawyer in the UK had commenced action against one of the insurers. One insurer sent a letter to the hospital via a courier company asking if the death certificate was genuine. It was signed by Dr Fard, and the hospital responded, confirming that Dr Fard had indeed certified the death.

I arrived in Tehran and the next day flew to Shiraz. My associate in Tehran originated from Shiraz, and his family lived there. It is an interesting city, and the inhabitants made me very welcome. I arrived during Ashura. This is when the Shia Muslims celebrate the martyrdom of Imam Hussein, the grandson of the Prophet Muhammad. Men and women march along the street dressed in black, chanting and banging their chests. Some undertake bloody flagellating rites, banging themselves with chains and cutting themselves with knives. In Shiraz, those I saw did not go to such extremes. That day I think I was probably the only Christian in Shiraz. I was told that part of the festival is to give food and drink to the poor. People kept offering me food and drink. My associate suggested that they thought I was poor as I was a Christian, but the locals all smiled when making such gestures. They were being humorous.

We started at the hospital. It was a vast place and is a teaching hospital. Staff claimed not to know Dr Fard but pointed out that hundreds of doctors passed through the hospital. We were allowed to examine the death register that contained the names of everyone who died there. We found an entry for Ghulam indicating he died on 2-11-92. He allegedly died in a car accident, his death was certified by Dr Fard, and he was buried in the main cemetery. The information tallied with that provided to the insurers. The record showed that his ID card had been cancelled before a death certificate was issued there.

We next went to the cemetery and found a record for the burial. We were shown the grave, and the inscription bore Ghulam's name, age and date of death. We then went to the address in Shiraz shown on the documents. It transpired that this was the address of his business partner. He provided detailed information about Ghulam and his death. He took us to see Ghulam's wife, parents and other family members. They all spoke about his death and burial. We spoke to neighbours and local shopkeepers. Everyone seemed to know that Ghulam died in an accident.

My associate told me that I was wrong this time and that it was a genuine claim. I suggested that perhaps I was not wrong. I insisted we returned to the hospital. We did and again examined the death registry. We commenced at the page showing Ghulam's death on 2-11-92. I asked my associate to examine all pages after that date. A while later, he jumped up and stated that Ghulam had died twice! He died in similar circumstances on 20-1-94. The only difference from the first entry was the name of the doctor certifying death; it was not Dr Fard.

We went back to the cemetery, and the man in charge was extremely helpful when I explained the situation. He examined all of the records and then realised that the grave space had been purchased on 2-11-92. The payment for burial was made in January 1994 when Ghulam really died. Payment had been made then for the grave to be inscribed, and the man in charge stated that someone must have bribed the staff to put a false date on the grave.

My associate was amazed and queried why I went back to the hospital. I explained that Ghulam's business partner appeared to be talking about a different funeral than Ghulam's family. In my opinion, the partner was inventing a story about a funeral for the fake death. The family knew nothing about the fraud and were telling me about the genuine death and funeral. There were some anomalies between the two stories. One person said that 30 people attended the funeral, whereas his wife said that 400 attended.

I was staying in a small, modern hotel, and my associate insisted that I had dinner at his family house. I went there that evening, and a beautiful young lady walked down the stairs and greeted me. My associate said I had met his sister earlier at the hospital. I had met someone dressed in black wearing the full burka, but what a difference! Moments later, another similarly dressed young lady appeared. He had twin sisters. I was then asked what I wanted to drink. Coca Cola perhaps, I said. But what did I want in it? Ice was all I could think of. Then I was asked if I wanted vodka, gin, rum or whisky? Subsequently to that, I had been offered alcohol by many Iranians in their own homes. I later staggered back into my hotel, hoping that the manager would not notice anything untoward and contact the authorities.

Being concerned that I might be stopped leaving the country and my papers relating to the death(s) might be confiscated, I gave my associate copies of all of them just in case. I was asked numerous questions by officials on departure, but they never examined any documents.

Ghulam's Two Graves

- - - - - - -

I have undertaken quite a few investigations in Iran, but one I particularly recall was a claim I investigated mostly in London. Mr Hossein took out a life policy with a cover of £266,000 on 20th April 2012. He did so via a telephone call to the insurer's Freefone. A few weeks later, his wife notified the insurer that her husband had died in Iran on 10th May 2012 after a fall. The death certificate indicated he had died from a stroke.

I interviewed Hali, the wife (or was she the widow?), at her tiny council flat in London. Present was a relative who spoke excellent English and a solicitor. It appeared that Mr Hossein had claimed political asylum in the UK, and his wife later joined him from Iran. He only did occasional part-time work, and they survived on benefits. However, they managed to go back every year on holiday to Iran. Mr

Hossein had also managed to obtain a new Iranian passport, despite claiming asylum in the UK!

The solicitor had told the insurance company that they could arrange for a post-mortem to be carried out on Mr Hossain. A ridiculous comment to make as the body had already been buried in Iran. This made me suspect that the solicitor was acting rather suspiciously. "No win – no fee" came to mind. The first items given to me were photographs of the body and the grave and a video of the burial. Clearly, they were out to impress upon me that he was dead. Not normal and, in my view, over the top!

Numerous documents were provided, including an email showing that Mrs Hali had changed her return flight from 26th April until 3rd June. When I asked why, she told me that after her husband's death, there were various formalities to attend to. But he didn't die until 10th May, so how could she know about his death in advance? It was an error, she said, and there were other reasons for this.

Later I rang the solicitor asking for the originals of certain documents, and he insisted I had already taken them. I had not done so. In Iran, all documents relating to a death, the family, their marriage, birth etc., if for use abroad, need to be translated by authorised translators and then legally notarised. All documents relating to his birth, passport, ID card etc., had been duly translated and notarised. Irrespective of whether he had died or not, these documents would not change. However, all documents relating to the death, such as post-mortem, police report, burial etc., had only been translated but not notarised.

There were numerous points telling me that this was not genuine. Mr Hossain took out the policy on 20th April 2012. His passport indicated he was in Iran at the time. It was taken out via a Freefone number. Since when did a UK Freefone number work in Iran? I was certain that someone took out the policy after Mr Hossain's death, and that person had been in the UK.

It proved very difficult to get a visa to go to Iran as my associate there had emigrated. Meanwhile, the family's solicitor in London had commenced proceedings against the insurer. I had been using a lawyer in Tehran to investigate travel claims, and he agreed to investigate this for me and travelled to the south of Iran. Yes, I had been correct. Hossain died on 20th April 2012 after falling at a shrine, and the cause of death was shown as a stroke. All of the documents produced relating to the death, those not notarised, were false. Within 2 hours of the death, someone rang the insurance company and took out the policy. Quick thinking indeed.

- - - - - - -

I have arranged for quite a few travel insurance claims to be investigated in Tehran. Surprising how many young ladies walk into a wall or fall over and break their noses. The "before and after" photographs are intriguing. Cosmetic surgery is a very successful business in Tehran. Of course, travel insurance only covers an emergency, not cosmetic surgery.

I have found Iranians to be very friendly, hospitable, intelligent people. Many eminent surgeons in the USA and Europe originate from Iran. I would love to travel around the country to see different regions. It is a pity that perhaps 2% of Iranians control the people and lifestyles there.

Chapter 12: Some Unusual Scenes

Note. I took some of these photos, and over the years, contacts have also sent some to me. If you recognise any of these, then please accept my gratitude.

I Gave This Place a Miss

Maybe I will take the bus after all

Who lost the ladder?

The name of a new town perhaps?

Didn't want a drink anyway!

Do you deliver to London?

Took ages to have a shower

A monkey wrench

A Big Mac please

The new iPoooooood

A road sign in Taiwan – can rats there read?

Hotel porter in Malawi

Big Kenyan melons

Snails in Ghana – a local delicacy (don't tell the French)

Farewell at a hotel in Tanzania

Armed guard at hotel in Tanzania

A roadside "café"

Well done or medium rare?

Lagos can be hazardous

What bridge?

A very special offer

Fascinating Havana

Think I will walk

Chapter 13: Nigeria- Travel Problems

I never thought I would go this far without another mention or four about Nigeria. I have just come across an article I wrote in 1994 and thought it worthwhile repeating part of it here. I was travelling regularly then to Nigeria and noted that fewer Europeans or Americans were venturing there. The Government banned foreign exchange bureaus, and currency could only be exchanged at banks, a procedure to test the patience of the most intrepid traveller. However, one scam used at a bureau was for them to say that one or more of your notes was counterfeit, so the manager had to ring the police. It was suggested that it would be a good idea to leave before the police arrived. Of course, the note(s) was not counterfeit, and they were hoping you would disappear, leaving your money behind. The official exchange rate was about 33 Naira to a pound sterling. Unofficially it was at least 65. The black market flourished, particularly among the Muslim traders on Victoria Island. Sometime later, the bank at the airport was robbed, so the authorities closed it—quite a clever idea in effect. To stop bank robberies, close the banks.

At times there were serious shortages of petrol leading to long queues at filling stations and fighting amongst customers. The country has oil but not the refining processes that regularly worked. Police officers had not been paid for months so regularly extorted money at roadblocks. I always sat in the back of a car and tried to conceal my white face. Otherwise, I would be asked to pay for a radio licence or a fine for the tyres having different brand names on them. Regularly in a hire car, my driver was stopped when entering Benin City and "fined" for not having a radio licence!

My enquiries often took me across the country to Benin City, Owerri, Calabar, Warri and Port Harcourt, and this was one horrific journey I made in May 1994. Calabar is close to the Cameroon border, and immigration checkpoints lie in wait for any poor foreigner who dares to travel in that area. Approaching Calabar, I was stopped at an immigration checkpoint and asked to produce my passport and visa. I was aware that there was no requirement to carry these with me, plus the possibility of them being stolen was high. I did have a copy of the passport etc., but to no avail. I had to explain to each immigration officer, in turn, the reason for my visit. Rather than ask me outright for money (dash), it was their way of forcing me to surrender and offer dash. I had to make a written statement, and they did not even read it. I was told I would have to wait there for two days while someone brought my passport from Lagos.

Eventually, I gave in and enquired how much they wanted. They said there were 16 of them, so they wanted Naira 1,000 (about £16). I was promised a safe return journey; I had to return on that same road from Calabar. As we approached the checkpoint on the return, I laid on the floor of the vehicle. As we passed them, officers pointed at the car and started shouting – they had lost Naira 1,000 that I am sure they planned to extort a second time. Luckily, they were not armed.

Soon after, we were stopped by a group of men who were armed. They placed wooden stakes containing nails across the road. This mob, most of whom spoke at the same time, told me I would need a sanitation certificate and special pass to drive through River State. I suggested they spoke to the driver, but it was clear that I was their target. They flashed various badges in front of me and claimed they were state officials. A gun was pointed at me, and local council officials are not usually armed! I was shown various documents detailing "motor sticker, advert, reg township permit, inter-state development, cooperative, mobilisation, occupational survival, municipal, oil and land erosion, pollution, mineral producing areas, express educational, trespassing, road maint (sic), ownership, capitation levy", and so on. I was told that the fee was 3,500 Naira (about £100 at the official rate). It was impossible to obtain any lucid response to my questions; they just shouted that I should give them money and pointed the gun in my face. I decided not to query the **capitation levy** in case they suggested they might have misspelt the word and missed off "**de**" at the beginning!

They claimed to be from the local government, and I asked to see their boss. I was told they could not leave their official post – a bench under a tree next to several empty spirit bottles. They became violent and removed the rear seat from the car. They opened the boot and started to search my bag. I stopped the man and asked him to be patient while I paid him the money. In the bottom of the bag was the equivalent of about £300 in Naira. In those days, credit cards were of no use upcountry, and everything had to be paid in cash. Before leaving Lagos, I always changed a large sum of money in order to survive, as in those days, changing money upcountry was difficult and dangerous. I still had hotels and food to pay for at least another three nights. Had the man seen the money, he would have stolen it all. When travelling in Nigeria, I always kept four £50 notes in my shoe just in case!

Having been stood in the sweltering heat for an hour, I paid them and then quickly replaced the rear seat and moved the wood plank from the road. The main man insisted that I signed the receipt before I could leave. However, one man still insisted that I paid him a sanitation fee. He handed me the receipt, and we drove off with his arm still in the window. He tried running alongside, shouting a demand for money; the amount decreased as we went further along the road! Looking back, I do hope he was not dismissed by the local government for failing in his duty! Bastard!

What was really written under "Mobile?"

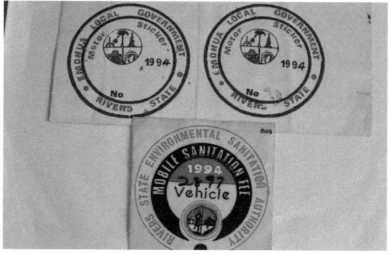

If such taxes were payable in River State, there would have been violent demonstrations with worldwide TV coverage!

I am now licensed to carry a toilet in River State!

After leaving this, we came across an army roadblock. I was told to wind down the window, and a drunk officer placed the muzzle of his machinegun close to my nose. He was sweating profusely, shaking, and there was a strong alcoholic aroma. There was a piece of string attached to the trigger and wound across his shoulder. He pointed to a large bottle of water on the floor and demanded water. Quite a reasonable request, I thought, in the circumstances.

My driver bought fuel on the black market from a man on the beach in Calabar. He had waited for 2 hours in a queue at a garage. When he reached the front, there was a power cut. In Benin City, we queued at a garage for an hour, and the fuel ran out as we reached the front of the queue. We found another queue, and when nearing the front, a Nigerian Airforce Officer drove past us and then reversed his car to the front of the queue. I pointed out to the officer the error of his ways. His response was that as a foreigner, I was being "bad-mannered" and he could have me deported. The petrol pump attendant asked me to keep quiet and not upset the man. He was worried that the officer might return with a lorry full of troops and beat up the staff, a regular occurrence, I was told.

On that eventful trip, I met a doctor who had obviously written a fake death certificate. He eventually admitted the errors of his ways and agreed to give me a written statement. However, he pointed out that it was the norm for doctors to charge a fee for medical reports, so he would only give me a statement on payment of Naira 10,000 (£160 unofficial exchange rate). I told him what he could do with his statement, but I doubt he followed my advice.

Chapter 14: Democratic Republic Of Congo (Zaire)

Zaire, now known as the Democratic Republic of the Congo, featured in one quite exciting investigation. Why do African despots include the word "democratic" in the title when renaming their countries? I have only visited Kinshasa, the capital, on one occasion. It was far more frightening than Nigeria. This was partly because they speak French (a sort of French anyway). In Nigeria, being mostly English-speaking, I could always try and use a certain amount of logic when confronted by people. Although I speak some French, I found the accent very difficult to comprehend in Kinshasa. I have since worked in a multitude of French-speaking countries in Africa. The locals never use two words to greet you when they can use 20! I often equate African French as similar to Chaucer's English. Clearly, the French, the Belgians in this instance, also taught Africans how to ensure that bureaucracy survived!

Anyway, I have proved a large number of deaths in the DRC to be false. I have briefed an associate there to undertake the enquiries in the past 3 or 4 years. This was because whenever I had a case requiring investigating there, civil unrest took over. Recently I wanted to travel there, but the road from the airport was closed, and it was not possible to move around Kinshasa. I have also proved claims to be false without the need to travel anywhere other than the UK and Ireland. In 2017 I proved that a lady who allegedly died in Kinshasa had been working in a hotel in Dublin after her alleged death. She had been using different names.

My one trip to Kinshasa was in late 1990. Mr and Mrs Boketa lived in south London, and in March 1987, they took out a life policy with a cover of £250,000, a very large amount in those days. Allegedly Mrs Boketa died of a heart attack in Kinshasa in January 1990. Numerous supporting documents were produced in support of this.

I never managed to interview Mr Boketa as he was always away on business, or so he claimed. I could only speak to his solicitor. There was a delay in dealing with this, so he commenced legal proceedings against the insurer. Our enquiries in London suggested this was a fraud. Their real surname was not Boketa but Mongo; I will continue here using the name Boketa. They were illegal immigrants who claimed asylum, lived on benefits and proceeds from thefts using credit cards. Mr Boketa was said to own an import/export company, but we could find no trace of any business. According to the solicitor Mr Boketa was informed of his wife's death by a telegram from Kinshasa sent five days after her death and after she had been buried. Most unusual!

I spoke to neighbours in south London, and the information provided by one lady proved later to be very instrumental in me eventually locating the "dead" lady. The neighbour said that whenever she spoke to Mrs Boketa, her husband would intervene and take her back inside their flat. The neighbour had not seen her and her two young children since December and had asked Mr Boketa about them. He maintained that they were inside their flat there; this was three months after her alleged death!

I was aware that Mrs Boketa had left London on a one-way ticket to Kinshasa just after Christmas. According to the neighbour, for about six days after Christmas, she returned home every afternoon in a taxi, carrying numerous bags from the best London stores. She had been to the sales. I established that Mrs Boketa had maxed out numerous credit cards and had no apparent way of repaying the debts. Also, the day she left London, her husband notified one card company that her card had been stolen. It seems that Mrs Boketa had no intention of coming back to the UK. The neighbour did say that Mrs Boketa was tall and glamourous, and she likened her appearance to Naomi Campbell. You will see the relevance of this later. Note: Naomi Campbell was not involved in this.

I went to Kinshasa and stayed at the Inter-Continental hotel (now called by another name), said to be the only safe place for foreigners. Whenever the national flag was raised in Kinshasa, one had to stand to attention if in that vicinity or risk being arrested. It was an offence to take photographs anywhere near a government building. A contact in the insurance industry had provided me with a name of a private investigator, and I met him at my hotel. This man had been a police officer in Kinshasa and had spent several months being trained by the FBI in the USA. However, he spoke only a few words of English, so my French came in useful. This investigator, Victor, suggested that it would take at least ten days to investigate the case, no doubt working out his fee for such a period. Eventually, I agreed to pay him for three days and then review the position. I forgot to mention that I worked 15 hours a day!

We started at the registry office, and there was a full record there of the death. Similarly, there was a record at the cemetery, but this did not show where the grave was. At the hospital, a record existed in the emergency room, but the record appeared not to be in exact chronological order. I met the doctor who had certified the death, Dr Bulu. He was a surgeon and recalled that the day Mrs Boketa died, he was in the emergency room temporarily, as the duty doctor was absent. He could not give any reasonable explanation as to why a surgeon would attend the emergency room on a Saturday afternoon; that is when she allegedly died. He told me he dealt with many deaths and could not recall the death of Mrs Boketa, so he could only rely on the medical file made at the time. I was shown the file.

I went to the mortuary, and there was a record there of the body arriving on 9th January, the day she died, and leaving on 10th January. The burial allegedly occurred on 13th or 14th January. The record was not clear, so where was the body kept? I interviewed the matron in charge of the emergency room, and she was very nervous. She told me that there was not a record of the death made until sometime later. She was told that a UK insurance company sent a letter to the doctor asking about the death. Dr Bulu gave her all the information about the death, and she made a record.

I had managed to obtain a completed questionnaire from Mr Boketa via his solicitor in London. This showed the person who witnessed the death, Mr Elo and provided his address in Kinshasa. I went there and met his brother, who stated that Elo had moved out and he did not know his whereabouts. The brother said he had never heard of Boketa and had no knowledge of any such death. We later located Elo at his workplace. My associate told him he was from the Ministry of Graves, or something to that effect. He added that he was trying to locate the grave of Mrs Boketa, and records showed that Elo was involved in her burial. Elo laughed and stated that she never died, and it was an insurance scam. Mr Boketa had set it up, bribed officials and was back in London. Elo knew that Mrs Boketa was in a rural village about 10 miles from the city. While this interview was taking place, I was sat outside in my associate's car. I observed him returning to his vehicle with a man in handcuffs. He had informed Elo that this was now a murder investigation, and he was taking him to the police station.

The police agreed to take action. Elo was put in a cell, and we set off for the village. This was about 8 pm, and it was dark. The police had no vehicle, so four officers crammed into the back of my associate's old car. We arrived at the village, and a large crowd quickly gathered nearby. Everyone was dressed in loincloths, old shorts etc., except one person. In the middle of the crowd was one very tall, beautiful lady dressed in designer clothing, and she walked through the mob as if on a catwalk. When spoken to by the police, she agreed she was Mrs Boketa. Police tried to arrest her, but the crowd moved menacingly toward them. Mrs Boketa agreed that she would attend the police station the following morning.

The mob turned violent, and numerous stones were thrown in our direction. By this time, I was lying almost on the floor of the car. My associate had always locked the vehicle, even when standing a few metres away. Such an old car, and I could not comprehend his logic until now. From under his seat, he removed a small machinegun and fired over the head of the rioters. The police returned rapidly to the car, and we sped away with two officers clinging to the roof. Was I delighted later that night to have a large Scotch or four back in the safety of my hotel!

Mrs Boketa did not show up at the police station the following day, so a large contingent of officers, now armed, went to the village and arrested several members of her family. Villagers were told that once Mrs Boketa attended the police station, they would be released. Not sure what legal procedure was being followed, but who was I to query their actions?

My associate told me that according to the police, I would have to remain in Kinshasa for a few days until Mrs Boketa turned up. Also, I was informed that I would be responsible for paying the police for their overtime. I paid my associate, telling him that I would need to change some more money the next day. Luckily that evening, he and several police officers had tickets for an international soccer match in Kinshasa. About half time I was on a flight back to Europe. Had I stayed there, I suspect that I would also have been held ransom until I distributed large sums of money. I often wonder if Mrs Boketa's family are still in custody there? Anyway, Mr Boketa fled the UK and is probably ripping off companies somewhere else in Europe under a new identity.

- - - - - - -

Another interesting claim involving Kinshasa came from a diplomat in London. He was accredited to an Embassy in London. He had insured his son, who then died at a hospital in Kinshasa after an accident. I tried to visit his wife in London, but she would not see me. Diplomatic immunity was mentioned, but I do not believe the 1961 Vienna Convention on Diplomatic Relations meant that insurance companies should not investigate such a claim.

Numerous documents were produced in support of the claim for the son, Jean, who was said to be a student. The agent for the insurance company was, I thought, the best person to interview in order to get some background on the son. I went to his house in London, and his wife told me that he had travelled that morning to Africa with his friend from the Embassy. The trip was arranged only that morning. It transpired that the insurance company had indicated to the agent that they were asking me to travel to Africa to investigate the claim. Talk about walking into a dangerous trap! I was extremely annoyed, or at least would have been, had I not acquired valuable information from the agent's wife. I asked her about Jean and his studies in Europe (I was guessing) and asked if she had met him. She said he was studying at the University of Liège in Belgium and had recently been back in London.

So, while the diplomat and agent were busy in Africa awaiting my arrival, I was on a flight to Belgium. I went to the student's union at the university and said I needed to speak to Jean but had lost his contact details. I had his passport photo, gave it to the representative and said that I would return to the union bar at 6 pm. I promised €50 to whoever could bring Jean along. At 6 pm I returned, and there was Jean waiting for me. He was the son of the diplomat, and I decided not to ask him if he had died. Clearly, he knew nothing about the claim.

The matter was reported to the police in London, and it was eventually agreed that the diplomat would meet with the police but not be questioned. He would only make a verbal statement. A complete waste of time in effect. His statement read along the lines, *"In 1972 my wife gave birth to Jean at the main hospital in - - (Africa). On the same day, my mistress gave birth to a son at a different hospital, and she also named him Jean. In March 1990, I went to the British Embassy in - - - - to obtain papers to travel to the UK as a diplomat. As I walked out of the Embassy, a young man asked me if I knew who he was. Yes, I said you are my other son Jean. He said he knew I was going to live in London and asked if he could travel with my family and me, and I agreed. Mr Saunders went to Belgium and met one of my sons called Jean. It was the other one who sadly died in an accident in Africa."*

The diplomat could not be questioned. I'm sure you can think of many interesting questions. How did Jean, the son with the mistress, know you were going to London? How did he know you would be at the British Embassy that day? How did he recognise you? How did two sons travel to London on the same passport? (Note: only one passport had been used for Jean to travel to the UK). The son seen in Belgium is the one in the passport photo, a copy of which you gave the insurance company when he allegedly died? Where was the passport then for the other son? How did one Jean travel to - - - (Africa) when the other one called Jean had his passport with him in Belgium.

This explanation was like something out of a fairy tale. However, the Ambassador swore an affidavit backing up this story. I believe that the diplomat was asked to leave London.

Chapter 15: India – Pakistan – Sri Lanka - Bangladesh

Over the years, most false claims have originated from India. It has a huge population, and many people of Indian origin live in the UK. I will devote the next few pages to India, Pakistan, Sri Lanka and Bangladesh. Andy Young and other colleagues use to undertake most of the investigations in these countries, but I have personally been involved with hundreds of cases and visited them all a few times.

I recall a few years ago travelling through the Pakistan Punjab area. There had been heavy rains, and rivers and waterfalls were in full flow. I was amazed by the beautiful countryside. I stayed in a hotel in Abbottabad and realised about a year later, when American troops flew in there in a helicopter that it was not far from Bin Laden's home. I have also spent time in Karachi, and there I played golf on a link's course. I was surprised to find such a facility there. However, the 19th was perhaps not as enjoyable as normal. Another orange juice, sir?

I have travelled long distances through Bangladesh, a country with an abundance of lakes, rivers and floods. In the UK, we refer to Indian restaurants, but many of them are owned by people originating from Bangladesh. A large percentage of Bangladeshis in the UK in the restaurant trade come from Sylhet in the northeast. Visit one of the hotels there, and you will hear Bangladeshi people speak with Geordie, Scouse, Cockney, Scottish etc., accents. The food is very enjoyable. However, the journey from Dhaka to Sylhet takes 5½ hours by road and is so dangerous. Coaches all seem to have a deadline to reach their destination, and if this involves overtaking on bends, forcing oncoming cars off the road, then so be it.

I always enjoy travelling to India so long as it is not Mumbai where one can sit for hours in traffic. The Sikhs in the Punjab in the north of India are particularly friendly, and they do enjoy a drink. I take a bottle of whisky for my associate there and have a drink with him and his colleagues. He removes the cap and throws it away, claiming, "we won't need that again!" Plus, the Indian food in this region is very enjoyable.

My first visit to Sri Lanka was during the troubles, and it was not safe to venture out in the evening. Many buildings had been bombed. Since then, I have been there on holiday and what a wonderful country. Forests, nature reserves, animal sanctuaries, parks, flora, long stretches of golden sand: I could go on.

Again, I have managed to prove claims from these countries to be false without needing to leave the UK. I recall a lady claiming that her husband had passed away in India in 2008. The claim was against a fairly old policy with a cover of £60,000, not a claim that would rise to the top of the suspect list. I interviewed her in England and had to go to the local library to find someone to translate. The man did an excellent job. He knew the deceased but suggested that the word "deceased" was perhaps premature, as the man was serving a sentence in Hull Prison in England! He was said to be an alcoholic, and it was known locally that his wife wanted to be rid of him. I am not sure that this was the best method, though.

The claim I am about to mention is a very sad case, and I ended up feeling sorry for the claimant. Mrs M took out a policy in August 2007 for £593,000. Later, her husband provided numerous documents to indicate she died in a car accident in Pakistan in April 2008. There were countless photographs of the accident scene, the car and the insured, plus 3 of her family who also died. I have seen numerous fake photographs over the years, but these were clearly genuine, and one of the ladies in the car was definitely the man's wife

When I went to meet the husband, there was a top of the range, fairly new Mercedes in the drive, and he told me he was the chauffeur for the director of a public company. Mr

M had three very polite, well-educated young children, two of whom appeared in a photo crying next to the wife's body. Mr M wanted me to interview them, but I refused. In conversation, he explained how his wife had converted to Islam from Hinduism 20 years ago, and her parents subsequently refused to speak to her. He said he had no idea where the parents lived, and they would be unaware of the death. He claimed his late wife's passport had been surrendered to the authorities in Pakistan. Something was not right here.

I managed to locate the parents, and they said that their son-in-law had, in fact, brought the three children along to see them and inform them of their daughter's death. They could not recall the date but thought it was prior to April 2008. I spoke to a neighbour of Mr M who also suggested the death was before April 2008. Mrs M's GP had not been informed about her death and had not seen her for some time. I was certain that Mrs M had died but suspected that there was something wrong with the claim. The lack of her passport being unavailable was unusual. It would not have been surrendered to the Pakistani authorities.

I went back to see Mr M. Instead of a new Mercedes, an old car was in the drive bearing a taxi licence plate. He was actually a taxi driver. Unlike my first visit, he was not expecting me. I suggested that he had, in fact, taken out the life policy after the death of his wife and had changed the dates on all of the documents. Eventually, he agreed. His wife died in April 2007. He returned to the UK and took out the policy in August 2007. A year after her death, he took all of the documents back to Pakistan, had them re-issued and had the dates changed to April 2008. He cried and then changed his mind insisting that she had really died in 2008. He did withdraw the claim. He and his wife were previously insured, but the policy lapsed through non -payment of premiums. I really felt for him and his young children.

A regular scene on Indian roads

The Pakistan Punjab – stunning scenery

A tractor in Pakistan

An Indian coach

A doctor in Sri Lanka claimed he treated a lady for 5 days as an inpatient, and then she died. This was his "clinic". One small room, no bed, no toilet. I think he was perhaps not telling the truth!

One of the most interesting but complex claims involved the death of a businessman in the Indian Punjab. I cannot really change the man's name to protect the guilty because, although a Sikh, he had a Muslim name, and this is very relevant to proving the claim to be false. He was using the name Aamer Gull, a Muslim name and his relatives all used the name Singh, a Sikh name meaning lion. Between February 2002 and November 2007, he took out life policies mostly to support mortgages on houses, hotels and other businesses. He allegedly died in a village in Punjab in India from a heart attack in November 2008. At this time, the value of his life cover was £2.2million.

His nephew submitted various claims assisted by a legal representative in Birmingham. My investigation lasted several months. I made numerous enquiries in the UK and India and interviewed a large number of his relatives. He had an Indian passport, and this was allegedly lost in the post when relatives sent it back from India, so I only received a copy of the main page. I visited the Indian High Commission in the UK and, after making enquiries, they agreed that the passport had been issued there, but there was a "discrepancy" with the paperwork. I was informed that Gull's real name was Sa---- Singh, there was no evidence of any official name change, and they were attempting to establish how the Gull passport was issued. They agreed that a Sikh could not be called Aamer Gull. Interestingly, the surname of some of his family was also Sa***. I was led to believe that Sa*** Singh was Gull's brother! Gill is a Sikh name, and it seems that somewhere along the line, his false name was misspelt as Gull. Interestingly Gull is a Muslim name for a female! Quite an error somewhere along the line!

His very elderly parents had lived in the UK for around 50 years but claimed not to speak English. I interviewed them with their legal representative, and they claimed they were in India when he died. They went into some detail, and the mother actually cried. I spoke to them, and many of the family members and no one could explain how they had a relative with a Muslim name. There was one exception. A family member said it was known amongst them that he had been using a false identity for years.

In India, I went to a large number of villages and met family members. The death was registered when a relative told the village headman that he had died. However, the village headman did not know Gull. In fact, he registered his death under the name "Gill", a Sikh name and was surprised when asked to change it to "Gull". Various family members insisted that Gull had died there, but there were numerous discrepancies in their recollections of events.

There was a medical death certificate issued by a Dr Maxxx at Bilga Hospital. This is a large, fairly modern establishment outside Phillaur set up by a charitable trust. I was told that Dr Maxxx had not worked there for some time and should not have issued a certificate using the hospital's letterhead. I rang Dr Maxxx, but he refused to meet with me. I managed to find the name of the clinic where he worked part-time, and I went there to see him. Eventually, he told me he had met a man at a function who said that a relative had just died, and he needed a death certificate. Dr Maxxx duly obliged him issued the certificate but never saw a body.

I managed to find elderly farmers who were related to Gull. They identified him from the passport photo and said he was Sa*** Singh. They had seen him in the Punjab in November 2008, and he had returned to the UK; he certainly never died there, they added.

Before reporting this case to the police in the UK, I received some interesting information. A representative of one of the insurance companies met a former employee who had arranged one of the policies for Gull. When he was told he had died, he laughed. His daughter, he said, was working at one of the premises owned by Gull, and he was very much alive and still running the business. I knew the name of the business and had informed the insurers of his whereabouts. It was decided to leave matters to the police.

The case was reported to the police, and after a long period of time, they decided not to take action as there was "insufficient evidence". I think it was too complex for them to handle. The claimant's legal representative tried to pursue the claims. I interviewed him at length and left him in no doubt that this was a fraud. However, some months later, I learned that he was trying to arrange probate. I spoke to the probate office, who said that if it was a fraud, then it was my duty to report it to the police! It rather frustrates me when so often I see fraudsters unchallenged by the authorities.

- - - - - - -

Another interesting claim also involved the Punjab. Ravi Singh, who allegedly worked in a shop in Northampton, took out 12 life policies, mostly via the internet, with a total cover of £2.22 million. This was in 2007, and he allegedly died later that year in Amritsar. A claim was initially only sent to one insurer by Ravi's employer, Jas. I interviewed Jas at length, and it was obvious that he was involved in fraud. He denied the existence of other policies, and when later confronted, he stated he had not had time to go through Ravi's papers. Ravi, according to him, was a distant relative. With one exception Jas was the executor and beneficiary of the policies.

We made enquiries in India, and as is usual, the death was properly registered. Someone had produced a medical death certificate from a hospital in Amritsar, and this proved to be a false document. Ravi's family was seen in India. His real name was Amand, but he had changed it to Ravi. He was at that time in hospital in Delhi as he had a liver problem due to excessive drinking. Someone from the UK had rung the family there and said that Ravi was going to be murdered. Subsequently, two men had called at the family home twice looking for him.

Ravi returned to the UK while we were on the way back from India. He appeared to fear for his life, as he had only just learnt about all the life insurance taken out without his knowledge. We met him, and he stated he only knew about one insurance policy; he had no knowledge of the ones taken out online. Ravi had recently changed his name by deed poll and obtained a new UK passport bearing his new name. He also registered with a new GP so that his record of alcohol abuse would be concealed. He said he wanted some life insurance so that money could go to his family in India in the event of his death. Ravi was concerned for his safety because he realised that his ex-employer, Jas, had insured him for a vast sum.

It is amazing that one can change one's name by deed poll and then obtain a passport in that name. To my knowledge, no official record is kept of such changes. I might try and see how easy this is, so see what name I use at the end of this book!

- - - - - - -

Now back to Pakistan for a claim in respect of a man dying in a traffic accident in Karachi. I will call him Hamay Khan, a 31year old man supposedly living in England for 3 years when he took out a policy with a cover of £775,000 in 2010. The policy was written into trust, and one of the trustees was a lawyer. I will call him Mohamed. Mohamed wrote to the insurer about the trust and, in the same letter, mentioned that Khan had travelled urgently to Pakistan to see his sick mother. Mohamed said he would keep the insurer updated. Must remember to tell my insurer when I next go abroad! Insurers would need thousands of extra staff if everyone wrote telling them about their overseas travels. Was this a warning that a claim was imminent????

Mohamed next informed the insurer that Khan had died in an accident in Karachi in January 2011. The policy had only been in existence for 8 months. I visited Mohamed, who had an office in a mosque in England. He explained that Khan was a student, helped at the mosque and had various jobs locally. Mohamed appeared to know few details about the death and actually asked if the insurer would pay for him to travel to Pakistan to obtain information. I do not believe he was actually joking. There was a file on his desk, and this suggested that research had been carried out with 12 insurers to obtain the best deal. I could not fathom why he would have these documents. It was also claimed that the passport was with the police in Pakistan. I believed nothing he told me, so off I went to Pakistan.

It was claimed that Khan was knocked over by a car about 6 am while on route to the mosque and died instantly. He was staying with his brother, who lived in Karachi, having travelled there from the family home in Dera Ismael Khan in the north of Pakistan. I first checked that the death registration certificate was genuine. It was, but I could not understand why the death was registered at an office 40 km from the brother's home there. The death had been certified at a small, private clinic. The body, as the death was accidental, should have been sent to one of 3 government hospitals there for a post-mortem, and the police should have been informed. No doubt a bribe prevented the man at the registry office from asking too many questions.

There was a document from a police station, and an officer there confirmed that it was a form issued allowing a body to be transported out of Karachi. There was no record there of any accident. The form was issued by a constable, and he was summoned to the chief's office. He recalled issuing the form and showed me the original medical death certificate that had been given to him by the deceased's brother. Most unusual, particularly that he happened to have this document handy when I arrived. Had someone at the registry made a phone call about my enquiries? That was the only enquiry made by that time.

I rang the brother and later interviewed him at my associate's office in Karachi. He stated that he was telephoned by his brother's friend, who said he had been knocked over by a car and was dead. This was around 6:30 am, and he was at Manxxx Medical Institute. The brother went there, arranged for EDHI to take the body to his home. He went to EDHI's office, bought a coffin and took his brother's body in the coffin back to their village on the roof of a public bus. He said the journey took 10 hours, and his brother was buried in the village late that evening.

In Pakistan, EDHI is the ambulance service. EDHI confirmed to me that they had not collected the body or sold a coffin that day to the brother. I later obtained written confirmation of this.

Later that day, I received an email from the insurer in the UK containing a police report from the station I had just visited. Mohamed, the lawyer, had just sent this to the insurer. The next day I returned to the police station, and the officer in charge confirmed that the report was false. I did, however, examine the station's date stamp, and it was identical to the stamp on the report. I was informed that the brother was at the police station and had admitted that Khan was not dead. There was a small mosque attached to the police station, and the brother was there praying. The senior officer said that the constable had just handed a phone to him, and there was a call from a lawyer in the UK. He told the officer that Khan was dead and asked him to take care of things. It was clear to me that the constable was involved.

I had been to the Mannxx Medical Institute, a rather posh name for a slum. The doctor was away from Karachi, and I had spoken to him twice on the phone. He said he would return early to Karachi to see me. He never asked why someone from the UK wanted to see him. Obviously, he already knew. The constable also appeared to be aware that I was seeing the doctor that evening because he said he would accompany me there, and the brother would meet us there. I interviewed the doctor, and he insisted that a body was brought in dead early one morning, he issued a medical death certificate, and the brother took the body away. He could not explain why he had not obeyed normal procedures, and not informed the police and sent the body to a government hospital. During this interview, the constable was present but kept leaving the doctor's office. Each time he left, the doctor received a telephone call, and it was obviously the constable ringing him, telling him what to say.

The body was not taken away by EDHI, and they supplied no coffin. The brother claimed that the body was taken on the roof of a coach and took 10 hours to arrive at Dera Ismael Khan, the family's village. The journey takes 18½ hours and is 1553kms! I was able to establish that bodies cannot be transported that way.

Dera Ismael Khan is in an area where I knew that the police would not allow me to enter. Terrorist activity prevailed there at the time. I decided to send my associate to the north of Pakistan to make enquiries there. He did so very successfully and, in the circumstances, proved to be brave. He located the family home, and all the neighbours said that Khan was alive, and they had seen him around in the past few days. At the family home, he met another brother who confirmed that his brother died as claimed. However, it appeared that he was notified of the death 2 or 3 hours before he actually died! The brother spent ages trying to bribe my associate. He claimed that I had told people in Karachi that I was a policeman, I had offered the police money, plus offered the doctor the equivalent of £7000 and a trip to England if he admitted the death was fake. I am not sure exactly how I could invoice the insurer for such an amount, so the brother must have been alleging that the insurance company was corrupt! The brother told my associate that British people were against Muslims and Pakistanis in particular. He was offered the equivalent of £35,000 to report that the claim was genuine. How bloody stupid! What about my enquiries in Karachi? There was no way this could be genuine. The brother spoke about Bin Laden, and my associate falsely gave the impression that his report would assist them – he was concerned for his safety and wanted to leave. My associate asked about the grave and was told to wait while they arranged to have a headstone made.

Very early the following morning, my associate went to the cemetery, and there was no record of any burial for Khan.

My associate saw the brother and other relatives approaching the cemetery, so he decided to leave and get away from that area.

The matter was reported to the police in the UK. Surprise, surprise! We were told that the CPS decided they could not take action unless we found Khan alive. Mohamed, the lawyer who submitted the claim, was making various allegations to the insurer and approached the Ombudsman, so it was decided to interview him again and make additional enquiries at the mosque. Near the mosque, I spoke to an Asian man who lived near Mohamed. He said he had never heard of Khan and that no one from the mosque had died in Pakistan. I then met Mohamed walking nearby. He was quite abusive and said there were several serious allegations about my conduct. He agreed that we would speak on the telephone later and arrange an appointment.

Later, I met the Mosque committee and was informed that Mohamed had been told to vacate his office there. There appeared to be a serious problem, but I will not go into that here. I was informed that the alleged deceased never worked or attended the mosque, and they knew of no member who had died as such in Pakistan. Had he attended there as was claimed by Mohamed, then special prayers would have been said if he had died. I was provided with a written statement.

I had also been provided with a letter provided by Mohamed about Khan's studies. I proved that the college mentioned in the letter had no record of such a student.

I rang Mohamed and agreed to meet him at his new office. He told me that he was using this office temporarily while his office at the mosque was being decorated. What a liar! He kept stating that I was corrupt, and he made several ridiculous allegations. I had, according to him, told everyone in Pakistan I was a police officer and offered people money. I pointed out that I had given everyone my proper business card and how could the Pakistan police think I was a police officer. I went through some of the evidence, but Mohamed was not interested. He just wanted to continue making stupid allegations.

I would love to meet this man again should he try and put in another claim. He is one of the most unpleasant persons I have ever dealt with, and it saddens me that he can continue to act as a solicitor!

- - - - - - -

Bangladesh might feel left out if I did not include a claim from there. Mr Ahmed took out a total life cover of £730,000 in 2009. His wife notified insurance companies that he had died in a road accident near Sylhet in Bangladesh in

December 2010. She provided a death certificate, police and post-mortem reports. I interviewed her at length and completed a questionnaire about his death (the death abroad questionnaire I mentioned at the beginning of this book). She provided information about the cemetery, names of his relatives, people who attended the burial etc.

It was clear that she and her husband were in debt. She agreed they had debts of £45,000, and she said she had to send £1,500 to Bangladesh for the funeral. I did not believe her and suspected that this was a false claim. Another suspicious pointer was that Mr Ahmed rang one of the insurance companies, said he was going to Bangladesh for 2 or 3 weeks, and asked if he would still be covered!

So off to Bangladesh. I met my associate in Dhaka, and the next day we took the bus to Sylhet. That night I stayed in a decent hotel full of very pleasant Bangladeshis from the UK with Scottish, Geordie, Welsh, Cockney accents etc. The food was excellent, plus they were allowed to sell beer in the hotel.

The medical death certificate and post-mortem report were allegedly from one of the largest hospitals in that area, Osmani Medical College. The Medical Director confirmed that the documents were false and there was no record of the death there.

I went to the police station and was eventually told that the officer who allegedly made the police report did not exist, and there was no record of such an accident. The claimant, on the questionnaire, showed the police officer in charge of the case as Officer Rahman, and she provided his mobile and office number. The office number belonged to the police station, and later I realised that when meeting the inspector, I had also met Rahman. I rang the mobile number and spoke to him. He agreed we had met earlier, and he insisted he knew nothing about such an accident or death. According to him, many people knew his mobile number!

At the cemetery, there was no record of the burial. I located the family's home and made enquiries in the vicinity. The family was well known, and their son from London, Ahmed, had returned there on holiday. People had seen him there recently.

I sent my associate to the house, and he spoke at the door to Ahmed's mother, who insisted that her son died in an accident. I then went and spoke to her, but she closed the door in my face. On the questionnaire were the names and addresses of people who attended the burial. I met most of them and was given varying stories about Ahmed dying there.

Eventually, I went back to see the mother and suggested that she might prefer talking to me than the police. She invited me in, and I met Ahmed's wife, the lady I had interviewed in the UK. She and her mother-in-law insisted that Ahmed was dead and accused me of harassing them and causing them ill health.

Later that evening, I received a phone call from Ahmed's wife. She was concerned that I would go to the police. She then agreed that her husband was alive. A police officer had telephoned them and warned that I was in Sylhet making enquiries; officer Rahman I assume. Her husband had left immediately and gone to Dhaka. She told me she was extremely distressed and had done this because they had no money in the UK. After submitting the insurance claims, she informed her parents in London, and they were angry with her. She said she intended to return to London in the next few days, and I promised that I would not inform the authorities in Bangladesh about her actions. A few weeks later, she rang me and asked if I could send her husband's passport to her as he wanted to come home!

- - - - - - -

A quick mention of Sri Lanka. You will recall the Boxing Day tsunami in 2004; thousands of people were tragically killed. The UK insurance companies were faced with a large

155

number of claims, but in most cases, the claimants would not manage to obtain any supporting documents for months. Along with the reinsurance industry, we set up a system to meet claimants, ascertain the relevant information, and settle the claims without the delay of waiting for death certificates to be issued. On many occasions after meeting with claimants, I drove home with tears in my eyes. Horrific stories, and I often wonder how people could get over such horrendous events.

Unfortunately, after such events, there are always people who try and cash in. After 9/11, I was informed that the police in the USA set up a squad to assist insurance companies in dealing with a large number of false claims for *missing* persons. I recall a ferry capsizing on a lake in Ghana, and a lady from London was reported as missing, presumed dead. I managed in Ghana to prove she was nowhere near that lake or ferry on that fateful day.

A lady in London claimed that her husband was killed in Sri Lanka in the tsunami. Our investigations in the UK suggested that this was unlikely. However, an investigator working for one other insurer, let's call him Tom, said that he had evidence that the man was alive. The other insurers who we represented put our enquiry on hold to see what evidence was available. Tom had contacted them from Sri

156

Lanka with news that he had proved fraud. The matter dragged on, and eventually, we saw what he described as 'evidence'. He had written a report stating that a man, not identified, told him he had seen him (the dead man), he thought he might have travelled after the tsunami, someone said he was a crook, someone thought he was in another area when the tsunami hit the coast, and he didn't believe he was dead. None of this would ever stand up in a court of law. There was no evidence, and the wife in London pursued her claims more vigorously with the help of a solicitor when it became obvious that the insurers had no evidence to refute the claims. We continued and made "proper" enquiries in the UK and in Sri Lanka, took written statements from witnesses and eventually, the claim was dropped.

Going back to the tsunami, another two men of Sri Lankan and Indian origin rang insurers reporting that a member of their family had perished in the Tsunami. I rang both of them, stating that I needed to interview them. Within days both notified insurers that their missing family member had turned up! Miracles!

Although maybe out of context in this section, the investigator Tom featured in another case later. He had approached an insurance company with ideas about how he could investigate their claims. It was that company, now no longer in business in the UK, who decided to engage him and first used him on the tsunami claim. Later, a claims manager I knew took over at this company and came to see me. They had a claim for a man who had died accidentally in Nigeria. Tom investigated it, and the company refused to pay on the grounds that it was a fraud. The family of the lady had issued proceedings against the insurer, and the court case would take place in London very soon. I proved that the claim was very genuine. Tom was a crook!

Chapter 16: Ex-Soviet Countries

Russia and various countries from the old Soviet bloc featured in my travels. I once had a claim for a death in Sakhalin, an island in the far east of Russia, just above Japan. It is now a major oil-producing area. The claim was for a ship's captain who lived there and was allegedly murdered. To get there, I flew to Moscow, transferred airports and flew for 8 hours across Russia. It was winter, and the entire journey was above snow-capped mountains.

I arrived there, and deep snow lined the roads. I checked into a new, very modern hotel that seemed to have been built about two centuries after the rest of the city. The claim was genuine, but the main concern was that the man took out the life policy, knowing that his life was in danger. This did appear to be the case, but there was insufficient evidence to really prove this.

The return flight to Moscow was full, and I sat in one of the eight business class seats at the front. In those days, I occasionally smoked, so I had to go to a seat at the rear for this. Most of the passengers were oil workers, and by the time we arrived in Moscow, every single drop of alcohol on the flight had been consumed. At the rear, there was a small section for smoking, but this was ignored. All ashtrays were overflowing, and empty bottles were being used as ashtrays;

in places, the floor covering started smouldering. By the time we arrived, a large number of workers had formed a choir and were in full flow. An eventful journey.

I also carried out another investigation in Moscow. A man there was acting as a financial advisor, selling small pension plans to locals on behalf of an international insurer. The pensions had a small life benefit, and quite a good number of people died. With one exception, they were dead, but people did not appear to realise there was a requirement to inform the insurance company at commencement that they were ill. The policies were being sold illegally on a Ponzi style scheme. Policyholders were promised that by introducing new clients, they would receive a commission that would pay their own premiums, plus an income. I realised that investors were mostly poor and were selling household items and their old cars to join the scheme. I interviewed the man behind this, an Azerbaijani and felt quite threatened when I left his office, followed by two henchmen.

A week or so later, I had meetings with international insurers based in the Isle of Man. I was ordering a coffee near the flight's boarding gate at Heathrow, and lo and behold, my Azerbaijani friend was behind me in the queue. If only I could have taken a photo of his face. He was en route to the Isle of Man to see if he could represent other insurers in Russia. I left the building there of an insurer as he entered. I don't speak Russian, but I think I could translate what he said. The second word was "off".

- - - - - - -

I travelled several times to Ukraine, and my first visit was to Dnepropetrovsk; I think this was where they first made the cruise missile, and it was some years before foreigners could travel there. Again, this was a claim for an international insurer, and the man had died from cancer. Only Austrian Airlines flew there at the time, and I arrived 2 days before my luggage. The airline gave me the equivalent of $100 in local currency to spend on clothes etc. I needed it as it snowed all the time I was there and was bitterly cold. Via a European insurer, I had made contact there with an employee of an insurance company who spoke good English. He took me to a huge, Soviet-style department store. On one floor I bought a toothbrush, on the next floor toothpaste plus a razor, on the next floor shaving foam and so on. I was there for nearly 2 hours. I did buy a fake Nike waterproof coat, they must have sold out of genuine ones, and 25 years later, I am still wearing it when gardening. With sufficient clothing and washing gear, I had enough local currency remaining to buy several beers for my new associate and me.

The city was extremely impoverished, apart from my hotel, an old building that had been modernised. It was difficult walking along the streets because one could not see the potholes under the snow. I recall an old lady sat on the pavement, dressed in rags. She had a bunch of bananas, about 7 in total, they were covered in snow, and she was trying to sell them.

I suggested that evening to my associate that we went to a typical Ukrainian bar for a beer. He said there were no such places, but during the summer, there were some bars near to the river that were busy. We went to such a place, and it was clean and comfortable. We had an excellent beer plus salmon roe (poor man's caviar) and snacks: very pleasant. In such places, I always like to see the bill before ordering more drinks. It cost under £2, so I ordered another beer or three. Suddenly loud music sprung up, and there was a rush of air behind me. It was a scantily dressed young lady doing a pole dance. "Perhaps we ought to have another beer", said my associate. Of course, I did not agree with him but did not want to risk incurring his wrath as we had to work together. After dancing the lady came to speak to us. By this time, she was wearing a fur coat. She wanted to practise her English and was an extremely well-educated person. She was a classical pianist and said that she had a young daughter, lived with her mother and could not survive financially without dancing in this bar. She had married an Asian from the UK, but he had, she thought, abandoned her. It transpired that he lived not far from me in England. I suspected that he was already married when he later married in Ukraine. I refrained from contacting him, but I was very close to doing so.

The man who died had failed to disclose his true medical history to the insurance company. This area was not far from Chernobyl, and the information given to me by doctors there about the number of persons suffering still from cancer was quite disturbing.

- - - - - - -

I had an extremely unusual, false claim for a death in Georgia (not the one in the US) and, a couple of years later, another similar claim with some of the same characters involved. In respect of the first claim, Angela lived for a while in Dubai with her partner, Vladimir. He was from southern Russia, and she was Ukrainian. He insured her for $300,000, and a short while later, she died while on holiday in Rustavi in Georgia. It was claimed that she had a sudden heart attack, was rushed to the main hospital in Rustavi but was dead on arrival. The pathologist carried out a post-mortem, the police were involved, and the body was shipped to southern Russia for burial in Rostov-On-Don, from where Vladimir originated.

I travelled to Tbilisi in Georgia and went with my interpreter by car to Rustavi, a journey of almost one hour. In the Soviet days, Rustavi was famous for having one of the largest steelworks in Russia and large chemical factories. It was known as "Metal City". The steelworks were vast and extended for a mile or so, but it appeared that the only part of them in operation was based in prison there. Most of the inhabitants of the city were unemployed and lived in large, basic tower blocks. The city was impoverished, to say the least. Alcoholism was rife, and vodka was probably cheaper than milk. When communism ended in Russia, parts of

Georgia seemed to end up in a time warp. To think that Angela went there from Dubai for a holiday!!!

I went to the mortuary at the main hospital, and there was a record thereof her death. A post-mortem was carried out, and the body was removed almost immediately. I interviewed the elderly pathologist, and he insisted that she had choked to death after eating. I went to the office of the Public Prosecutor, and a young officer recalled the death and showed me his record. He remembered that it was the pathologist who rang him about the sudden death. By the time he arrived at the mortuary, the body had been removed, and this was unusual. However, the pathologist insisted that there were no suspicious circumstances.

I established that there was only one undertaker's office there controlled by two elderly ladies. They still seemed to think they were working under a communist government and claimed they were not permitted to give me information. Eventually, they decided to assist and informed me that coffins had to be obtained from their office. I indicated that the claimant had stated that the body was shipped to Rostov-On-Don in southern Russia on a train for burial. The ladies said that permission would be required from them, but they had no record of Angela. They stated that the train journey took at least 20 hours, and apart from needing official forms signed by them, they would have needed to buy a coffin.

Vladimir had provided the address where he said Angela was staying with relatives. It was an apartment, but we only had the block, not the actual apartment number.

It was quite a run-down place surrounded by muddy streets. I must have knocked on every door, but no one had heard of Angela or of the death of a young lady from Ukraine. I went there several times. A group of men, all unemployed, sat at the rear of the apartments every day drinking vodka. They promised to ask around about Angela. Unfortunately, I returned there the second day after lunch. They were all drunk and incapable of uttering a single, coherent word. The following day I went there before midday, and they were almost sober. A very sad state of affairs, and I did have a lot of sympathies as there was no work in that area.

I went back to the pathologist and interviewed him at length, but he would not change his story. He was driving a fairly modern Mercedes car, and I was informed that he had just imported it from Germany. The cost would have equated to several years' salaries! He spoke some English, and I had a quiet word to one side. It was obvious. I said that he had been paid to issue a false certificate. His response was that if he stated as such, he would be killed.

I also interviewed staff at the office where the death had been registered. When staff members examined the register, they seemed a little perturbed. Eventually, someone recalled that the man who registered the death was a police officer from a town about 10 miles away. I went there and was pointed in the direction of the officer's home. This place was as poor as Rustavi. In the midst of poverty was a new mansion, a real oasis in the desert, and it belonged to the officer who was the chief of police. I went to his office in the police station and interviewed him very briefly. He claimed to have no knowledge of the case or the registration and said I was speaking to the wrong man. I decided to leave as I felt somewhat ill at ease, particularly when he laid his gun on the table in front of me. Outside his office, my interpreter, a rather nervous lady, said she was glad I believed him as she was afraid. I said I never believed a single word he said but could see that she was shaking with fear, so I decided to end the interview.

I had several meetings with the Public Prosecutor. He gave the impression that he did not believe the death was genuine but seemed reluctant to act.

Later I interviewed Vladimir in Dubai. There were many discrepancies in his explanation of events. The claim was not paid, and Vladimir, he had left Dubai, hired a "no win no fee" lawyer there. The lawyer submitted numerous documents to the court there. There were statements certifying that the death certificate issued in Georgia and the subsequent registration documents issued by the registration authorities in Tbilisi were genuine documents. There was a marriage certificate issued by an orthodox priest in Donetsk in Ukraine stating that Angela and Vladimir were married there, forms showing she was buried in Russia, declarations about her passport and so on.

Such documents must be legalised in order to be produced in a court in the UAE. This means:

- Documents should be certified by the public notary in the country from which they originate
- All documents should be in English or Arabic

- Diplomas of higher education must be certified by the Ministry of Education

- Certification is required in the UAE consulate in the country that issued the document

- Certification in the UAE Ministry of Foreign Affairs in Dubai

- Translations must also be legalised in the country in which they are translated.

So, the lawyer produced a large number of official, legalised documents. The courts seemed to believe that Angela had to be dead because of what was written on these legal documents. The fact that there was not one word of truth in them was irrelevant. They were all legalised!

I went back to Georgia and obtained further evidence, and this had to be legalised. I made enquiries in Donetsk in Ukraine. There I located Angela's real husband. He was a miner, and they were not divorced. I interviewed the orthodox priest who had certified that Vladimir and Angela were married by him. Perhaps he was tricked, was his defence. He first insisted that he had married them, but he could not be sure as his office had burnt down, and all marriage records were destroyed. Very convenient!

It was becoming an expensive investigation as there was in those days no UAE Embassy or Consulate in Georgia or Ukraine, so I had to arrange to have all the papers attested and legalised in Moscow. It was like a competition; who could get the most legalised documents?

Vladimir lost his case, but his lawyer appealed, and the case went to court in Dubai. We arranged for the Public Prosecutor in Rustavi to travel to Dubai to give evidence. The case was about a week before Christmas. On the first day, the case was adjourned due to translation problems. Everyone in the small courtroom spoke fluent English, but the proceedings had to be in Arabic. This dragged on, and I feared I might have to spend Christmas there.

The case started, but the court only sat for about 3 hours a day. Vladimir did not have to attend. Surely cross-examination of the claimant in such circumstances would assist the court to make a decision. I was giving evidence about all of my enquiries when the judge stopped me and, in English, said, "Mr Saunders, if Angela is not dead then why did Mr Vladimir produce a death certificate?" I was totally shocked and could see that the various lawyers in the court were of a similar disposition. My response was, "Sir, so that he could steal $300,000 from the insurance company."

171

I managed to get home before Christmas, and the insurer won the case. I have no faith in justice in the UAE. Recently I had another case in which a wealthy member of one of the controlling families in a smaller emirate died. However, I proved that he omitted to mention on the application form that he smoked 60 cigarettes a day, had a heart operation, and had numerous other health issues. The claim was refuted, but there was an appeal. I was asked to send a copy of my report to the court. I duly printed one from my computer, signed it and sent it by courier. This was not acceptable as my signature varied slightly from the original and was in a different place. They insisted that I again copied the original. I tried to explain that the report was on my computer. When I printed a copy and signed it, this became an original. No, I was told we must have a copy of the original. This went on for some time!!

- - - - - - -

I could not believe it when later I was sent another claim for a young lady dying in Rustavi. She had lived in America and was insured with several companies for the equivalent of about £500,000. A man originally from Georgia claiming to be her husband, let's call him Lawrence submitted the claims. She, I will call her Alexa, had allegedly fallen into a river when out walking. It was the time of the year when the snow melted in the hills, so the flow of the river was rapid. Her body was allegedly located an hour or so later downstream, where it had been washed up on the rocks.

So back to Rustavi. It was the same pathologist and the same public prosecutor's office. At the mortuary, I was shown a small file and allowed to take a photo of the picture of the lady, Alexa, allegedly lying on the mortuary slab soon after the accident. Do you notice anything about the photo?

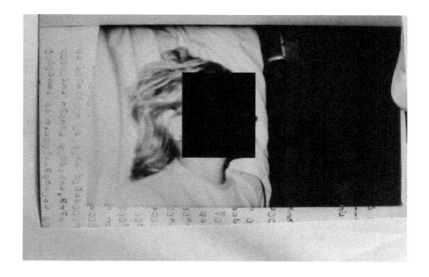

She is still wearing at least one earring; her hair was not dishevelled and plus her face appears to be unmarked. Yet, she was swept downstream in fast-flowing water and ended up on the rocks. The photo is insufficiently clear for an expert to state that this is not a dead person, but several medical examiners have expressed their suspicions.

I went to the public prosecutor's office, and once again, no official there had actually seen the body at the mortuary. The pathologist had reported the death to the police, and they spoke with the next of kin, Lawrence and treated the death as an accident. I went to the cemetery, there was only one there, and the man in charge informed me that his office had recently burnt down in the middle of the night, destroying all the records. Very convenient! He could not fathom out what might have caused such a fire. This man was genuine and was really suspicious about that fire.

His destroyed office

The following day my translator received a call from the manager of the cemetery stating he had located Alexa's grave. One of the workers told him he remembered where the body was buried. The grave was unmarked. I pushed a

174

stick into the ground, and there did appear to be a box down below.

As the claim was in America, I had not been able to interview the claimant and obtain information about family members and addresses in Georgia. I did get in touch with Lawrence who was in Georgia and met him at the Sheraton Hotel in Tbilisi. He was extremely aggressive and made various accusations about my investigation. I could not establish how he could have any details of my investigation unless someone I had met had been in touch with him—the worker at the cemetery, of course, who knew the whereabouts of the grave. Lawrence acted like a member of the mafia and insisted on showing me his gun. I had arranged for someone to follow him to try and establish where he stayed in Tbilisi, but he left the hotel at speed and was clearly not wishing to be followed.

I returned to the mortuary and obtained from the register details of other bodies there at the same time as Alexa. I then examined another register that showed bodies being removed to the cemetery. Alexa's body was shown. However, an elderly lady had died, was in the mortuary but there was no record of her ever leaving there. Clearly, she had left as her body was no longer there. I managed to find out where this lady had lived and spoken to neighbours. She was an alcoholic, had no family, died at home, and her body was removed to the mortuary. No one attended any funeral, and they had no idea what happened to her body. It was assumed that the state must have arranged her burial. I made further enquiries at the mortuary and in the office that arranges to take bodies to the cemetery. The old lady had disappeared. No, it was obviously her grave I had seen! As she had no family to attend her burial, it was a simple task to remove her body from the mortuary under the pretext that it was Alexa's. I tried to convince the public prosecutor's office, had meetings after meetings but could not get them to be very active. I mentioned exhuming the body and was told it could be done but would take time.

The parents of Alexa in America were only told about the alleged death by Lawrence after I commenced enquiries in Georgia.

It was necessary to return to Georgia. By this time, I was aware of the name of the small village where Lawrence's mother lived. I went there one morning with a driver and my interpreter. In the village, no one appeared to know anything about Alexa or a death. We were informed that the mother had just caught the bus to go into Tbilisi. We caught up with the bus, and when it stopped, my interpreter boarded it, spoke to the mother, and she agreed to see us that afternoon.

We followed the bus at a distance, and when she alighted in Tbilisi, my driver followed her on foot. After about 10 minutes, he lost her, but during all that time, she appeared to be having an animated conversation on her mobile.

We returned to the village that afternoon and spoke to the mother. She was somewhat vague but insisted that her daughter in law had drowned as claimed. I did not believe her.

At some stage of my investigation, I was informed by one of the insurers in America that Lawrence had previously claimed for the death of a lady in Georgia. The young lady took out a life policy with the assistance of Lawrence and fell from a balcony of a building in Georgia (not Rustavi). This was witnessed by Lawrence's mother, and eventually, he was paid. The insurer had tried unsuccessfully to investigate via diplomatic channels.

I was in the process of returning to Georgia to arrange exhumation of the body. I received a call from my interpreter, who had been contacted by the public prosecutor. Lawrence had removed the coffin from the cemetery and flown it on an aircraft to Ukraine. He had managed to go to court and obtain legal authorisation. I believe I was informed that the coffin was removed very early morning before the manager at the cemetery could realise and ring the public prosecutor.

Corrupt officials were obviously involved in both claims in Rustavi. The pathologist was involved, but I think that they had to be complicit with someone within the public prosecutor's office.

Sometime later, I was informed that Lawrence had made a complaint about my actions. He claimed he moved the body because I had been there, poking sticks into the grave. In my opinion, had we opened the coffin, we would have found the corpse of the old lady whose body went missing from the mortuary.

It was also alleged that I had dragged his mother off a bus, broken her leg and beaten her. He produced photographs of his mother with her leg in plaster and marks on her face. Added to this was a full medical report from the hospital detailing all of her injuries, and it was dated and timed about 3 hours after I had interviewed her. I was annoyed even to be asked by an insurer if this was true. My interpreter for this investigation was a young lady, a lawyer who spoke excellent English. She was introduced to me by a contact in an insurance company in Tbilisi. She was with me all the time of the alleged beating. Hopefully, one day Lawrence will write a book, but it would be found in the fiction section of the library! I was never informed about the eventual outcome of this claim but did not believe it would have been paid.

- - - - - - -

Back to Ukraine for a very unusual claim. Mr Atla took out a policy online in the UK with a cover of £490,000 in May 2016. In early 2017, his wife notified the insurer that he had gone missing in Ukraine and his body had been found near a lake in the south, about 50kms from Odesa. Her claim was that he went on holiday to Kyiv in January, stayed at a hostel and after a few days, she lost contact with him. On a Ukrainian police computer showing photographs of unidentified bodies, she saw a picture that resembled her husband. She travelled to the south of Ukraine, identified his body and had the body cremated there.

Mrs Atla was in Ukraine when I wanted to interview her. She and her husband held both Hungarian and Ukrainian passports and lived in Ukraine, close to the Hungarian border. She arranged to return to London, and I met her in an office at a block of flats in east London. She spoke no English and a friend of her husband, let's call him Aleks, acted as translator. Aleks said he lived in that block of flats. Mrs Atla said her husband had been in London for a couple of years, owned a company (it never traded), but she had no knowledge about his business. He travelled, but again she did not know where he went. They rented a flat, and her husband paid the rent to someone. She had no idea who, and he paid the utility bills.

She reiterated the story about him travelling to Kyiv on holiday. She added that as all hotels were full (in Kyiv in mid-January?), he could only stay in a hostel. When she lost touch with him, she flew to Kyiv to visit the police. I pursued this point, and it transpired that she was already in Ukraine at the time. According to her, he was a teetotaller and in good health. I did not believe her, but she was not very bright. It was my impression that Aleks was not just the interpreter and friend, but he was actually answering my questions.

I went to Odessa, a very interesting, historic town. The next day I travelled with a translator to the area where the body was located. It was near a lake in a rural area. I met the local mayor who recalled the body being found. He said that no one in the village had ever seen the person before, and it was assumed he was a tramp. He arranged for villagers to show me the place and pointed out that in January, it was snowing, and the ground would have been frozen for days. He recalled that the body was frozen and took several days to thaw out.

He allowed me to copy the photo he had taken on his mobile.

Where the body was found

The mayor called the local police officer who dealt with the case. I learned that in that area, there were around 120,000 inhabitants. Since 2001 there had been around 70 unidentified bodies. Later the pathologist gave me a much higher figure. The police officer told me that when there was an unidentified body, a photo was taken and placed on the national police computer. She received a telephone call from an officer in Kyiv who said that a lady thought this might be her husband. Subsequently, Mrs Atla arrived, identified the body and had it cremated in Odessa. She said that cremations were unusual, but the wife said she could not afford to ship the body back to the Hungarian border for burial. The police officer thought that the pathologist saw the dead man's ID card and passport. Later the pathologist told me that he thought the police had seen these! Mrs Atla claimed her husband had been carrying $ 7000 but the police officer said he was obviously a poor man. Nothing whatsoever was found on his body.

I met the pathologist who had carried out a post-mortem, and he said that the deceased had been an alcoholic for at least 3 years, and the cause of death was alcohol related. Interestingly the man who took out insurance claimed he was a teetotaller, and Mrs Atla confirmed this to me! The pathologist and the police officer both asked the wife for details of relatives in order to carry out DNA testing.

According to her, they were all dead, but this was not what she told me when I interviewed her. I was provided with a photo of the corpse and later obtained a copy of the insured's identity card.

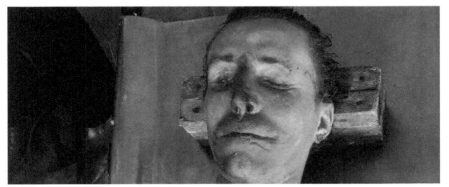

The same man?? The corpse

Husband's old ID card

The wife had registered the death in the main town near the lake. She had surrendered his Ukrainian passport. Interestingly, she had told me that she had never seen his Ukrainian passport. He had not travelled with his Hungarian passport, and she had proof that she had surrendered this at the Hungarian Embassy in Kyiv. So, where did his Ukrainian passport come from if she never saw it and there were no documents found on the corpse?

I went to Kyiv and met the lady who ran the hostel. Her story differed completely from that given to me by Mrs Atla. The lady told me that Mr Atla arrived there very late one night. He had less than the equivalent of £2 in local currency and said a friend would be giving him money the next day. He said he was looking for work on a building site. The lady was taken back by this as in January, it was freezing, and very little happened in the construction industry. The hostel consisted of a room for eating and 3 bedrooms, each sleeping 14 people. The cost was the equivalent of £9 a week. The manageress said that he appeared to be sober, a drink was not permitted in the hostel, and he never joined the conversations at mealtimes. He was there for 3 days and left suddenly one morning.

The lady was able to describe him and his clothing. He only carried a very small bag that could not have contained any additional coat. I showed her the photograph of the body, and she was adamant that this was not Mr Atla, and he had not worn such clothing.

The police informed me that Mrs Atla reported her husband missing. She complained that they were not trying to find him so was invited to the station to examine photographs of unidentified bodies found since the date he disappeared. There were numerous such photos at that time. She thought that one of the men might be her husband. The following day she returned to the police station and said it was her husband. According to her, he was an alcoholic, and his family were all dead. She stated he also had a serious heart problem. The problem with lying is that one regularly finds it difficult to recall the original lie!

Mrs Atla returned to London to meet me again and had the same interpreter, Aleks. I had found out that Aleks was really George and rented the flat where the Atla's had lived in London. He lived there when they were allegedly there and put the utility bills in their names. He originated from Ukraine, was intelligent and ran a successful business. Mrs Atla returned to Ukraine, and nothing further was heard from her. I think I know who set this up, don't you? So, if you go to Ukraine, you will find thousands of photographs on a police computer of unidentified bodies. It might have been a good idea for Mrs Atla to have established the cause of death before positively identifying the body. Even if it had been her husband, the fact that he was an alcoholic would have resulted in a case of medical non-disclosure.

Chapter 17: Central & South America

Time to move on to Central and South America. Some years ago, European international insurers were selling life cover to residents of Argentina and Colombia. Colombia, being the largest supplier of cocaine, was, particularly at that time, an extremely violent country. We had heaps of claims where the policyholder was shot. It was almost as if a bullet through the head while waiting in a car at a red traffic light in the rush hour was a natural death!

In those days, Andy regularly travelled to Colombia. Some deaths were fake, but often the insured's true occupation and lifestyle had not been declared on the insurance application. I recall a case where a man died and was insured for a significant amount of money. The cause of death was not suspicious, and the policy had been in force for some years. The insurer did not want to pay for Andy to travel to Bogota but asked if he could arrange for our associate there just to confirm that the man was dead. Our associate, a lady who is still working for me, rang Andy late one evening and was very upset. She had only visited the cemetery and the church. Later that same day, there was a knock on the door. She opened it to find a man pointing a gun at her. He advised her to stop asking questions.

Andy flew to Bogota and, within 3 days, proved the claim to be false, and he returned home. You can see why we do not want our overseas associates to conduct the enquiries. They have to live in that country. We often lie about the hotel we are staying in and leave the country as soon as possible. Our associates can say that they are merely employed as translators.

I made one trip to Colombia. The death was in the north near Medellin, and the man had lived about 20 miles from there. I flew from Bogota to Medellin but was informed that it was far too dangerous to travel 20 miles by road to the man's home city. I would have to fly back to Bogota and then take another plane. As it transpired, I found sufficient evidence in Medellin to refute the claim.

- - - - - - -

I travelled many times to Buenos Aires in Argentina, a city I enjoyed visiting. Wonderful architecture and the 'parrillas'', bbq grills are magnificent. I had one fake claim there but there were so many other cases where the true medical background had been concealed. One claim involved a young, recently married man who died suddenly. His death was Aids-related. It transpired that he was gay, and his wealthy parents, afraid of the social stigma, paid a young lady to marry him. He omitted to mention his HIV infection on the insurance application. Hopefully, such attitudes have now changed in Argentina.

A parrilla

The main fake claim I investigated was the death of Oscar. Although fairly young and allegedly healthy, he died suddenly, and the doctor showed heart attack on the death certificate. I interviewed the doctor at length and asked why the body was not sent to a government hospital for a post-mortem. How could he certify the death as a heart attack? Eventually, he admitted he had never seen a body but was pressurised into issuing the death certificate. It seems the doctor was gay, and thugs had threatened to expose his lifestyle. The body was taken by a funeral home to a place about 40kms from the city. There was a church service, and he was buried in the grounds of the cathedral.

I met the priest, and he showed me various documents about the funeral. I believed him. He showed me the grave there as well. I interviewed the funeral director, and there were discrepancies in what he told me. Later back in the city, I interviewed the brother, a real thug. Again, there were numerous discrepancies, and I indicated that the claim was false. I do believe that local people attended the funeral service and really thought that Oscar had died. As for the coffin, I suspect it was full of old books. My interpreter was brilliant and could translate while I was speaking normally. At one stage, the answer to my question was stupid, and I remarked, "what a bloody liar". I might have perhaps used another word. Anyway, she translated it immediately, and the man got up from his seat and threatened to hit me. My translator remarked that perhaps she was not meant to translate everything I said. We both smiled.

- - - - - - -

I investigated a couple of claims in Brazil. One involved a businessman who had taken out a large number of accidental death plans, and he was shot dead when leaving his local bank. I became involved because the policies were reinsured in Europe. It did not make sense for someone to take out so much insurance cover for just accidental death and not to cover natural death. The evidence suggested that the man had arranged for two people to shoot him.

- - - - - - -

Some years ago, I travelled to Honduras. A man from London, George, had been living there for a while and allegedly died. He had some relatives in the UK, but they appeared to know little about his life in Honduras. I travelled to the capital city Tegucigalpa classified some years ago as the most dangerous place in the world. I had a problem finding a translator and noticed that the armed police officer at the front door of the hotel spoke good English. He told me he had lived in the USA, and if his inspector agreed, he would accompany me on my travels. His inspector did agree for Pedro to assist, no doubt receiving part of the translator's fee I was paying.

The following day I made several enquiries in the City, and it did appear that George had not died there. A doctor stated he was given the name of someone who he was informed had died at home, so he issued a death certificate. The death had been registered, but some official documents were missing.

George, I established had been staying on the Caribbean coast, near La Ceiba, so early the next morning, we drove there, a journey exceeding 5 hours. As we left the city, Pedro reached under the car seat, took out a gun and placed it on his lap. He pointed out that the road was famous for armed robbers, so he wanted to be prepared. Anyway, we arrived at the coast and proved that George had left a few days ago, quite a while after his "death". We returned to the City and luckily did not have a rendezvous with armed robbers!

- - - - - - -

There was a case in Honduras that ended up as headlines in several UK papers. Anthony McErlean was staying in Honduras with his Honduran wife and allegedly died in an accident one morning. He held an insurance policy for accidental death cover of over £500,000. He was, at the time of his alleged death with an American friend who wrote a statement for the UK insurer. It was claimed that he left home early with his friend to visit a site to take wildlife photographs. Their vehicle had a puncture, and while fixing it, he was run over by a truck carrying cabbages.

His wife, via a friend in the UK, dealt with the insurer. Apparently, Anthony was cremated, a rare event in such a Catholic country. We asked for a large number of documents, and the wife kept maintaining that they were not available. I carried out enquiries in the UK. I spoke to his daughter in London, who was not aware he had died. Anthony had lived in Faversham in Kent in southern England, and I spoke to the person who had bought his house there plus neighbours. It was known that Anthony had left behind substantial debts.

I was asked to travel to Honduras but decided to wait until the various documents requested arrived in the UK. One day I received a telephone call from the person who had bought McErlean's house. He had been given my card by a neighbour. He had just seen Anthony and his wife in Sainsbury's in Canterbury in southern England! I contacted the police, and eventually, McErlean was arrested. Police found his fingerprints on his own death certificate!

He was sentenced to 6 years in prison, later reduced to 5. After his release, he defrauded a pensioner out of a significant sum of money and was sent back to prison.

Conman who faked death in 'hit and run' with Honduras cabbage truck

He impersonated wife to claim £520,000

McErlean: His prints were on death certificate

-- - - - - -

In 2005 a man originally from Ecuador called Alfredo Sanchez allegedly died in Costa Rica. He was insured in the UK for over £1million, including a death in service benefit from his employer here. His English wife, Sophie, was given funds by the employer to travel to Ecuador for his funeral. Enquiries suggested that Alfredo had moved to Costa Rica to start a new life mainly because of the debts he had in the UK.

Again, I only needed to make enquiries in the UK, and various people seemed to know that he was not dead. I spoke on the telephone to the family of Sophie who lived in Farnham in England. They knew nothing about his death, gave me their daughter's phone number in Costa Rica, and I rang her. The claim was then dropped, but the case was reported to the police. Again, the death certificate contained the fingerprints of the dead man!

Eventually, Sophie was arrested when she arrived in London from Australia for a family wedding. She was sentenced to 2 years in prison.

£1m insurance scam man is found – then goes on run again

His fingerprints were on own death certificate

Anne Barrowclough Sydney

A man wanted by British police for a £1.25 million insurance scam has been found living in Australia with his four children.

Alfredo Sanchez allegedly faked his own death to obtain the money but was caught out when police found his own fingerprints on his death certificate. Police say that Mr Sanchez and his wife, Sophie, from Farnham, Surrey, planned the fraud to cover huge debts. Mrs Sanchez was arrested last year

Alfredo Sanchez has been living in Australia with his children since

Later Sanchez was arrested in Australia.

Briton arrested over 'faking death in £1.25m insurance scam.'

Hugo Sanchez taken into custody in Australia after police allegedly find his fingerprints on 2005 death certificate

And in 2012-newspaper headline

A FORMER Farnham resident who faked his own death to fund a new life abroad has been jailed for five years.

Hugo Jose Sanchez, 57, formerly known as Alfredo Sanchez, was extradited from Australia in March following a five-year police inquiry.

He admitted 12 counts of fraud worth a total of £850,000 at Oxford Crown Court in April and was sentenced at a separate hearing on May 28.

Mr Sanchez, who worked as a web designer for HMV, took out numerous loans and life insurance policies covered by payment protection insurance (PPI) whilst living in Farnham in 2004.

Later that year, his wife Sophie contacted HMV to claim Mr Sanchez had died of a heart attack during a holiday in Ecuador.

Mrs Sanchez provided the firm with a death certificate and received a death benefit payment of £112,000, along with pension payments.

Chapter 18: East Africa

I travelled regularly at one stage to Kenya and countries in east and southern Africa. Kenya Airways had an excellent network out of Nairobi. I could leave London on Sunday evening, arrive early Monday in Nairobi and be working in Tanzania, Zambia, Uganda etc., by early Monday afternoon. I could make enquiries in 2 or 3 countries and be home in 7 or 8 days travelling between various countries on Kenya Airways.

UK insurers on the mainland and offshore used to do a lot of business in Kenya, insuring some of the wealthy businessmen of Asian origin. I had one false claim in this category but numerous claims involving medical non-disclosure. I regularly visited the 3 main private hospitals in Nairobi and knew most of the best specialists there and in Mombasa. The majority of those persons insured underwent medical examinations, but with some of the earlier claims, the quality of the examinations left much to be desired. Too often, the patient was related to the doctor or took medication to lower their blood pressure and so on. I interviewed a number of excellent doctors and set up a panel for the insurers of those who could be relied upon to undertake accurate and thorough medical examinations.

When applying for insurance, people there would show the name of their regular doctor. However, they only ever visited such a person for colds and minor ailments. They would normally have a specialist who they would see for their blood pressure, heart problems, diabetes etc. If they died when the policy was fairly new, the challenge was to locate the doctor holding their main medical record.

Later, when the situation in Uganda improved, and Asian businessmen returned there, a similar problem emerged. This also occurred in Tanzania, Uganda and Zambia. I can recall my first visit to Uganda, a beautiful country ruined for a while by Idi Amin. As an aside, I recall my days in Customs at Heathrow soon after Amin had deported most of the Ugandan Asians. I stopped an African male who had a Ugandan diplomatic passport. He was extremely pleasant but clearly lacked the intelligence one would expect from a diplomat. I asked him what he did before Idi Amin took over. His response was, "I was de lift operator".

Anyway, when I did my first claim in Uganda, there was no such thing as the rush hour. There was hardly any traffic, and the centre of Kampala resembled a ghost town. In the centre was a large showroom that had once sold cars. In the midst of this was a man with a small desk and a chair plus a used tyre and battery. He was there to sell these items. Not the chair and desk, but had I made him an offer - - - - -   As the years went by, traffic in Kampala became a congestion nightmare as more and more businesses started up.

- - - - - - -

I recall a claim in Kenya when a man died of Aids 6 months after taking out a policy and testing negative for HIV. I interviewed the doctor in Mombasa who did the original medical. He recalled that he examined the man and told him he would have to return to the lab at the hospital the following day for an HIV test; the medical was late in the day, so the lab was closed. The man said that he had to travel away on business early the next morning, so he had been to the lab for a test earlier that day. Sure enough, the test result arrived later on the doctor's desk. It was negative, so the doctor sent off the medical examination and tests to the insurer. A clever ploy. When you go to a lab and ask for a test, no ID is asked for. If it is for insurance medical, then a passport is required. The lab did not realise the test was for an insurer. It was the insurance agent who had the HIV test! The person applying for insurance would obviously have failed such a test. I had exactly the same set of circumstances later in Dar Es Salaam.

I was regularly in Kenya from around 1993 until 2002, investigating such claims. Claims for persons of African origin started around 2002, and I went there multiple times on such cases. One visit is still vivid in my memory. I had to see a pathologist in the main mortuary in Nairobi in 1993, just after the Nairobi to Mombasa train fell into a river killing over 100 people. This was my first visit to the mortuary. Staff gave me directions to the pathologist's office and told me to walk the entire length of the mortuary. After a short distance, I heard laughter behind me and saw the staff watching my progress. There were not just bodies lying all over the floor, but the place resembled a huge jigsaw puzzle, body parts everywhere. I took a deep breath and continued in the same direction staring at the ceiling. After speaking to the pathologist, he tried to send me back the same way. I wasn't falling for that again. I have now been there numerous times and certainly know my way around the mortuary!

I recall a claim for a man from the UK who lived in Mombasa and died there. I will call him Ray. He had a Kenyan wife and ran a small business in Kenya. He had taken out a life policy with a cover of £165,000 in England and died about a year later. The cause of death appeared to be alcohol related. The man's family in the UK were quarrelling over his estate. Eventually, I went to investigate his death in Mombasa.

I had met the chief pathologist in Mombasa many times, Dr Mandaliya, an absolute gentleman and excellent pathologist. He recalled the death and told me that he never needed to pickle the man's organs. They were already pickled as he was an alcoholic.

I met the deceased's wife and friends there. I was told that Ray could not get out of bed in the morning and open both his eyes until he drank a flask of vodka. Late morning, he would visit countless pubs in Mombasa. I inquired how he could have passed a medical exam in England less than a year previously. I was told that the insurance agent was a friend and arranged an early morning medical. Friends arranged for Ray to wear a new suit, have a haircut and get up early. After consuming a quantity of vodka, he was taken for a medical. When it was finished, he rushed outside for a drink.

I made enquiries in Moi Avenue in Mombasa, the main street in the town where there are a large number of bars. At the first one, the barman said he remembered Ray. Every morning he used to go there, have 2 pints of lager and leave with a flask of vodka. He did not believe he had a drinking problem as he only had 2 pints. I went to the next bar, and yes, the barman remembered Ray. 2 pints, and he took away a flask of vodka. I obtained the same story in 5 adjacent bars. A very sad case indeed.

- - - - - - -

I had a case where a man died in Lamu, an island off the coast of Kenya about 150 miles north of Mombasa. One arrives by aircraft on the mainland and takes a boat across to the island. There were only two vehicles on the island, only one of which actually worked. It is a very historic and amazing place, and hopefully, one day I will return there for a holiday. In some ways, it resembles Zanzibar (see later on in this chapter).

The man had fallen, hit his head and died. He had a policy that paid out a vast amount of money in the event of accidental death. It was a difficult enquiry as I had to walk everywhere as arriving at meetings on a donkey did not appeal to me. Not good for my image either! At times I had to walk long distances when the tide came in, forcing me to divert inland.

I interviewed the man's wife, and she agreed that he had been suffering from cancer, but this was not related to his death, according to her. He had fallen late at night down concrete steps and hit his head. She told me he had recovered from cancer. I went to the hospital and met a medical assistant who had examined the body. He insisted that a head injury had caused his death. He could not explain why the body was not sent to the mainland for a post-mortem. I interviewed the local registrar and the relevant police officer, and they all insisted that it had been an accident. In such a rural area, the local chief had to make a written statement, and this related to an accident. I interviewed the chief, who said that the man died from cancer. He started making a written statement, stopped and asked how much I was paying him. When I stated I did not pay for statements, he demanded a large sum of money. He grabbed my briefcase and destroyed the notes I had made.

There were numerous discrepancies in all of the stories, and I was convinced that no one was telling the truth. As Lamu is a Muslim place, persons of other religions have to be sent to the mainland for burial or cremation, normally to Mombasa or Malindi. I was certain that a foreigner dying there would have to undergo a post-mortem, so I telephoned Dr Mandaliya, the pathologist in Mombasa. He immediately recalled the case and told me that the man died from cancer; there were no injuries. He later sent me a copy of the post-mortem report and the real death certificate. I was amazed that so many people could lie in order to assist a foreigner with an insurance claim. However, with respect, the deceased and his wife were very highly thought of on the island and had probably helped quite a few people there.

The airport for Lamu on the mainland

The boat to the island

Arriving on the island

Donkey – the main form of transport

In most of the fake claims for African Kenyans living in the UK, the common denominator was London. They all lived and worked around the London area, and there were 5 false claims in a period of 2 years. In each case, the insured had poorly paid jobs, lived in squalor but were insured for amounts ranging from £250,000 to £1.17m. One of the "deceased' persons was wanted for a serious crime in London, so he had good reason to return permanently to Kenya. In all these cases, while the various documents produced were false or at least issued under false pretences, family members and friends in Kenya insisted that they were all dead.

One man, I will call him Toyo, insisted that his wife had died in a hit and run accident in Mombasa. Toyo lived in one room in part of a house near Heathrow Airport. It contained a bed, broken furniture and masses of rubbish and junk. I had to sit in the midst of this on a broken chair when interviewing him. Toyo appeared to be using his first and middle names as surnames. He was in debt, and his wife was said to be a student. Enquiries indicated she rarely attended any courses. Toyo and his wife were each insured for £250,000. He produced a large number of documents from Kenya in support of the claim.

I started in Nairobi as he had supplied a letter from the Ministry of Foreign Affairs confirming that the death registration certificate was an original and genuine document. No Ministry could say that such a document was genuine without carrying out an investigation. The lady at the Ministry confirmed that the letter appeared to be written on a genuine letterhead, but it was false. It was not her signature on the letter. Plus, there were many spelling mistakes and typing errors. One would think that if trying to steal such a large sum of money, one would at least pay an educated person to write proper English.

Enquiries of the police, cemetery and medical authorities in Mombasa showed the claim to be false. There was a medical death certificate from the Mombasa Hospital. This is the best hospital in Mombasa and is private. A victim of a hit and run would not be taken there but to Coast General, the government hospital. There my friend, the pathologist, Dr Mandaliya, would have carried out a post-mortem.

The address I had for the claimant's father was false, but I thought the area might be correct. I spoke to some people in the area, and one lady said she thought she knew the family. She knew a man locally called Albert whose brother lived in London, and he had recently been on holiday in Mombasa with his wife. She was certain the wife was still alive. Later she located Albert, and he told me his brother and wife had returned to the UK after a holiday in Mombasa.

The lady obviously gave the family my contact details as I received a telephone call that evening from Toyo's father and he asked to see me. We met up, and he was insistent that his daughter in law had been killed in a hit and run accident. According to him, I could not trust anything that his other son, Albert, said as he was a drunk! Naturally, when I asked the father details of the hospital, mortuary, police station and so on, he said he had not asked his son such questions.

The family home in Mombasa

- - - - - - -

Another Kenyan living in London was Max, who was married to a girl from Eastern Europe. Max had insurance

209

cover of about £1.17m. I seem to recall that he was a bus driver who decided on a career change. He was about to become a rich property developer. What a shame he "died" before achieving his dream. I interviewed his wife, who told me they had been on holiday to Kenya. She returned to England alone and then had a problem contacting her husband. Eventually, she received a call from his uncle, Sam, to say he had been shot in a robbery and was in the hospital. This part of her story transpired to be true. She did not know the uncle's number, so she had no way of contacting her husband as his mobile was stolen when he was shot. Eventually, the uncle rang to say he had died in the village from pneumonia. During the interview with me, the wife regularly cried.

She told me she flew to Kenya, stayed somewhere in a rented flat in Nairobi and attended the funeral. Uncle Sam had given her all of the documents relating to the death. I asked her if she could describe the cemetery. She couldn't. He was allegedly buried at Langati. This is at the top of a hill just outside the city, close to the National Park and domestic airport. Quite stunning scenery and difficult to forget.

So off to Nairobi for what turned out to be a very lengthy enquiry. So many people in the village told me about his death, but none of their stories tallied. A medical assistant had provided a written note confirming the death because someone told him about it. He never saw a body. There was also a written statement from the village chief about his death. The problem was that none of these documents could be used officially in order to correctly register the death. The death registration certificate produced was a forgery. Plus, there was no record of the death at Langati cemetery.

The wife had given me the mobile number of Uncle Sam, and when I rang the number, I spoke to another family member who spoke little English. After I completed my enquiries in the village, I received a call from Sam asking me to go to the village to see him. Rather than walk into a potential trap, I agreed to meet at an outdoor coffee shop in Nairobi. When we met, he insisted that Max was dead and went into great detail about the circumstances. Yet another different story! I told him that he was not dead and that it was a fraud. Initially, he cried aloud, and other customers and passers-by all stared in his direction. He then stood up and started shouting at me about his poor, dead nephew and the nasty man from England who had come to upset the family and steal from them. Most of what he said was in Swahili, and a large crowd gathered and angrily pointed in my direction. My driver and I decided to make a very quick exit.

The matter was reported to the police here, and I do not think the insured returned to the UK unless he had a new passport! It transpired that he was wanted by the police for another matter.

The registry in the village

Uncle Sam before he commenced yelling at me.

- - - - - - -

When several life insurers sent me a Kenyan death certificate for Alan Pike, alarm bells rang instantly. It turned out that in late 2002 he had taken out life policies with 4 insurers with a total cover of around £894k. He allegedly died in a traffic accident in Nairobi on 19th January 2003. A solicitor in the northeast of England representing Pike's wife, Kerry, sent a death certificate to the insurers.

My colleague at the time was in the northeast of England on another claim, so he went and saw Mrs Pike. Her story was that her husband was a financial advisor for offshore companies. She appeared to have very little knowledge about what he did. She stated he went to Nairobi with his friend Michael in connection with his business. Michael rang her to say he had died in a car accident. She stated that in his will, he had written that he should be buried, "wherever he hung his hat", so she told Michael to have him buried in Nairobi. Kerry had no idea as to which hospital he went to or where he was buried. She was told that they were in a taxi in Nairobi and it crashed. The driver and Michael sustained minor injuries, but Alan died. They were taken to a hospital, but Michael discharged himself soon after arrival there. According to her, Alan's sister, Susan, flew immediately to Nairobi.

Kerry said she was seeing her solicitor the following morning along with Susan, so my colleague agreed to meet at the solicitor's office. When they met, the sister said she arrived in Nairobi and met Michael, who left Kenya on the plane on which she had arrived. She was given little information by Michael and was unable to establish the hospital her brother went to, details of the police who attended the accident or the cemetery where he was buried. She explained that officials there were very unhelpful, so she flew home.

My colleague spoke to Michael on the telephone, and he was extremely vague when asked for details about his friend's death. He said that Alan took him to Nairobi with a view to him starting an office there for dealing with offshore investments.

The various explanations were unbelievable, and the certificate produced had to be suspect. Although it was the correct type of document, it could not have been issued officially. The date of death was 19th January 2003, a Sunday. Had he died in an accident, his body would have been taken to the government mortuary, where the official pathologist would have carried out a post-mortem. She did not work on a Sunday, so the post-mortem could not have been done until Monday. The system is such that documents would not arrive at the central registry for several days. The death could not have been registered on 21ˢᵗ January, as shown on the certificate. The informant on the certificate should have been the pathologist. It was not. Plus, the cause of death was medically incorrect.

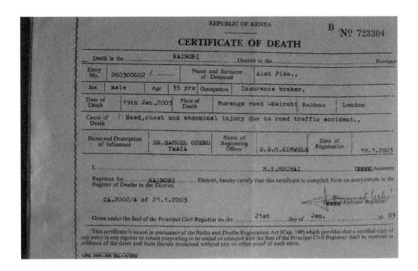

Various documents relating to the death were with a different solicitor, one who handled only criminal cases. My colleague was told by someone he met in the area where Pike lived that Pike had problems with HM Customs. I rang an ex-colleague and mentioned that I was dealing with a claim for Pike. If my enquiries were of interest to anyone in HM Customs, then perhaps someone could ring me. Very soon after this, I received a phone call. Pike was on bail and due to appear at Canterbury Crown Court in England on 10ᵗʰ February 2013 on a charge of money laundering. His death certificate had been produced to the court, and the case was dropped. The charge was related to Pike having been stopped at Dover when travelling by car to France with his sister. He was carrying £55,000 in cash and had apparently stolen over £100,000 from an offshore insurance company.

This was a commission fraud, and we had investigated many such frauds on behalf of insurers in the late 80's early 90's. A person obtained a contract to act as an advisor for an insurance company and is paid commission only. To give a basic example, let's say he sells a policy for life cover or a pension, and the monthly premium is £100. In the region of 12 months premium is paid as commission upfront, £1,200. Should the monthly payments cease and the policy lapses within, say 15 months, then the commission has to be repaid. When an advisor is a genuine person, the repayment would be taken from a new business commission.

However, with fraudulent cases, you arrange for friends, relatives to take out large policies. Once you receive a large commission payment, all of the premium payments cease. The insurer is owed a considerable sum of money but cannot locate the advisor. Sometimes he has traded using a false identity. He might register a company using puppet directors who cannot be traced. A false address was normally used.

Pike had taken commission from an offshore company based in the Isle of Man. Normally it takes time for an insurance company to realise that there is a fraud taking place. It works the same as is known as a long firm fraud. Initially, the business is good. Many new clients are introduced, and only the odd premium lapses are to be expected in normal business circumstances. The number of new businesses increases, and then a few policies start lapsing. Suddenly they all lapse, and the advisor has been paid perhaps £100,000 commission that the insurer wants to be returned. However, the advisor has disappeared, or the company he worked on behalf of cannot be located. This is what Pike had been up to, and when stopped by Customs, he was carrying a large amount of cash, part proceeds of his crime.

I went to Nairobi, and it soon became clear that this was a scam in order to steal money from life insurers plus avoid attending court. I established that Pike and his friend Michael had stayed at an international hotel. However, Pike checked out on the morning of 19th January, the day he allegedly died. Michael did not check out until 2 days later, yet they were meant to be returning together to the UK. The sister checked into the same hotel on her arrival in Nairobi, and she was alone. Enquiries at the airport showed her leaving on 25th January along with a man with the same

surname as her, and this was perhaps her husband, or - - - - -
. There had been no mention of him travelling to Nairobi,
plus he never stayed in the same hotel as the sister.
Furthermore, according to airline records, this person needed
wheelchair assistance. I wondered if perhaps part of his face
was bandaged. Was it perhaps claimed he had been in an
accident? So, who was this person?? I will leave it to your
own imagination!

Upon my return to the UK, I rang different offshore
insurers in the Isle of Man and Switzerland. A number had
dealings with Pike, and he and his own offshore company
had been paid millions of dollars in commission. I
experienced a problem trying to explain that they were being
ripped off. Some said that there were a few lapsed policies
but nothing to worry about. I left my number and suggested
they rang me when all the policies lapsed. It was not long
before I was investigating the loss of over $10m by
international insurers.

Pike and others had sold policies to UK nationals
allegedly working and living in West Africa, several
countries in East Africa, Indonesia, Philippines, Malaysia
and so on. The majority of the policies were investments and
pensions with premiums of £200 to £300 a month. The
policyholders were said to work for various international

companies. Some of these companies never existed. Others had no knowledge of such employees. The organisers had office addresses in several countries. I visited some of them, and they were all Regus serviced offices. The "investors" had to supply a copy of the main page of their passport for money laundering regulations. One common denominator was that most of the individuals were born in the northeast of England, where Pike lived! It took me a while to deduce how the premiums were being paid as these people could not all have bank accounts in overseas countries. The money was received by insurers from a bank in Nairobi. That bank received all the funds from an exchange control business in Nairobi. They were being paid mostly in cash. I spent 2 days going through their records, tracing all the payments.

Eventually, Pike was arrested and appeared before Canterbury Crown Court, where he was sentenced to 5 years in prison. Had he just used the false death certificate to explain his non-appearance in court, the chances are he would have succeeded. With a large sum of money from the international scams, why was he so greedy in trying to steal from UK insurers?

The international commission fraud was initially investigated by the police on the Isle of Man, but the matter was eventually dropped. I think that apart from the complexity of the enquiry, it would have involved perhaps expensive travel to several countries in order to gather the evidence.

- - - - - - -

Over the years, I visited Uganda a couple of times and noticed how the economy gradually improved. I have been fortunate enough to travel around the country, a beautiful place once described by Churchill as the pearl of Africa. My first claim there involved a long journey from Kampala to Mbale, close to Mount Elgon and the Kenyan border. I believe the first known case of Ebola was in the mountain, and the patient was taken from there to Nairobi.

Michael was a Ugandan living in London, and he claimed that his wife, Emma, had died after an illness in a hospital near Mbale. Michael appeared to be involved in property in London, and his solicitor was really pursuing the claim that Michael's wife had died in Uganda. Enquiries here plus an interview of Michael threw doubt on the authenticity of the claim, but we needed firm evidence, so I travelled to Uganda.

There I hired a car and driver and travelled over 4 hours to Mbale. The place of the alleged death was a rural hospital in Budada, a small community in the hills about an hour from Mbale. The doctor there insisted that Emma had died as claimed, and he showed me a medical record. He was unable to explain why a lady from Mbale would seek treatment at such a rural establishment an hour away from her home.

Most of my enquiries were in extremely rural places in stunning countryside. To travel to one village, I had to take off my shoes and socks and make a bridge from stones so that our car could cross a stream.

Having got the car across, we soon realised we could drive no further, so we started walking. A group of boys came out of the forest. One of them grabbed my briefcase, put it on his head and indicated to us to follow them to the village. It was very hot, but what a stunning place, with multi-coloured shrubbery and numerous colourful birds. Upon arrival, I met the village chief. I was in the wrong village. The one I wanted to go to had a very similar name. But what the hell! Eventually, I located the correct village, and the residents had no knowledge of the deceased or her burial there.

There was sufficient evidence to show that the claim could not be genuine. Early Saturday morning, I was going to return to Kampala. My driver then told me that the previous evening he had been approached by a lady who asked if he was driving the white man who was looking into the death of Emma. She asked him to take me to her on Saturday morning. She was living just a short distance from my hotel.

I met her, and she said she was Michael's mother. She insisted that Emma was dead. According to her, Michael had given me the wrong name of the place where Emma was buried, and the mother wanted to take me to her grave. I told her that if I proved she was not truthful, then she could find her own way home. It was a fairly long journey and involved driving across fields as in places there was no road. So off we went to another remote village, and the mother said her family originated from there. Upon arrival, locals immediately took out a bench and asked me to sit down. They had positioned it in front of a grave. How could they know I was coming to see a grave? It was so new that in places, the concrete was still wet. The headstone did have details of Emma inscribed. Around the grave, I could see a white powder, so I followed the trail. The trail ended adjacent to a bag of concrete in a shed nearby! Had I arrived a little earlier, I could have helped them to make the grave!

The new grave

So off back to Kampala, stopping for lunch in the town of Jinja overlooking the source of the Nile. Another mesmeric site.

When making enquiries in London, I had completed the death abroad questionnaire with Michael. This showed that his sister attended the funeral, and she worked at a bank in Kampala. I went to the bank and interviewed her. She was holding a small piece of paper and appeared to be relying on this to answer my questions. I pointed out that the funeral allegedly took place in midweek, so she must have taken leave from the bank to attend, and she agreed. I suggested that if I made an enquiry at the bank as to whether she was at work that day, I would have to explain the reason I was asking. If she was lying, then I doubted if the bank would be too keen on employing someone who was assisting a fraud in the UK. She started crying and begged me not to speak to the management. She told me that her mother had telephoned her over the weekend, stating that an Englishman was making enquiries about Emma. The sister claimed she knew nothing about any death, and her mother told her what to say to me if challenged. Hence, she kept referring to the piece of paper in her hand, which she agreed to give to me along with a written statement.

The sister did give me some interesting information about Emma. She was a diplomat working in an African Embassy in London. Upon my return, I rang that embassy and spoke with Emma; she was shocked to learn what had happened. After a disagreement with her husband, she had moved away from the family home. Hence she was not there when I met her husband. It had taken her some time to get her passport back from her husband. Now she could understand why he needed it. She still officially used her maiden name.

Michael was arrested by the police and sent to prison. His wife definitely had no knowledge about what he was up to.

- - - - - - -

In 2011 Rose Ndadaye, living in London, took out life cover close to £3m. She then wrote to insurers stating that she had checked that it was not illegal to take out policies with several companies. She claimed that she was born into poverty and, should she die, she never wanted her own children to suffer as she had. In the letter, it was also mentioned that she was about to travel to Uganda to see her children, and she wanted to check that the policies covered her while abroad. She might well have told them that she was about to die! One insurer eventually cancelled her policy, but a total of £1.7m remained at risk when she allegedly died in a hit and run accident in Kampala.

She was said to be a childminder, plus she owned a private school in Kampala with an income of £75,000 a year. She had written the policies in trust in favour of her brother-in-law, John Katege. Soon after she sent the letters to insurers, another one arrived from John headed, "very sad news". It referred to her death in Uganda. Well, it must be genuine; she told us she was travelling there! Do people really think insurers are so naïve?

I made various enquiries in London and later interviewed John, a schoolteacher, or so he claimed to be. He stated that when he received a telephone call from Uganda, he flew there, identified her body in the mortuary and attended her funeral.

His story did not ring true, plus there seemed to be discrepancies in his responses concerning Rose's background etc. According to him, when Rose travelled to Uganda, she asked him to look after her insurance policies. She told him that she had taken out several in case an insurer failed to pay out in the event of her death. He went on about a car insurer not paying his claim. I asked him why at the beginning of the interview, he failed to mention details of all the policies. His response was that I might have thought she had too much insurance. This was one remark made by him with which I did agree!

The results of enquiries in London threw further doubts on the validity of the claim. I believe that Rose might originally have claimed asylum here. It was also my belief that a handful of persons might have used that identity. There appeared to be no business run by Rose and no trace of any income or job.

So off to Kampala where I discovered that the death had been registered by John Katege, soon after he arrived there. His photograph was attached to the registration. John had told me that he had identified her body at Mulago Hospital, the largest hospital in Uganda. There was no record there of the death, plus the post-mortem report produced by him was false. Death was apparently certified by Dr Lubega Lukande, and his mobile phone number was in the file. There was no such doctor working there, but I rang the number, and the man who answered would only give me his name once I said why I was calling. Yes, he said he was Dr Lukande, and he remembered the death. However, he claimed to be too busy to see me for at least a week. Eventually, he agreed to meet with me outside the office of the Medical Director. Surprise, surprise, he did not show up, and his phone remained switched off.

The police documents were false, but the letter from the village chief about her burial was genuine. The chief could not recall much about the death, did not know if Rose had any family in the village, and he could not remember where she had been buried there. With no family originating from that village, she could not be buried there. He recalled that Rose was related to a man called **Jamil**.

I had names and telephone numbers of witnesses. When I contacted them, they were all away on business, or so they claimed, apart from Florence. I met with her, an extremely intelligent young lady, and she told me that her husband, **Jamil** was the best friend of John Katege. She went into detail about the death and funeral but never saw the body.

Florence told me she converted to Islam when she married Jamil. Interestingly it was claimed that Rose was married to a Muslim who died, and her 4 children had Muslim names. Florence said she had to finish our interview as she had to go and pray. I hope the word "forgiveness" featured in her prayers!

The matter was reported to the police in London, and John Katege was arrested and charged. I recall his court case as the Medical Director of Mulago Hospital gave evidence via video link. It was John's claim that he must have been tricked. When he identified the body in the mortuary, he only saw the feet! I wish someone would try and trick me into receiving £1.7m. That would be quite a "feat!"

News › Crime

Jailed: fraudster who faked sister-in death in Uganda car crash

PAUL CHESTON | Friday 11 September 2015 |

85

John Katege faked his sister-in-law's death *City of London police*

A fraudster who faked his sister-in-law's death in a bid to claim nearly £3 million from life insurance companies was jailed for seven years.

John Katege, 31, forged documents and even wrote his own post

- - - - - - -

What follows is certainly one of the most unusual claims. In fact, it is 2 claims, both involving Uganda. Mr and Mrs Singa (again, I am changing names to protect the guilty) had a life policy for £500,000 that was increased to over £760,000. Two years later, Mrs Singa was on holiday visiting friends in Uganda when she was taken ill and died.

I rang Mr Singa but had to wait several weeks before I could meet with him as he said he was travelling to India to spread his wife's ashes there. When we did meet, he claimed his wife had gone to Uganda to meet a friend called **Manish** (the reason for highlighting this will soon become obvious). She lost her passport and reported this to the police in Uganda. He showed me a copy of the relevant report. His wife was ill and admitted to Kibuli Muslim Hospital but eventually died. He produced reports from the hospital, a post-mortem report allegedly done at the main hospital, Mulago, cremation documents and receipts from an undertaker.

A short while later, I received a claim relating to the death of Manik in Uganda. He was insured for over £270,000, and his wife was the claimant. Manik had gone to Uganda to visit his brother, **Manish.** He was taken ill and hospitalised at Kibuli Muslim Hospital and eventually died.

To save me typing too much, read again what allegedly happened in respect of Mrs Singa. Yes, an identical story, with the exception that the ashes were scattered in Kampala and not India. When I interviewed Manik's wife, I asked about Mr and Mrs Singa and told her that Mrs Singa had died at the same hospital as her husband. She said she had never heard of these people.

So off to Kampala. Both deaths were registered at the central registry in Kampala, but certain documents seemed to be missing. At Mulago Hospital, there was no record of either body being in the mortuary. I had post-mortem reports, both done by a Dr Kali. Staff told me he was abroad, someone rang him, and later Dr Kali rang me. He insisted he did both post-mortems on behalf of Dr Lago at Kibuli Muslim Hospital. Staff at the mortuary examined the post-mortem register, and both cases had been recorded. Mrs Singa was shown in the register the day before she actually died! The staff member who kept the register recalled that he was told by Dr Kali to enter these cases. Had there been post-mortems, then there would have been charges. Enquiries at the account's office there indicated that there were no records.

The Medical Director at Kibuli Muslim hospital, a fine establishment that stood amongst scenic surroundings on a hill, was extremely helpful. There was a record thereof Manik being admitted, but 7 days after his autopsy! A first for sure! Dr Lago's signature was on all of the documents, and he did work there but was off duty. His mobile was turned off, and the Medical Director asked me to ring Dr Lago later and report back to him. I did so, and he said he was in Nairobi. He was not, as I knew his mobile would not have worked there. When I rang him again, he said he was ill. Later he told me he never treated either person but was asked by someone to recommend a pathologist.

At the undertakers, the man said he did not have the records there but recalled arranging the cremations. An elderly man sat at the back of the office said that he was talking nonsense. They had not done such work. Later I did get a written statement from the owner indicating that he had provided an estimate to an Asian male, and he suspected that this had been copied and altered. They had not arranged the cremations. Enquiries at the Hindu Temple revealed that the documents produced were false.

Two names featured throughout my investigation, Dennis and Manish. I had a number for Manish, rang him, and he said he was just entering the Congo by car and was about to lose connection. I asked about the journey he was doing, and he explained it to me. I felt like telling him that if you intend to lie first, get your geography correct. Clearly, he did not know his Congo from his a---!

I also had a PO Box address on one of the forms and was able to establish the area to which it belonged. Eventually, I met someone who knew a man called Manish who ran a small shop there. He had not travelled as the man had seen him an hour earlier, with his brother, Manik, who was from the UK. The dead Manik, no doubt. I spent ages making enquiries in that area. Some people said they had seen both men earlier. Others said that Manish had travelled to the Congo, and one man said that Manik was dead. I left my local mobile number with some people along with the message that if I did not receive a call from Manik by 9 am the following morning, I would go to the police.

When I awoke the following morning, I had 20 plus missed calls on my mobile. When I rang the number, I spoke to Manik, who begged me to meet up with him. I did so, and he explained the reason he had "died".

He stated that his brother in Kampala was approached by a man who he met there in a restaurant. The man was called Singa, and he asked for the brother's telephone number. Later Singa rang Manish and said he might get a call from someone about Mrs Singa dying there from malaria. He asked him to confirm the death, and if he did, he would invest in his business in Kampala. Manish found out that it was an insurance scam and spoke to his friend Dennis who agreed he had helped. Manish rang his brother in the UK, and they were both livid that Manish had been used in such a way.

They did not know Singa's full name or address, so they then came up with a plan to expose him to police in the UK. Manik was going to take out a life policy (he already had one in existence), get the same documents from Dennis that had been supplied to Singa and submit a claim. He was then going to inform the police that if they could locate an insurance claim with identical papers, then it was a fraud. Manik agreed he had to pay for the fake papers and said he had borrowed around £14,000 from his bank. I asked him if it had been worthwhile investing such a large sum of money to become a private investigator? Complete rhetoric, of course, so I did not expect a response!

There were a few holes in his story. Why had he still not notified the authorities in the UK about the fraud? When I met his wife, I told her I had a claim for someone relating to the same hospital in Uganda. Was that perhaps not a clue that I knew who was involved in a fraud? Why not just tell the police that someone was putting in a false claim and give them the information already known to him. Why take out a new policy when he already had life cover? Why had his wife kept ringing the insurance broker asking when the claim would be paid? Why borrow so much money from the bank? But mainly, why then insure that loan and then submit a death claim to the bank? I could go on, but I think you get my point

Manik returned to the UK, and I interviewed him and his wife under legal caution and took a written statement. I interviewed Mr Singa under similar conditions. He admitted the fraud and said that it had been the idea of Manish, who he met in Kampala. This I believed. Mr Singa held a responsible position in a large UK business.

Both cases were reported to the police here. If I asked the reader to guess the outcome, you would be wrong. In respect of Singa, the police said they were too busy to take any action. You will recall that he tried to obtain £760,000 and had made a full admission in writing under legal caution. In respect of Mr and Mrs Manik, they were given a police caution. So, who lost out? When I interviewed Mr and Mrs Manik, it took longer than expected, and I received a parking ticket. I ended up paying a £30 fine. No doubt reduced for good behaviour!

- - - - - - -

More recently, I have had four claims relating to deaths in Uganda. In each case, the claimant has produced a death registration certificate from the Central Registry. Such documents appear to be easily obtainable. If genuine, then numerous other documents should also be available. I have met the claimants, asked for these documents, and 3 of the claims have gone away. Clearly, they were not genuine.

Often, people think that if they get one certificate, then it will suffice for an insurance pay-out. Regularly, in cases of traffic accidents, I ask for a police report. Fraudsters can obtain the death registration certificate but have no access to fake police and post-mortem reports.

One claim was from a Ugandan dental hygienist in London. She took out substantial personal life cover, and one policy provided cover for a child. On the application where it asked about foreign travel, she disclosed that she went every year to Uganda to see her young child. Yes, the child died a while later in Uganda, and a claim was submitted for £5,000. Totally fake!

- - - - - - -

I have travelled many times to Tanzania. When I first went there, the country still bore the effects of Julius Nyerere's socialist rule. While it is still a very poor country, there have been some improvements. Unfortunately, as in many countries in Africa and elsewhere, of course, corruption has slowed progress.

My first visit there was in 1993. It was in relation to an international policy, and the man had died in Dar Es Salaam. The insurer used an investigator from Kenya, and he had been two or three times to Tanzania. The claim did appear to be false, but there was a clear lack of real evidence, just lots of rumours and innuendos.

There was a rumour that the dead man was actually in Dodoma, and he did have family there. Had I commenced my enquiry in Dar Es Salaam, then no doubt word would have reached Dodoma before my arrival there. I arrived at Dar Es Salaam airport and found a driver to take me to Dodoma. In those days, there were no flights to Dodoma. The drive took around 8 hours, and I passed some stunning scenes across the Rift Valley. I particularly recall huge pineapple plantations. Arriving late evening in Dodoma, I could only locate one hotel. The reception appeared ok, so I booked in. The room was basic, to say the least. The bed had a large mosquito net over the top. The toilet and shower consisted of one large hole in the ground. Nowhere to sit in comfort, that is in the room, not even the toilet. I went to the bar and ordered a meal. When it arrived, I was somewhat put off by the livestock crawling in the cabbage. However, the site of a large glass-fronted fridge full of Castle beer from South Africa lifted my spirits. The other occupant of the hotel was a fellow Brit working there in respect of telecoms. Obviously, sitting in front of that fridge was preferable to lying under a mosquito net, getting up in the night for a pee and disappearing down a dark hole. My fellow Brit agreed, so we stayed at the bar until the fridge was empty. Years later, the Dodoma railway station was featured in the book and TV programme "Pole to Pole" by Michael Palin. I think he stayed in that same hotel.

The following day enquiries suggested that the "dead" man had gone back to live in Dar Es Salaam. I interviewed his relatives, and they all told me a slightly different story. Back in Dar Es Salaam, I went to the cemetery where the man was allegedly buried. The previous investigator had also been there and was told by staff that the dead man was buried there. They showed him his grave and marked headstone. The staff at the cemetery told me the same story. I established that the cemetery belonged to a local mosque, and there I met the mosque secretary, Mr Chaki. He assured me that the man could not be buried in their cemetery as he was from a different Muslim sect. We returned to the cemetery, and Chaki had his driver remove the headstone, and he put it in the boot of the car. I did not understand what was said in Swahili to the workers but believe that one or two were instantly dismissed. Later, Chaki confirmed that an elderly lady who died some years ago was buried in that grave.

Anyway, when the enquiry was finished, I paid my driver, and he left the hotel. A few minutes later, he ran through reception holding a large grave headstone above his head and shouting, "Mr John. You forgot Mr Z's headstone". Hotel guests stood still, looking in amazement at my driver.

The headstone

The doctor who certified the death was a prominent physician who treated government officials. I interviewed him, and when I went back to see him, he had "gone on safari". This means he had travelled, and this was a phrase I heard many times in subsequent enquiries in Tanzania. The relatives of the "dead" man came from a prominent family in the city. They also went on safari. By the time I concluded my enquiries, there was ample evidence of fraud, plus numerous persons wanting to go on safari! By the way, I came across the same physician a year or so later when he had issued suspect documents, a fake claim. Once more, he went on safari!

As an aside, I was staying in the Kilimanjaro Hotel in Dar Es Salaam. Unfortunately, it had gone downhill since its prowess in the old colonial days. The AC in my room would not work, and several times staff told me that it was being fixed and would be finished any moment. Mr Chaki loaned me a fan for the room. The AC was never fixed. The following year I had to return to Tanzania and asked Chaki to check if the AC was working. He was told they were working on it, and it would be fixed that afternoon. It transpired that it had not worked for two years!

I forgot to mention that Chaki was a loss adjuster and has worked for me ever since our first meeting. A very religious, wonderful, generous man who looks after people irrespective of their religion.

- - - - - - -

Since then, I have been back several times to Tanzania and have been driven many miles across the country. One trip was to a small town close to the border of Malawi called Songea. It is possible to fly there, but this would have involved my staying there for 2 or 3 days, awaiting a return flight. The journey by car took about 15 hours, and the distance is 585kms. I arrived Saturday afternoon in Dar Es Salaam and decided to arrange a car and driver. My friend Chaki was abroad at the time. I found a man with an old

Mercedes. He told me he came from Songea and knew the road well. After financial negotiation, at the start, he must have thought I wanted to buy his car. I arranged to leave at the crack of dawn.

My driver, I will call him Sam, arrived and off we went. Sat next to him was a young lady, and he told me she was a friend who he would drop off near Morogoro. The drive was through Morogoro National Park, and I saw a variety of wildlife. I did point out well after Morogoro that he had forgotten to drop off the young lady. No, he said he had changed his mind, and she was coming with him the whole journey. We did stop off overnight, surprisingly they shared a room, and we arrived at our destination the following lunchtime.

It was a fairly straightforward enquiry involving a critical illness claim, and the man had omitted telling the insurer some of his medical history. We finished at around 5 pm, so I told the driver we would start back to Dar Es Salaam and find a hotel on route at about 8 pm. At this point, he told me about a mysterious fault in his car. He was lying in order to have an extra night away from his wife with his girlfriend at my expense.

Most people think that Africa is always baking hot. Not in the hills at night in the cool season on the road through the

Rift Valley. I was freezing and asked the driver to put the heater on. He looked perplexed and asked what heater. He had claimed to be from this region, another lie. Anyway, we located a hotel, well a place with a bed and toilet. I had left most of my main baggage in the city but went to bed wearing everything in my possession. Wow, was I cold? Thank goodness the car problem had disappeared!

On another trip, I had to travel to Mwanza on Lake Victoria and was able to fly there. My friend Chaki arranged for his contacts there to meet me and arrange a hotel. My hotel was a boat on the Lake. Difficult getting up in the night and wondering why everything was moving. Certainly, something different. At this hotel was a garage full of old, vintage cars. An enjoyable trip - - - I think the claim was false!

My Boat Hotel

Vintage cars

- - - - - - -

In 2007, I investigated a claim relating to a young Tanzanian lady dying in a road accident just outside Dar Es Salaam. She had insurance cover of over £400,000, and the claimant was her sister in Japan. Numerous supporting documents were produced. This was another of those claims that was clearly suspect, as there was no one to interview in the UK, and the insured's background history in the UK was very sketchy. Had the person only been in the UK temporarily? If so, how could she expect to keep paying insurance premiums when living in Africa?

I interviewed at least 12 officials in Tanzania who had records relating to the death. The police officer had statements from witnesses and sketches of the road plus photographs. The hospital had a lengthy file, and three doctors recalled the death: one of them did the post-mortem, or so he claimed. Neighbours, where the lady was staying, told me they also recalled the death. This is a case that had I sent it to my associate there, he would have reported that it was genuine. The body was cremated in a small town about 120 miles away from the scene of the accident and nowhere near the person's residence. To cremate an African is very rare -- that is apart from in false insurance claims' scenarios! The "deceased" was said to be a well-known person who had a programme on local radio.

I interviewed the police officer at length along with the officer in charge and pointed out different anomalies. I formed the opinion that the most senior officer was also involved. The following morning my associate received a call from the police officer. He asked that I did not refer the matter to his hierarchy in Dar Es Salaam if he told the truth. He said it was an insurance scam, and he had been trying to help his sister. Later a letter arrived from the officer in charge stating that there had been no death. I refer to this case because I cannot recall another fraudulent claim with so many supporting documents and witnesses. To come across several doctors and police officers involved in one case is unique.

- - - - - - -

On two occasions, I travelled from Dar Es Salaam across the sea to Zanzibar, a fascinating place to sample the ancient buildings and the new (tourist hotels). The main town is Stone Town, with narrow lanes, old, carved wooden doors, and beautiful mosques and buildings. It is like stepping back in time. Sit in a hotel or restaurant bar on the front with a cool drink, watch the youngsters dive into the sea and fishermen repairing their nets. I think that one day I might return for a holiday.

The first claim related to the alleged death of Lilly. A few months after taking out a policy with a life cover of around £140,000, she died after a short illness at the main hospital there, Mnazi Mmuja. The claim came from her fiancé, Nesmo (later, he was described as her husband), who lived in Tanzania. Lilly appeared not to have relatives in the UK, and very little information was available here.

I travelled to Dar Es Salaam and then took the short flight to Zanzibar with my good friend Chaki. The Central Registry confirmed the validity of the death registration certificate. Death had been registered upon production of a medical certificate from a doctor at the hospital.

The cemetery was divided into Muslim and Christian sections, and Lilly was said to have been buried there. I met the man in charge, and he kept no records. According to him, relatives brought along written permission from the church or mosque, paid money, and he dug a grave. Most graves had wooden crosses bearing a name. However, many had been moved from graves and were scattered about the place. According to him, local farmers kept tying their cows to the crosses, and the cows pulled them out of the ground. There are two Christian churches there that can give permission for a burial. There was no record of Lilly's death at either. The fiancé, Nesmo, had produced their marriage certificate from the Catholic Church and this proved to be false.

There was a report from Dr Julian, who had a clinic in a coastal village. I will call the clinic Memo. It was extremely impoverished with few facilities but in a beautiful coastal area. Dr Julian explained that Lilly was staying at a hotel along the road, was taken ill, and he treated her. He sent her to the main hospital and was later told she died on the way there. I had been informed that although Lilly had a very English name, she was of African descent. Dr Julian could not recall her skin colour! During the interview, he received several text messages and kept going outside to talk on his phone. It was obvious that he was taking instructions about what to tell me. The doctor never asked why I was there asking him these questions. Obviously, he knew, and I suspect someone at the registry had contacted the person behind the fraud. Memo Clinic belonged to Dr Hari in Dar Es Salaam, who operated a tour business there.

I went to the local hotel where she had allegedly stayed, and staff could not recall anyone staying there who had died. The records were with the manager who was away. They spoke to him on the phone, and he told me that the lady stayed there and died on the way to the hospital. The records, he said, were locked away, and the man with the key would not be back there for several weeks. Very convenient!

Next stop was the main hospital. The medical death certificate bore the name of a Dr Komo, and he was off duty. There appeared to be no record of the death, but the mortuary attendant eventually found a record in the mortuary. He said he recalled the death and thought that the body had been shipped to the mainland by Memo Tours. That company, he said, arranged for transportation of corpses of foreigners. I later established that the mortuary attendant was a friend of Dr Hari, the owner of Memo Tours. Eventually, I was sent a letter from the hospital confirming that there was no record of the death. When at the hospital, I saw genuine records containing the signature of Dr Komo, I was certain that it was his signature on the medical death certificate.

Back in Dar Es Salaam, I went to the office of Dr Hari at Memo Tours. On the wall were certificates from various embassies confirming that when one of their nationalities died there, this company would arrange the transportation back home of the corpse. The staff there said they had never heard of Lilly and had no records relating to her death. They rang Dr Hari, and he told me he had gone on "safari" and was nearly 200 miles away. He insisted that Lilly had died in Zanzibar, and he had arranged her burial there. I rang him again the following day, and he stated that the insurance claim would not go ahead. Nothing further was heard. I still do not know if Lilly actually existed.

A visitor to my hotel room

- - - - - - -

A person called Kasim took out two life policies with a cover of £136,000, and soon after this, she notified the insurer that she had changed her name by deed poll to Arafa Nassib. Later, her 17-year-old son notified the insurer that she had died in Zanzibar on 14th April 2016 after a road accident. My colleague interviewed him in Birmingham, and there were many discrepancies in his explanation about his mother's death, various family members and how he was informed about the death. His continual response when clarification was sought was, "I am confused". This was another typical case when a person decides to put in a fake death claim, does not expect to be questioned, so is not properly prepared. It was obvious that there were financial problems and discrepancies about his mother's employment and income.

So off to Zanzibar again. Mrs Nassib was allegedly buried in Bumbwini in the north of the island. Enquiries there indicated that only someone from that area could be buried there with the permission of the local Sheha (Chief). There were 3 Shehas in that area, and conveniently for me, they were all at a local authority meeting. I went there, met them and they all denied knowledge of Nassib. They said that if she was from abroad, then she would have to be buried at the main cemetery in Stone Town.

The local Shehas (I am on the left)

Main cemetery Stone Town – no record of her there either!

The accident, according to the medical papers, had been reported to the police at Makadara Police Station. I went there and discovered that an accident had been reported by Arafa Abdiy Nassib *Mduruma* (another name, but it had the

254

correct age alongside) and the entry in the station diary read –:

22/5, 4pm Arafa Abdiy Nassib Mduruma, *female,* Age 47. *Tribe* Mshiraizi Wa (Note this is a tribe in Zanzibar). Makadara. *The accident happened on 22nd May at approximately 3:30am. She was hit by a wing mirror of an unknown vehicle. She damaged her right shoulder. Accident happened* in Darajani Stone Town. *Action PF3*

Note: PF3 is a form issued to the complainant in order to be treated at the government hospital. So, have you noticed anything odd here??? She was meant to have died in a traffic accident on 14th April, according to the documents produced. Yet on 22nd May, she reported having been hit by a wing mirror of a car.

Next to the Central Registry and, as expected, the death registration certificate was a genuine document. Staff had accepted the medical death certificate from the hospital as being a genuine document, so registered the death. The medical document is actually sent to the registry by staff at the hospital, which would suggest that someone at the hospital is corrupt. The son in the UK had provided the address where his mother was staying in Zanzibar, but this did not exist.

So back to the main hospital.

At the hospital, I established that the doctors named on the police and medical reports worked there but were currently away. There were no records at the hospital of the death or of any treatment there.

Finally, an enquiry of the authorities in Zanzibar paid dividends. There was an immigration record showing that she arrived there on Emirates Airline on 8th April 2016 and departed on 5th May 2016, economy class rather than in a coffin!!

The case was reported to the police in the UK. Mrs Nassib was sentenced to 2½ years, and her son was given a 12-month community order.

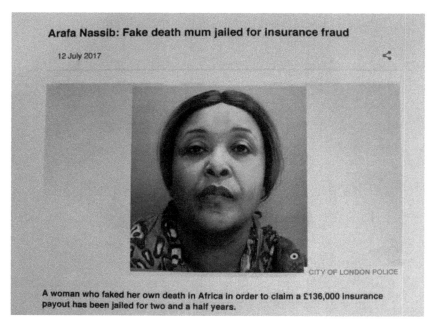

Arafa Nassib: Fake death mum jailed for insurance fraud

12 July 2017

CITY OF LONDON POLICE

A woman who faked her own death in Africa in order to claim a £136,000 insurance payout has been jailed for two and a half years.

First-class travel in Zanzibar!

257

Twice I was fortunate enough to visit Moshi in the north of Tanzania at the foot of Mt Kilimanjaro. On one occasion, I went there by car from Nairobi, an eventful journey through different landscapes. Approaching the border, numerous Maasai warriors line the street hoping you will want to take their photo for $20; inflation knows no borders!

On one occasion, I slept in a hut at a small rural hotel on the outskirts of Arusha.

I had a car and driver from Nairobi and, after finishing an enquiry in Moshi, I thought it better to drive back across the border to Mombasa in Kenya than return to Nairobi and catch a flight. On the map, it looked fairly straightforward, but there are numerous winding roads, many of which are dirt tracks. It is at least a 7-hour journey covering nearly 400kms. I saw some amazing sites, especially as we crossed Tsavo National Park. However, it was the dry season, and red dust covered everything. When I eventually arrived at my hotel, I emptied my suitcase and asked the porter to wash it for me. I peeled off my red clothing, had a shower followed by a bath and then another shower. Eventually, I looked once more like a white man! I would make that journey again, given a chance.

- - - - - - -

When I started investigating death claims, Zimbabwe never featured for some years. I then had in1997 – a claim when a nurse living in south London allegedly died of Aids in Zimbabwe. She held several life policies in respect of mortgages. I could not find any relatives in London and spoke to a neighbour and employer who all seemed to think she had been a very healthy lady. So off to Zimbabwe, and my investigation took me to Bulawayo to Harare to Mutare. Her relatives were not aware of her death, and the doctor who signed the death certificate said he never saw a body but was told she had died suddenly of Aids. Fancy using AIDS for a fake death!

I established that the lady was living with her husband in Johannesburg. Eventually, I obtained a telephone number, and while passing through South Africa on my way home, I rang it and eventually agreed to meet her husband in a hotel there. He assured me that his wife was dead. He was from Nigeria and lived in London. I suggested that I had never had a claim before involving Zimbabwe, but as the lady was married to a Nigerian, then I realised why I was dealing with my first fraudulent claim from Zimbabwe. The man said he would take legal action against me in London. I promised to pick him up at the airport when he arrived and take him to a lawyer - - - or perhaps a police officer! I never heard from him again.

- - - - - - -

Zimbabwe was a beautiful country, with friendly people, a good education system, sporting prowess, wonderful agriculture and infrastructure. I was lucky on that trip to see so much of the country. I read a book about Robert Mugabe, the Prime Minister. One sentence was, "And yet Mugabe's moderation, pragmatism and apparent sympathy for his opponents, have utterly mystified them. (The Americans, British and Russians – see ***). How things were to change after this book was published in 1981! I now read it and make a cross with a red pen where Mugabe's opinions and promises vastly changed. Every page is covered in red crosses!

Many Zimbabweans fled the country and went to South Africa and the UK. Suddenly I had a regular flow of fraudulent death claims involving Zimbabwe. Many of these came from people who had claimed asylum in the UK, obtained a British passport then returned to Zimbabwe to "die". Most of the medical death certificates were stolen from government hospitals, and never did I have a doctor who acted dishonestly. A multitude of claims allegedly involved road accidents, and numerous police documents were produced. I never interviewed a police officer who had written reports that were false. Someone had managed to print blank death registration certificates, and never did I come across anyone in the registry who had acted dishonestly.

Between 2003 and 2009, I regularly travelled to Zimbabwe and had a total of 15 false claims. I think this was related in many ways to the economy that was sinking under Mugabe's control, or rather mis-control. It saddened me to see what was happening, and every time I went there, the situation became worse. The infrastructure was being destroyed, poverty and starvation became rampant. Anyone in opposition to Mugabe suffered. Farms that had produced plentiful supplies of food were being taken over by Mugabe's cronies and were often used as just weekend retreats. Numerous farm employees were living under canvas, under sheets of plastic and were jobless. Yet Mugabe and his corrupt wife, Grace, became wealthy. Grace had a house built in the upmarket Harare area of Borrowdale. It is said that only the sand and cement came from Zimbabwe; everything else was imported from abroad. It was claimed that the funds to build this monstrosity were stolen from a social housing fund.

Grace would often travel to the Far East and return with large quantities of designer clothes, handbags, jewellery etc. Air Zimbabwe suffered and eventually went out of business.

Mugabe would regularly board an Air Zimbabwe flight and change its destination. Who would want to travel on such an airline? You might book a flight to London and end up in Libya! Mugabe sold out to the Chinese. They took over many of the country's mineral deposits in exchange for a broken-down aircraft and two buses that hardly ever worked.

It was not my intention when starting this book to become at all political. But Zimbabwe is a country I fell in love with, and I was deeply saddened to see how people there suffered under the rule of a man who became a tyrant. I met probably around 300 African Zimbabweans all over the country with whom I engaged in conversation. When not in earshot of others, they asked if the British would perhaps invade and restore credibility. Only one of the people I spoke to had a decent word to say about Mugabe. I was also visiting Uganda and Tanzania when Mugabe visited those countries, and I could not believe how he was given a hero's welcome by their leaders. When he died, I mistakenly believed that things might improve but then along came another tyrant, Mnangagwa.

*** This was a remark from an excellent book entitled 'Mugabe' by David Smith and Colin Simpson.

- - - - - - -

In 2012 Mr & Mrs Bhebhe took out life cover of £397,000. They lived just outside London and were both employed as nurses in London. In August 2016, Mrs Bhebhe claimed that her husband had died suddenly in Bulawayo, Zimbabwe, from a pulmonary embolism.

She produced many documents and, from my experience of making enquiries in Zimbabwe, I doubted if they were genuine. For example, there was a document addressed to the pathologist requesting a post-mortem, and it had been completed by one person. It should have been completed by two different people. There was a document from a "Fenerals" (sic) home. Unusual for such a business to make this spelling mistake. The address of the funeral home did not exist in Bulawayo. However, there is such an address in the area in Johannesburg from where Mrs Bhebhe originates.

My colleague interviewed her, and other suspect points arose. According to her Facebook page, on the day she was meant to be in Zimbabwe arranging the funeral, she was in a theme park in South Africa with her daughters. Investigations rarely come as easy as this one. I rang Charing Cross Hospital in London and was eventually informed that the day he died in Zimbabwe, he was at work in London. In fact, the day I rang the hospital, he was there at work.

The police arrested both persons, and they were taken to court. Mr Bhebhe claimed he had no knowledge of the insurance claim, even though a copy of his death certificate was on his phone and his fingerprints were on his death certificate. His wife pleaded guilty.

Nurse faked her husband's death to claim nearly £400,000 in life insurance

16th March 2021

Husband's death faked

A nurse who faked her husband's death to cash in a £400,000 life insurance policy was given a suspended two-year jail sentence. Thulile Bhebhe claimed Bekezela Bhebhe, 54, died in Zimbabwe in 2016 but he was working at Charing Cross Hospital. Bhebhe, 51, of Hayes, admitted fraud at Inner London crown court; her husband was cleared.

The insurer said:-

"Fortunately, it was quickly detected by our expert investigators, and we're pleased to see justice has been done. This is also very good news for our genuine customers, who ultimately bear the cost of fraud through their premiums. In this case however, it's Mrs Bhebhe who will pay the cost for her crime."

- - - - - - -

I travelled several times to Malawi, a beautiful country. I had a few small false claims but nothing special interest apart from one that features below. I really enjoyed staying in Blantyre, a place still with many interesting colonial buildings. I was fortunate enough to travel three times to Lake Malawi, and I have always promised myself a holiday at the lake.

I had a significant claim where a lady from the UK had burnt to death in a car accident. Her husband in the UK originated from Malawi and had family and friends living there. He took his English wife there on holiday. He hired a car and travelled around the country. He was returning very late at night to Lilongwe, where they were staying, when he hit a tobacco lorry parked at the side of the road. He managed to get out of the car and allegedly had just a bang on the head. The car caught fire, and his wife burnt to death.

There were aspects of this claim that required further examination, so I travelled to Malawi. On the way from the airport to my hotel in Lilongwe, I saw a large black area of the main road that had clearly been burnt. I established that this was where the accident happened. My enquiries at the main hospital showed that a medical attendant, there was no qualified doctor there, had been shown a large bone and was able to say that it was from a female human being. This was allegedly all that remained of her body. I saw the police, but they could only say that there was an accident, the car caught fire and the lady died. That was the total extent of their enquiry.

What was interesting was my examination of the car that had been hired. The owner told me that soon after the accident, the police must have checked the registration number, found out he was the owner and rang him. He arrived at the scene of the crash very quickly. The inside of the car was ablaze, but a passenger in the lorry said that after the car hit the lorry, he got out and, although the inside of the car was on fire, he saw the face of a white lady. The owner said that the car had only hit the rear of the lorry with minimal impact; I examined the car, and there was very little damage at the front. The owner said that the fire inside the car was intense. However, the petrol tank never exploded. He showed me the car and asked for my opinion. I was amazed as the engine compartment was intact. The paint on the inside of the wings and the bonnet was unblemished. How could a fire burn for so long inside a car, leaving only a human bone? This was equivalent to the heat in a crematorium. I was informed that a burnt-out petrol can was found inside the car.

I interviewed the claimant again and obtained full details of his journey that day. I returned to Malawi and undertook the same trip. I failed to comprehend how the claimant had ended up in the early hours of the morning on the main road approaching Lilongwe. Where on earth had he been during darkness? How could the inside of a vehicle burn so badly unless, of course, there was an accelerant involved?

The case was referred to accident specialists in the UK. One of them said that if asked in court if the accident was, in fact, accidental, he would have to say that there was a 1 per cent chance. The insurer decided to settle the claim.

- - - - - - -

I have visited Zambia several times and have investigated several false claims, mostly in the area of Ndola in the Copper Belt. It is a beautiful country, and parts of Lusaka are very modern plus fairly expensive. The false claims always involved false documents being produced to the registrar, and I do not recall any doctor or official being party to the frauds.

As with many African countries, the Chinese have provided *aid* to obtain the minerals there. I put the word aids in italics as I fail to see the benefits of building a football stadium next to a football stadium. Aid relating to medical

268

treatment or education would be more useful. Zambians in the Copperbelt are not very fond of the Chinese staff who have arrived there. I recall the news on Zambian TV when I was there a couple of years ago, plus the comments from locals. There had been many instances of thefts at night from mines, so the Chinese chained security guards to the equipment overnight. Local workers were also mining without adequate footwear or helmets, and eventually, a Chinese manager was murdered. I seem to recall that the authorities did not work too strenuously to investigate this. I recall being in a Chinese restaurant in Lusaka, and a group of Chinese, with their feet on the table, all started smoking next to a "No Smoking" sign. They ignored complaints and made out they did not understand English.

The flight from Lusaka to Ndola is less than around an hour on an assortment of light aircraft. Turbulence on that route is significant. On one flight, I was in the toilet relieving myself when the aircraft dropped some distance suddenly. My feet left the ground, and my head touched the roof. All remained intact, and I never missed! I was at Ndola airport when the flight to Lusaka was called, but I could not see any commercial aircraft.

Along with 3 other people, we were taken to a small Cessna. I sat next to the driver - - - I mean pilot. Once we took off, he pointed to a cool box and told me I was the steward for the day and to serve the drinks. An amazing flight!

Chapter 19: Missing At Sea

Over the years, I have investigated several cases where a person has allegedly gone missing at sea. In one year, I had 3 cases, all UK nationals, and you will be glad to know that they all eventually survived!

I will start with "Canoe Man", as John Darwin became known in the UK media. John was a prison officer who allegedly enjoyed canoeing, not true though, and lived on the coast near Hartlepool in northeast England. One day his canoe was washed up along the coast. The Coroner said that any suggestion that it was a deliberate disappearance had no merit: the potential financial awards available were *insufficient* to make it viable. The Coroner also said that the possibility he may be alive was minimal, "say about .0001%".

He was insured for around £195,000, plus there were various employment benefits, clearly an *insufficient* amount. There were a few debts, and we were convinced he was not dead. In our opinion, the police were also not convinced. When the Coroner ruled otherwise, and a certificate was issued, the insurers paid out.

Mrs Darwin worked in medical practice, and staff there later became concerned about her travels abroad. It was thought that she rarely travelled beyond the south of England, but suddenly she had fallen in love with Panama and obtained property there. Her colleagues suggested she did not know what language they spoke in Panama. This appeared to be a person who thought that the Isle of Wight was overseas!

I was speaking to the insurers about travelling to Panama with a view to finding Darwin and trying to locate assets as he was obviously living there. However, suddenly he walked into a London police station in 2007 and claimed he had no idea where he had been for the past 5 years. He did know his name and date of birth. It appears that when buying a property in Panama, he allowed his photograph to be taken, and someone recognised him. Mr & Mrs Darwin seemed to believe that they were going to be caught.

It transpired that after his fake death, he lived in a concealed room in the family home near Hartlepool and regularly left via another exit. We had suggested undertaking surveillance on the property soon after his disappearance, but when the death certificate was issued, the idea was dropped by insurers. If only! It transpires that fellow prison officers told the police that they had seen him at the market after his disappearance, but we were not informed of this.

He was sentenced to 6 years and his wife to 6 ½ years. I do have a certain sympathy in respect of their sentences. Agreed they had been paid out, whereas the cases I refer to in this book were attempts and fraud proven before payments were made. However, you have seen the number of cases involving substantive amounts and where no action was ever taken.

The press later reported that the Darwins divorced, and he was living with his girlfriend in the Philippines. I wonder if she will die, I mean disappear?

John Darwin

- - - - - - -

The next case I am going to mention is about the disappearance at sea of Russell Causley. I could almost write a book just about this man and his activities. To date, I think I have featured in 3 television programmes about his disappearance and the murder of his wife. The latter matter came to light later when the enquiry about his disappearance was underway.

Russell lived in Bournemouth in southern England with Patricia Causley. They were not married, his real name was Packman, but he took on her surname. One Monday morning in October 1993, I received a telephone call from a person I knew who worked in a claim's team for a large insurer in the south of England. She said that she had heard on a southern TV news programme that a man called Russell Causley had gone missing from a yacht off the Guernsey coast. She told me that a man of the same name had taken out a life policy for a large amount, and his solicitor had rung the insurer just before that weekend to put the policy on risk.

I made a series of calls and established that Russell was insured for nearly £1m. I rang the police in Guernsey and was informed that a yacht set sail late on Wednesday 20th October, and a lady on board had raised the alarm at around 2 am the following morning, claiming that a man had disappeared. The lifeboat and a helicopter searched but to no avail. The yacht was towed back to Guernsey. Onboard was Patricia Causley, described as the wife of Russell, Anthony Hackett-Jones, a solicitor and Georgia, a friend of Patricia's who lived in Bermuda.

I flew to Guernsey and met Sgt Phil Falla. He had arrived on duty soon after the return of the yacht to the port. In his view, something was wrong as Patricia just wanted to leave for the mainland. I then made numerous enquiries, and it was obvious that this had to be a fraud. Russell had worked abroad over the years in the aviation business with his wife, Carole Packman. He later bought a house in Bournemouth and became an insurance broker. He started an affair with Patricia Causley, who was said to be his PA. Patricia moved into the family home, and eventually, his wife left, never to be seen again.

Russell had proposed for a large life policy to cover a mortgage in respect of buying a house in London, in SW1, one of the most expensive areas of London. Later it was claimed that details of the property, the mortgage and the whereabouts of the funds to pay the deposit were only known by Russell. Patricia later told me that the information had "gone to a watery grave". I could find no trace of any funds available to him to buy such a property. Furthermore, why did his solicitor, Hackett-Jones, who was also the skipper of the yacht, ask for the policy to go on risk so early? Normally such cover goes on risk when funds are released for the mortgaged property.

Russell Causley was selling his house in Bournemouth, and it was under offer. At this stage, he took out a policy covering the remaining amount of the mortgage left on the property. It was due to be paid off in a few weeks, so why insure it? He also took out other policies, some covering accidental death. He had finance on expensive vehicles, and this was covered by insurance.

I established that the Causley's regularly claimed from insurance companies. It was said that every time they went to the USA, they were robbed and lost expensive watches. Hackett-Jones actually submitted a claim for the designer watch that Causley was allegedly wearing when he went "overboard". I spoke to many people in Bournemouth who knew him. No one thought he was dead, and the general opinion was that it was one of his little ploys. A jeweller told me that if Russell was dead, then it would affect his business: most years, he replaced expensive watches lost by Russell and Patricia while on holiday. I found one claim for the loss of a gold cigarette lighter; none of them, to my knowledge, were smokers.

The yacht was hired from a company in the Hamble, a yachting specialist village near Southampton, on the south coast, and I made enquiries there. Patricia and Hackett-Jones had given their proposed route to the Guernsey police after the incident. They said they were going to Ushant, off the coast of Brittany. The owner of the yacht company explained that had they completed such a trip, then they would have returned the boat several days late. The occupants of the yacht had only removed a few personal effects when they left it in Guernsey. The owner indicated that they did not have suitable attire to carry out such a trip. There were also suspicious circumstances surrounding Hackett-Jones arranging the hire, but he did have the qualifications to sail the vessel.

I interviewed Hackett-Jones and, for a solicitor, I was surprised that he could be so inconclusive and vague. His reason for arranging to put the life policy at risk defied economic sense. Also, he was at that time on bail for his own fraudulent mortgage-related activities.

The house in Bournemouth was sold, and Patricia rented a property in Lamberhurst, a rural village in Sussex. She lived on a long, narrow lane, and I am convinced that this location was selected as surveillance would be extremely difficult. We tried surveillance with cars at both ends of the lane plus someone in a nearby field. Patricia was driving at varying speeds along the lane, between 10 and 50 miles an hour, an obvious ruse to establish if she was being followed. Surveillance is an expensive procedure, so it could only be conducted for a short time.

The other person on the boat, Georgia, was Patricia's friend, and she lived in Bermuda. Georgia originated from the Bournemouth area, and I located some of her relatives. They were all amazed that she was on a yacht undertaking such a trip. Apparently, she hated the sea and suffered from seasickness. I classified her as "rent a witness".

I interviewed Patricia in the presence of her solicitor in Kent and took Phil Falla, the Guernsey police officer, along with me. She was a brilliant actress and had fully convinced her solicitor that she was a grieving widow. However, her display of apparent grief did not impress me. It was clear that she was lying, and there were many discrepancies in her account of events on the yacht and their finances. The following morning, I received a call from her doctor. He told me that she was suicidal, and if she committed suicide, then he would hold me responsible. What an act!

I had reported the matter to the police in London, and we had spoken in confidence to a local resident of Lamberhurst. I believe that this person phoned the police to say that

Patricia appeared to be moving. I was later informed that Patricia, after a glass of wine, too many told someone about the fraud. Later the police told me that they drove to the village and arrived as Patricia turned into the main road, obviously satisfied that she was not being followed from the lane in which she lived. She then drove to a pub and had lunch with Russell, who was arrested. I never got to meet with Patricia again but did have a length of rope ready to assist her should suicide become a possibility.

Russell was sentenced to 2 years in prison in respect of the fraud. The solicitor got 3 years and Patricia a 12-month suspended sentence.

During the investigation, Phil Falla and I became convinced that Russell's wife had been murdered by him with assistance from perhaps Patricia. We met with Samantha, Russell's estranged daughter. I will not spend too much time on this subject as it has been covered in-depth on television, newspapers and many articles are available on the internet. Samantha referred to me at one stage as "that nasty John Saunders telling me he was not dead". Her husband eventually explained what I meant, and she was very helpful. I felt very sorry for Samantha and think it was despicable the way that her father and Patricia had treated her. To her credit, she has made something of her life, and her son is actively involved in attempting to find the truth about his grandmother. I wish him well. There is no doubt that Russell was a violent man who would attack family pets, children, anyone who got in his way!

Both Phil and I were convinced that Russell's wife, Samantha's mother (Carole Packman) had been murdered. She disappeared in 1985. Phil managed to make enquiries abroad, and the results suggested that Carole Packman had disappeared off the face of the earth. Her real name was Veronica, but Russell didn't like this and made her change it. He had been a nasty, control freak and even made his daughter watch for Carole's return while making love to Patricia at the family home. One day Patricia took Samantha to London. When she returned home, her mother was no longer there and never seen again. A note appeared later from a police officer in Bournemouth saying that Carole went to the police station and said she was not missing, as had been reported, but wanted nothing to do with Russell or her family. The officer, unfortunately, died a while later, but it was suspected that this person might have been wearing a wig. I will leave it to your imagination to work out who this might have been!

The house in Bournemouth was in joint names, so this would present a problem for Russell selling the property. In

1990 Carole Packman removed her name from the deeds of the property. The signature was not hers. It was thought that it was Patricia who signed the document. Many people in several countries were seen by the police. Russell appeared to have told numerous different stories about his wife's whereabouts.

Eventually, Russell was arrested, charged with the murder and sentenced to life in 1996, one of the few occasions when a successful prosecution had taken place when a body was not found. Russell had confessed to a fellow prisoner. Later the verdict was challenged and quashed. He was retried, and it seems that his sister stated that he had admitted the killing to her. In early 2020 Samantha' son was trying to stop the authorities from releasing Russell as he has not admitted what happened to the body. I still wonder if Russell had help from anyone when he killed his wife!

Setting sail

Insurance
fraudster
faked his
own death
at sea

- - - - - - -

Another disappearance at sea and once again Bournemouth features. Paul Earley was a builder from South London. He built his own yacht on the south coast of England, a real craftsman. Apart from the insurance on his yacht, he had two life policies totalling about £118,000. One was fairly recent when his wife reported him missing. He had taken the boat to Spain and contacted her to say he was returning to the UK and would be in touch when he reached Lisbon. She claimed she never heard from him again.

The insurers told me there was no need to make enquiries as his wife could not obtain a death certificate for 7 years. Wrong; she went to court and was granted leave to swear death. Enquiries indicated that when Earley finished building the yacht, he took his wife out to sea in it. She had placed lots of china ornaments inside, and a rather heavy sea took care of these; they ended up in pieces on the floor. She was very seasick, so Paul turned the vessel around. When he arrived at the shore, his wife was alleged to have said that France looked just like Bognor! It was Bognor! Paul took the boat to the Mediterranean, but she still felt seasick. It did seem that perhaps Paul needed to dispose of the vessel.

Paul on his new yacht he had built

Mrs Earley was said to be living at her mother's address in south London. I went there, and her mother told me she was staying with her father-in-law in Lymington (on the south coast of England). She said she knew she was out but would later ring her and get her to ring me.

I already had the telephone number of the father-in-law in Lymington, rang the number and there was no reply. A moment later, Mrs Earley rang me, said she was in Lymington, and her mother had just rung her there. This was in the days before mobiles, so I realised she was not telling the truth and was not in Lymington. She agreed to see me but wanted the interview in the presence of her father-in-law's solicitor in Christchurch, near Lymington and Bournemouth. I insisted that the interview was at 3 pm.

I suspected that she was living near Christchurch. Enquiries showed she was using her maiden name and living in High Howe, an area of Bournemouth. The reason I insisted on 3 pm was that she had two young children at school, and I wanted to see who would pick them up, so I arranged surveillance. They would have attended the same school as I did a few years earlier, alright, quite a few years. I used to live about 400 yards from where Mrs Earley was then living.

During the interview with her solicitor, she kept crying, the solicitor put his arm around her, and we had to stop while she had tea. She was very convincing.

After the interview, I drove to the property in High Howe. My associate informed me that Mrs Earley had just returned with an older man (her father-in-law). A man believed to be Paul Earley had collected the children from school and was still in the house. As the children had called him "Dad" at the school, it was very likely him.

There was a police station nearby, and the police were brilliant. They went to the house, spoke to Mrs Early and suggested that her missing husband was there. She invited them in, but there was no sign of Paul there. The officers left, and I told them that surveillance had been conducted since Paul returned and he had not left. When they knocked at the door, there had been some delay before Mrs Early answered. The office recalled that the bed in the main room had been at a slight angle. The officers returned, and guess where Paul was?

He was in a hole under the be

He actually said the magic words, "It's a fair cop, guv". Police also found his DIY fraud kit (see above). Paul had gone to a cemetery, found a grave where the deceased person was born around the same time as himself and took on that identity. I believe that was used in the book "The Day of the Jackal!". Paul was spending time doing building work on the bungalow, and neighbours thought he was just a good friend of Mrs Earley. He did have an address elsewhere in Bournemouth. He was charged with the fraud plus a good number of false benefit claims. Along with his wife and father, they all pleaded guilty and were jailed. Sometime later, the boat was located in Spain by the loss adjuster working on behalf of the boat insurer.

- - - - - - -

And yes, one more disappearance at sea but nowhere near Bournemouth this time. Cusworth allegedly disappeared in 1992, and his small fishing boat was found near Felixstowe on the east coast of England. His wife submitted claims on two policies for around £200,000. Enquiries indicated that he was in debt in relation to his property business. The previous year he had claimed a substantial amount of money from an insurer in respect of a burglary.

An informant came forward to reveal Cusworth's whereabouts. He was living in a caravan site under a false name. It was known that his wife was visiting him, and surveillance on her led to him. She met him one day, and when asked if it was her husband next to her, she responded, "It might be. I can't remember faces".

In the caravan, police found all the items allegedly stolen a year earlier from his house and for which he claimed. Cusworth had three sons, and they had absolutely no knowledge of what their parents were up to.

Chapter 20: China

I had, over the years, made various enquiries in Hong Kong but not in China until 2009. A lady in the UK, Ms Li, applied to take out a policy for £1m in connection with a mortgage. The insurer eventually agreed to insure her for £800,000. Five months later, she allegedly died from a sudden heart attack in a remote town in China. The trustee and beneficiary was her ex-husband in the UK; they had divorced.

I could locate no mortgage, and the property mentioned in relation to her large mortgage had recently been sold to a Chinese man for around £140,000. Ms Li had various debts, plus her small takeaway business had closed down. The ex-husband produced a large number of supporting documents, but there were inconsistencies in his story.

So off to China and having spent a night in Guangzhou in one of the many new, international hotels, it was off to the rural areas. My translator I and spent several hours travelling to a small town called Zhenan and went to the medical centre there. It was small, very basic, and run down. Staff checked the computer and confirmed there was a record of Li dying there on 14th August 2009.

I met the Medical Director and his assistant, and both claimed they recalled the death. They showed me a file that indicated that Li was brought in dead after midnight. They suspected a heart attack, issued documents, and the body was removed. They insisted that there had been no need to call the police. They failed to provide to me a logical explanation as to how they could certify her death as being a heart attack. I spent ages interviewing them, but their story did not alter. They could not recall who took the body there, whether it was a man or woman and who removed the body.

It was claimed that Li was en route from Guangzhou to Luoding when she died and her body was cremated at Luoding. I went to the crematorium there, which is some way outside the town in an attractive, rural setting. This is the only crematorium in that area, and staff informed me that all of the documents relating to the alleged cremation there were false. There was no record there, plus had she died as claimed in Zhenan, the body would have been taken to a crematorium in a different city. Plus, there should have been a police report if it was sudden death.

Li was said to be on route to stay with her cousin in Luoding, and I only had the cousin's mobile number. My associate rang it, explained I wanted to see her, and she claimed to have travelled. Our enquiries showed that she owned a medicine shop in Luoding. We went there, and it was closed. Neighbours told us the cousin had closed early and left around 30 minutes ago, which coincided with my telephone call. Anyway, I did eventually meet the cousin later that evening. According to her, Li rang to say she was coming from Guangzhou and wanted to meet with her in Zhenan. She never asked why. Most odd because Zhenan is out of the way. One can take a coach between Guangzhou and Luoding but not Guangzhou and Zhenan.

The cousin said that they met at the roadside in Zhenan after midnight. Li was ill, so she took her to the hospital on the back of a motorcycle. I asked if she was dead when she arrived there. Her response was, "I don't know. She was talking nonsense". I must have been presumed dead a few times after too many beers at Twickenham on rugby occasions! In that state, however, I never tried to ride pillion on the back of a motorcycle!

The cousin said they took her body to the crematorium, and she was cremated the next day. She could not recall who removed the body from the hospital or how it was transported. She, in fact, seemed to know very little. What she did tell me mostly contradicted what I had been told at the hospital.

The following day I returned to Guangzhou and tried ringing various family members there, and, yes, they had all travelled away from Guangzhou! However, I located the business run by a cousin, met him and obtained another completely different story.

This was my first claim involving China but not the last.

When we returned to Guangzhou, my interpreter suggested that I should go to a small, local bar where there was music and good beer. I did so, and suddenly, a partially dressed young lady started dancing on a small stage with this enormous snake, possibly a python. I'm not certain that I suffer from ophidiophobia (I never learnt that word in China!), but I hate snakes. Anyway, later I was sat at the bar having a drink and watching football on the TV above the bar when - - - - -something was moving near to my ankles. It was the snake, and I froze. Luckily the young lady realised that she had lost her "pet" and collected it from around my feet. It's harmless, she said. At least, I think that's what she said in Chinese. An unusual takeaway!

- - - - - - -

In 2008 Ms Yi wanted to take out life cover of £1m. She was living in the UK with her sister and brother-in-law, and they also wanted a large life cover. They lived in an expensive property and owned multiple businesses. Because of this, the insurer agreed to cover the sister-in-law for £800,000. Ms Yi, though, only appeared to be a home help for her sister.

The brother-in-law, I will refer to him as Jao, notified the insurer that his sister-in-law had died in China from a heart attack, and this was 17 months into the life of the policy. I arranged to meet with Mr Jao to discuss the claim. I have interviewed claimants from all walks of life in run-down flats, squats and large, modern homes. Never had I met a claimant living in such an expensive, stunning property. I cannot go into too much detail in case it reveals the man's identity, but he was probably one of the most intelligent, well-educated claimants I have ever met. However, I never believed a word he said about the claim and really enjoyed the challenge.

Jao had retired from a high-profile position and helped his wife run her businesses. His sister-in-law had come to the UK a few years ago to assist his wife. I could find absolutely no reason why she would want to pay a very hefty insurance premium for such high cover. Her income was small, and she appeared to have no assets. Jao explained that only his wife and he in the UK were aware of the death, and he requested that enquiries were not made of his elderly father-in-law in

China as he was ill and unaware of the death. Also, he and his wife were the beneficiaries of the claim, but he assured me he would send the money to family in China. I was probably 99% certain that this was a fraud. It would be rare for me to suggest to a claimant that he or she was lying unless I had proof. Often it is necessary to travel abroad to the place of death to obtain that proof. If I was to challenge a claimant without strong evidence and be proved wrong, the ensuing publicity could harm the insurer's reputation and would probably have left me unemployed! The place of the alleged death was remote and possibly cut off by heavy snow at that time of the year. Not a journey I wanted to undertake.

In this case, there was not quite sufficient evidence to further challenge Jao. Instead, I gave him a lengthy list of documents to obtain, plus additional questions to be answered. By this time, I was in his office, and he was copying documents and making notes. He made so many remarks leaving me with the impression that he was making excuses should this turn out to be a false claim. He mentioned his age and suggested that when I was his age, I would realise that one's memory is no longer the same. I told him that I disagreed, my memory was fine, and I was 4 days older than him!

A couple of days later, he rang me. "You won't believe what happened, Mr Saunders?" he remarked. He went on to say that he rang the family in China to ask for the documents I had requested. The phone was answered by his dead sister-in-law. He claimed, "I have been tricked". I asked him if he would give them my details because I had spent my life trying to find someone to trick me into being paid £800,000! That was the last I heard from him.

Should this book be printed and sold, certain people reading the title might consider purchasing it to see if they are mentioned. Yao should you read this. I would like to mention that I really enjoyed meeting you. I did not believe you were really a dishonest man, and I am glad you saw the light.

- - - - - - -

I have investigated a couple of other UK claims relating to China, and these claims were also dropped as they were obviously false. I also made an enquiry for an Australian insurer, and although fraud was proved, it transpired to be somewhat unusual. A young Chinese male living in Australia, Wang took out a life policy there in October 2011 for the equivalent of around £400,000. The executor and the beneficiary was his Chinese girlfriend in Australia.

In March 2012, she notified the insurer that he had died in China from cancer after a short illness. She sent in supporting documents plus a certified copy of his passport. Enquiries in Australia revealed no significant medical history. His passport indicated that he was in China from 22nd July 2011 until 4th September 2011. The policy was taken out in October 2011. The next stamps in his passport showed that he went back to China on 29th December 2011; he died on 17th March 2012.

I travelled to Beijing and stayed there overnight. My good friend in Beijing, KT (I am not concealing his real name- this is his nickname), arranged an interpreter and booked a hotel for the first night. I arrived there late, checked in to be told that I was in one of the extensions, about 400 metres along the road. I eventually located my room but experienced a problem sleeping. This was because I have never before slept in an ashtray. Everything stunk of smoke, the curtains, linen, bed coverings and pillow. Revolting!

Anyway, the next morning I left my ashtray environment, met my interpreter and took the bullet train on a 3-hour journey to Zhengzhou, quite an experience. This is a large city that has a vast factory making iPhones and trucks. There is a new section of the city with smart walkways, a canal and plenty of new international hotels.

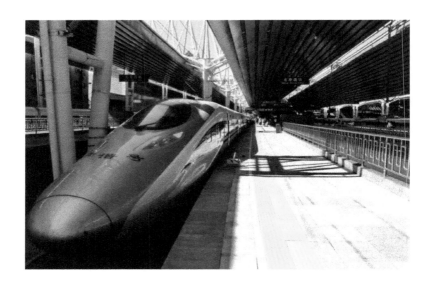

I made enquiries at several hospitals there and later
back in Beijing. Wang was diagnosed with cancer in July
2011 and was being treated at various hospitals in China up
until his death. He could not have been travelling as shown
by the stamps in his passport as he was in hospital in China.
The insurer checked with Australian immigration, and
Wang last left Australia in July 2011, so he was not in
Australia when the policy was taken out. I examined the
documents and suspected that his girlfriend had applied in
his name and forged his signature. The copy passport
produced had been certified by a lawyer. The insurer never
updated me on the outcome of a meeting with him.

I made enquiries of his sister in Zhengzhou, and her
explanation of events was incorrect.

I established that Wang's father took out a life and
critical illness policy on his son with a Chinese insurer in

August 2011 and later submitted a claim when he died. The insurer refuted the claim as they established that Wang's cancer was diagnosed shortly before that date.

- - - - - - -

Prior to leaving Beijing, I met up with my friend KT. He works for an international insurer and had visited my UK office to learn about areas where we had problem claims, etc. In Beijing, KT gave me a book and assured me that it contains a chapter about my work. I keep meaning to take it to my local Chinese takeaway to have translated. KT assured me that he had been complimentary. I thought I would also be complimentary as KT is a great character and very good at his job. However, should I find out that he was not so complimentary

- - - - - -

My friend KT and the book

I had a few hours before leaving for site seeing.

Chapter 21: Togo & Ivory Coast

Time for a bit of West African humour – no, not Nigeria and Ghana, they feature again later. Togo, a tiny ex-French colony next to Ghana. More than one insurer received a claim relating to Alomatu having been knocked down and killed in a hit and run accident along the coast road in Togo. He had taken out 5 different policies, all just for accidental death and with a total cover of around £720,000. The claimant was Washa, again I have changed his name, but you will see later why I have not changed the name of the alleged deceased.

I interviewed Washa in his flat in east London, but he had been very reluctant to see me in his home. I was not surprised as it was one room containing a bed, old sofa and desk. There was a tiny kitchen and a small bathroom. He had a laptop, and this was worth more than the rest of the entire contents of the place. I carried out numerous online searches and could find nothing in Alomatu's name, apart from the insurance policies and a bank account held jointly with Washa and used to pay the premiums. Washa and Alomatu had been directors of a limited company, but there was no sign that it had ever traded. I could start a company tomorrow and show Donald Duck as a director; it probably would never be queried!

Washa was a strange character. Apart from having a weird dress sense, he was almost as wide as he was tall. I asked about his relationship with Alomatu as, according to him, they lived together in this tiny place. He told me they were business partners and a "couple". Alomatu, he said, had lived in the UK for 8 years. I asked for the name of his doctor and was informed he never had one. They both preferred "traditional medicine". Both originated from Ghana, and he told me that Alomatu went to Togo via Ghana to visit a friend and his own mother, who both lived in Lome (the capital of Togo). His father had died many years ago.

Later his friend there, Ouatra rang to say he had been killed in an accident. He told him that he went out but did not return, and later, Ouatra located his body in a hospital along the coast. Alomatu always said he wanted to be cremated within 3 days of his death and wanted his ashes sprinkled in Africa. I refrained from remarking that it was a good job that he died in Africa, or else the cost - - -. He had requested this in his will, and he had left everything to Washa. Not many young people prepare a will when they have absolutely no assets, no next of kin or family, nothing in the bank and have only insurance policies for accidental death. Washa said he went to Togo for the cremation. His passport showed he was there for only 3 days. It is a very expensive flight on Air France travelling directly to Lome.

I asked about Alomatu's personal effects, and he told me he took them with him to Togo and gave them to the mother. He denied having paid excess baggage, and this would suggest that Alomatu's total possessions fitted into one case. According to Washa, Alomatu's passport was with him when he died, so it must have been stolen. He never drove, so he had no driving licence. Washa had no photographs of his good friend and no documents relating to income tax or national insurance.

I began to suspect that perhaps Alomatu might never have existed, and this is something that is often difficult to prove. Washa's date of birth was 3-9-68, Alomatu's was 6-12-68. Have you spotted anything here of interest? If you want to remember a false date of birth, then add a figure onto your own, 3 in this case. 3rd becomes 6th, September becomes December and keep the same year.

I told Washa that I was interviewing him on behalf of X Life, and he insisted that there was only one policy. After a short chat with him, he corrected himself and admitted there were claims with several insurers.

So off to Togo. I flew via Ghana as it was cheaper, plus I expected to end up making enquiries there as well. My good friend in Accra, Boat, drove me to the border, and there was a long queue of people waiting to cross. I was ushered

303

to the front of the queue. I did not imagine I was about to receive VIP treatment and guessed what was coming next. I had a visa but was obliged to pay an additional fee, probably entitled "white man crossing charge". I had arranged with a contact to meet an interpreter at my hotel. I speak some French, but as mentioned earlier in the book, African French can be very difficult to comprehend. My translator never showed until the following morning. When we met, I explained the purport of my visit, and he got up, said it was far too dangerous and left. Eventually, I found a young lady who worked in the shop at the hotel, and she spoke French, was from Ghana, so spoke English as well. She was quite adept at her task, but I did ask if the next day she could perhaps dress a little more conservatively. While interviewing people, they were all men up until then, they appeared somewhat mesmerised, staring at her ample bosom falling out of her dress. She smiled and took on my advice the following day.

Cremations there are arranged via the Hindu Temple. Africans are not normally cremated, and the ones I have come across have all been insurance scams! There was a record of the cremation, and I had to return the next day to meet various government officials. An undertaker had been engaged to collect the body from the mortuary at the hospital in Aneho, along the coast where he allegedly died. I was informed that Africans are never cremated, so officials wanted to see the deceased's passport plus his original will. A copy was faxed to them, but they insisted that the beneficiary from London travelled there. Hence the reason Washa travelled to Togo. He had to take the will to allow the cremation. According to him, the passport must have been stolen from the scene of the accident. How much cheaper it would have been to have buried his friend in Africa! I visited the undertaker, who confirmed that he collected the body for the cremation. He was still owed money.

Aneho is about 30 miles along the coast of Lome. The registrar operated from an office there, plus from a hut in a nearby village, and that is where I met him. It did appear that the death had been registered on the strength of the medical death certificate issued at the hospital.

I went to Central Hospital in Aneho, a very poor establishment and met the doctor who certified death. He explained that he was a general doctor but also acted as a pathologist. I attempted to establish his system for recording receipt of bodies, their identities, cause of death etc. and realised there was no system. He explained that if the police knew the identity of the deceased, they would give him a name which he would write on a tag and attach it to the toe of the corpse. Sometimes it might be a while before the police knew the identity, so they would give him a piece of scrap paper bearing the name of the corpse. He showed me his record, but Alomatu's name did not appear. In fact, there were very few names alongside the entries in the record. He said he could not recall the death as he dealt with so many. Regularly unidentified corpses went to a pauper's grave. He did identify his signature on the medical death certificate.

Next, I saw the police in Aneho, and the officer I met recalled the death. He told me the parents of the deceased took the body away, but he never recorded their names. When their son went missing, they went to the mortuary, where they identified him. There were no documents on the body when it was found on the highway. The officer explained that villagers regularly came out of the bush to cross what was the main road. Cars travelled at speed, and there were a host of such accidents.

It will be recalled that Washa told me in London that Alomatu went to Togo to see his mother and his friend, Ouatra. I rang Outara and eventually interviewed him in Lome. He told me he met Alomatu in 1996 in Ghana and kept in touch. Alomatu's mother lived somewhere in Sunyani, in the north of Ghana, not in Lome. Alomatu stayed with him when he came to Togo. He appeared to be in possession of very little information about his friend, such as where he came from, his job, marital status etc.

In respect of his death, Alomatu took a bus to Aneho where there is a large lake to see. He was due back at lunchtime but never arrived. At about 3 pm, Ouatara was in the market by the bus station in Lome and heard people talk about a young man having been knocked down in Aneho. Ouatara was worried that it might be his friend, so he took a taxi to Aneho, spoke to the police, went to the mortuary and found Alomatu. He said the police had not been able to identify him as he was carrying no documents. He had left home that morning with his passport, so it must have been stolen. Ouatara said he rang Washa in London and was informed that Alomatu wanted to be cremated. Ouatara told me that he had not met Alomatu's parents, did not know how to contact them, and they did not attend the cremation. Yet the police officer told me the parents took the body away!

I returned to see the police officer, and while interviewing him, he kept referring to a note that he was holding under the desk. The officer told me this time that the parents had identified the body at the scene of the accident, but the officer forgot to put the deceased's name on his report. The parents had taken the body away for disposal.

307

Finally, he confirmed that they often had unidentified bodies from such accidents.

There were numerous discrepancies, such as the police officer told me the parents identified the body and took it away. Ouatara said he identified it, he did not know where the parents lived, and they did not attend the funeral. Washa had told me that Alomatu went to Togo to see his mother, who lived there. When he went for the cremation, he handed the mother Alomatu's personal effects.

I returned to Ghana and made further enquiries. I established that Alomatu, or at least someone using that name, arrived in Accra from London on a Ghana Air flight on 17th August 2003. He was using a Ghanaian passport issued by the Ghana High Commission in London. I know from past experience that a Ghanaian can go to the High Commission in London, claim they lost their passport and be issued with a replacement. It was my belief that someone had travelled one way to Ghana using the name Alomatu.

Had a person called Alomatu lived in London for a few years, as claimed by Washa, then then he must have previously had a Ghanaian passport. To get a passport, he would have needed to have a birth certificate. I had been told that Alomatu's father died years ago. As described above, there were discrepancies about the whereabouts of his mother. I told Washa that the insurers would require to see Alomatu's birth certificate, and one had to exist if he had previously travelled to the UK.

Eventually, Washa sent this letter to insurers. I found the comment about having no photographs interesting.

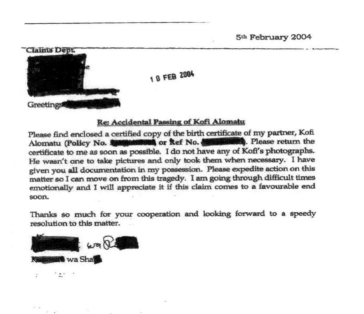

5th February 2004

Claims Dept.

1 0 FEB 2004

Greetings

Re: Accidental Passing of Kofi Alomatu

Please find enclosed a certified copy of the birth certificate of my partner, Kofi Alomatu (Policy No. ███████ or Ref No. ███████). Please return the certificate to me as soon as possible. I do not have any of Kofi's photographs. He wasn't one to take pictures and only took them when necessary. I have given you all documentation in my possession. Please expedite action on this matter so I can move on from this tragedy. I am going through difficult times emotionally and I will appreciate it if this claim comes to a favourable end soon.

Thanks so much for your cooperation and looking forward to a speedy resolution to this matter.

wa Sha

Republic of Ghana

C № 1014530

CERTIFIED COPY OF ENTRY IN REGISTER OF BIRTHS

Entry No.: 21467		Registry: Adjabeng
CHILD Name in full (write first name first and surname last.	Kofi Alomatu	Sex Male
FATHER	Name: Komi Alomatu Occupation: Teacher Nationality: Ghana Religion: Christian	
MOTHER	Maiden Name: Vivian Aku Awanyo Nationality: Ghana	
When Born	6th December 1968	
Where born. (write address, fully possible e.g. number of house, name of Street, name of ward or part of the town.	Korle Bu Teaching Hospital Accra	
Signature in full or Name in full and mark, duly witnessed, of informant and relationship, if any to the Child.	Komi Alomatu (Father)	
Date of Registration	11th December 2003	
Signature of Registrar	M. Y. Fiagbor	
Margin	BRA/02 01/11/12/03/66201 BRA/11/12/03/66128	

I, M_____ Accra

in the _____ Accra _____ Registration District in Ghana do hereby certify that this is a true copy of
entry No. 21467 in the Register of Births for the said District and that the Register is now legally in my custody.
Witness my hand this 11th day of December 2003

Registrar of Births for Adjabeng

_____ Registrar of Births and Deaths for Ghana do hereby certify
that the above Signature is in the handwriting of _____ Registrar
of Births for Adjabeng _____ in the Accra _____ Registration District in Ghana.
Given under my hand and SEAL in Accra in Ghana this 11th day of December 2003

B.D.R. Form Vbr

Registrar of Births and Deaths
L.S.

This is the birth certificate issued in December 2003, yet he allegedly died in September 2003. This is not as stupid as it might at first seem. In Ghana, it is possible for relatives to swear affidavits about someone's birth years after the event. In the affidavit, they give details of where and when the person was born, full details of the parents and state that as the birth was not registered, they are now requesting for it to be registered. I saw the Registrar of Ghana in Accra, but unfortunately, he could not locate the affidavits. However, if the birth certificate was not issued until December 2003, then how could this person have previously acquired a passport to travel to London? I had been informed that Alomatu's father died years ago, yet he is shown as registering the death in December 2003! I asked Washa to explain how he had obtained this certificate. He had told me he did not know the location of the mother and the father was dead. I still await an answer.

According to the certificate, Alomatu was born in Korle Bu Teaching Hospital, the largest hospital in Ghana. Staff managed to locate the relevant records from December 1968 when he was allegedly born. There was no record of his birth.

Almost the perfect crime. Cremating the body prevents any future exhumation, so it negates potential DNA testing. Every time I have had a claim where a person of African origin has been cremated in Africa, it has been a fraud.

Almost a perfect crime, I said. The problem is that you have to be born before you can die!

Scene of the alleged accident

Registry

Crematorium

- - - - - - -

Twice I have visited Ivory Coast to investigate claims. Being French-speaking and very bureaucratic makes it an extremely difficult location in which to work. The first claim was in respect of a man called Yves. He had a life policy for £200,000, and it was nearly 5 years after taking out the policy that he died. Most unusual if this was to be a false claim. He held a French passport and had died in a car accident when returning with friends from Ghana to Ivory Coast.

He and his family lived in poverty in a small flat in London. He was said to be unemployed yet managed to afford to travel to Abidjan. I interviewed his wife, and she was very vague when asked about the death and burial. She was even vaguer when asked when she came to the UK. She stated that a man brought her on a plane, handed her papers and told her she was on her own. She did not know where she was, spoke no English but somehow ended up in south London.

I went to Ivory Coast, and it was very difficult trying to establish the facts from various officials. The officer named on the police report appeared possibly not to exist, but the police said they were making enquiries into this. Three years later, they were still making enquiries. In other words, they did not want to admit that there was corruption somewhere in that station.

There was no record of the death at the hospital shown on the medical death certificate.

The registration certificate was fake, and I did get a statement stating as such. Other documents appeared to be genuine but could not have been issued correctly. The best information came from the cemetery. They had a record of the death, had a metal plaque made for the headstone, but it was still in the cupboard there as the body never arrived for burial.

I had the telephone numbers of Yves's friends and relatives there and rang them. Naturally, they had all travelled and would not be back in Abidjan for ages. I managed to ask them questions on the phone, and I think they were all talking about different events. Nothing in their stories tallied.

There was ample evidence that the claim was false, and the matter was reported to the police in London, who later decided against taking any further action. It would have been difficult for the police to travel to Ivory Coast and get the evidence there. The problem with reporting cases such as this to the police is that if they do not proceed, then the claimant alleged that if it was a fraud, they would have been prosecuted. Therefore, they allege that the claim has to be genuine so expect payment to be made.

The claimant managed to engage a "no win, no fee" solicitor and obtained many new documents. One document was from a court in Abidjan stating that Yves had died at a certain hospital, his death was certified by Dr X, and it was the court's decision that he was dead. The solicitor suggested this was proof, and the claim should be paid immediately.

As I was travelling to Ivory Coast on another enquiry, I did further work there on this one. The court document referred to the doctor who certified the death, but no medical

315

certificate from him was produced to the court. I proved that the doctor did not exist, but the court document was genuine. How could any court issue such a document with no evidence to back it up? I believe it would be possible to go to court, swear that my name is Donald Duck and that Mickey Mouse died in my presence, and they would issue me a legal declaration. I kid not!

One of the new documents produced was a letter and statement from the wife requesting that the plot in the cemetery be leased for an additional 10 years. There was no plot there, and when I went back again to meet the staff, they showed me the documents that had been sent to them by the authorities. They were perplexed, to say the least! The body had still not arrived!

This time family members did agree to meet with me. They made written statements about the death, and what they told me completely varied from what the wife in London was claiming. The statements were sent to her solicitor, and there followed accusations about my treatment of the family members I met. Apart from having 2 witnesses present, one was my interpreter; the interview took place in the lobby of an international hotel.

The claim had now been dropped, so I expect Yves to return soon and ask for back payment of his State benefits and insurance premiums. I believe it wrong that an insurer has to pay so much in legal fees in order to combat a "no win, no fee" solicitor who has nothing to lose. Often, they only pursue a claim hoping that the insurer will make a small settlement in order to avoid high legal fees.

But the body never arrived!

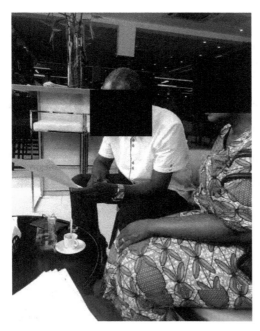

Yves relatives "under pressure"

- - - - - -

I cannot at the moment comment in too much detail about the second claim in Ivory Coast as it was still ongoing at the time of writing this section. It has no UK connection, apart from me investigating it, and you will be surprised to learn what one can claim from a travel insurance policy. I have mentioned this to several people in the industry, and they were surprised that such a claim could be made.

Let me call the insured Pierre, a person originating from Ivory Coast but resident in France. He took out a travel insurance policy as we all do when going on holiday. We

318

know that it covers us for emergency medical treatment, loss of money, credit cards and personal effects, but there is something else - - - -

It is claimed that one evening Pierre was walking along a street (dirt track) in Abidjan when he heard noise from some rowdy individuals who were approaching him. It was dark. There were no streetlights there, so he started to run. He knocked into a lady, and she fell into a 3-metre hole. He somehow managed to get her out of the hole and take her to a local clinic, where she died soon afterwards. She had identification, and the clinic called her husband, let's call him Jean. He came, and her body was removed.

The next day Pierre contacted his travel insurer in France and said he would need legal help as the police were about to interview him about an accident in which someone died. In fact, it was 2 days later when the police were informed, so Pierre must have had a premonition.

Jean engaged a lawyer in Abidjan and in France and is taking action against Pierre for causing his wife's death, around €240,000. He has produced documents, seemingly from a non-existent company showing that his wife had a considerable income.

I have made enquiries in Ivory Coast, and these are ongoing. There is a grave with a headstone. The cemetery records did not tally and were clearly made well after the date of the alleged burial. There are statements from 2 witnesses who are reluctant to be interviewed. There were numerous discrepancies, and once more, I think there might be a "no win, no fee" lawyer involved. Watch this space.

There was no record of the grave's location in a huge cemetery, yet a worker took us immediately to the grave.

321

Chapter 22: Middle East

Over the years, I have travelled many times to the Middle East. Countries include Turkey, Israel, Syria, Saudi Arabia, Yemen, Egypt, Jordan and the UAE. I have covered my trips to Lebanon and Iran in chapters 10 and 11.

I will start with Egypt, a place I have visited several times. My first enquiry there was in the early 90s. An Egyptian who had lived in London for years died in Egypt in a small village in the Nile Valley north of Cairo. It soon became clear from enquiries in London that the man was involved in mortgage frauds along with the executor and beneficiary of the insurance policies. The life policies were all related to mortgages on properties that had clearly been overvalued to obtain fraudulent mortgages.

At that time, the Egyptian Government was trying to encourage Egyptians abroad to return there and farm along the Nile. I went to the farming village where the man allegedly died, and a doctor insisted that he had examined the body and written a death certificate. The local registry had a record of the death, but there were anomalies.

The claimant in London had provided very little information about the death or about the deceased's family and friends in Egypt. Along with my interpreter, we went through the Cairo telephone directory ringing everyone with the same name. Believe it or not, it was not long before I actually spoke to the "dead man". He did not know that he was meant to be dead.

We later met up, and he admitted that he had been involved with his friend in mortgage frauds. He knew he had one life insurance policy but thought that was needed to get the mortgage. It had never been discussed that he was meant to die so that his partner could claim around £1m. He told me that a solicitor from London had recently visited him in Cairo and asked him to sign an undated will. The man was very angry, made a full written statement and said he would willingly return to London and give evidence in court, even if he was charged with mortgage fraud.

The actions of the solicitor were clearly suspect as she was involved in helping the claimant deal with the insurance companies. She knew that the man was meant to be dead when she asked him to sign his will. There was also evidence against a surveyor who was providing false values for properties. The UK police decide against taking any action.

Me with Abdel

In 2005 the owner of a nursing home in the Isle of Wight, Masser, allegedly died with his wife in a traffic accident in Cairo. There were many insurance policies, although his wife only had accidental death policies. The total was around £2.8m, and an Egyptian doctor from the Isle of Wight submitted the claims via his solicitor there. I carried out quite a lengthy investigation in the UK, and eventually, both the solicitor and I thought the events very suspicious. The man was in debt, and this is one of the main reasons that people commit such fraud. Unusual to get a claim where the claimant's solicitor expresses his concern that it is a potential fraud!

Our enquiries were extended to Cairo, and we found that most of the addresses given did not exist. There was a lawyer there said to be acting for the claimant, and when

324

interviewed, he insisted that the various letters bearing his name were false. The death registration certificates were also fake, and we ended up at a Ministry being advised by the Assistant Minister of Police that as we did not have work permits, we could not carry out an investigation. Being slightly deaf, the enquiry continued, and everything proved to be false. Masser's wife did not exist! Somehow, he had managed to get various records in her name in the UK. The fact that she only took out policies for accidental death was perhaps a clue. Few, if any, questions are asked when such policies are taken out and rarely is one's identity checked.

Being an Arab country meant that it was difficult to get anything in writing from the authorities confirming that the documents were false. However, we did go via the Egyptian Embassy in London, and they were super-efficient. They provided official evidence for the police in the UK to take action.

Undercover near Cairo

- - - - - - -

Over the years, I have investigated around 8 false claims in Egypt. One was for an insurer in Japan and was most unusual. A young man had accidental death cover for around $1m and was found dead one morning in a Cairo park. Documents produced indicated he died in a mugging, and many his personal effects had been stolen. The truth was that he hung himself from a tree, a very sad case. I never established how a police report had been obtained suggesting that he had been mugged.

- - - - - - -

I travelled a couple of times to Syria, a place I always enjoyed visiting. The people were extremely friendly. It was then a safe environment that is apart from when in a moving vehicle, and there are so many historical sites to see. Damascus features in the birth of Islam and Christianity, and I wonder what it is like nowadays. I have travelled long distances there by car and seen some amazing sites. On one occasion, when I finished in Damascus, my driver took me across the mountains to Beirut. I do not suppose one can safely undertake such a journey nowadays.

I investigated a substantial claim in Syria relating to multiple sclerosis (MS). Mrs Ali took out two small life and critical illness policies with an international insurer in 2006 and 2007. In June 2008, she took out a policy for a cover of $650,000, far in excess of the original policies. Her husband took out a policy with a cover of $500,000. For such amounts, the insurer asked a lot of questions about employment and income. When taking out the previous policies, she was described as a housewife. By 2008 she owned 4 shops, 2 parcels of land, and 5 houses. These were acquired, she claimed in January that year. She rented out the properties, had an annual income of $190,000 and assets worth $1.8m. She produced bank statements showing amounts of €600,000 and $634,000 in deposit accounts. Her husband claimed to own a travel agency and had a rental income of $300,000 a year. On the face of it, a couple with substantial income and assets, so the insurance cover was deemed suitable.

In May 2009, Mrs Ali submitted a claim for MS and submitted a relevant report from a neurosurgeon in Damascus. I was asked to travel to Syria and undertake enquiries.

The story was that one morning in November 2008, she awoke with no feeling in her leg or arm on one side. Mr Ali rang their local doctor, who suggested that she went to see Dr Khalid, a neurosurgeon. They travelled across Damascus in the rush hour, met Dr Khalid, who carried out various tests, and after a 30-minute consultation, he diagnosed MS. Normally doctors need to carry out a multitude of tests over a period of time before being able to diagnose MS. It can take months. Her initial symptoms, no feeling down one side, could be indicative of a stroke, and I doubt if any doctor would start looking at MS. I could not understand why the family's doctor would suggest sending her on a lengthy journey across Damascus to see a neurosurgeon. I would have expected heart-related tests to have been conducted without delay and, therefore, at a medical establishment nearer to her home.

There were numerous discrepancies in the information supplied by the couple about their finances. Mr Ali did not own a travel agency. He worked as an accounts clerk for an airline earning around $12,000 a year. He did not appear to own any property. I interviewed him and his wife twice. One major problem when lying is to recall those exact lies at a later stage. Mrs Ali claimed to have recently inherited a large fortune from her late father. Enquiries suggested he was not "late". I asked Mr Ali for recent statements in relation to his wife's two large deposit accounts. They were not available. He refused to accompany me to the banks in order for me to verify the existence of the accounts. Clearly, the accounts never existed. There was absolutely no evidence available to suggest that the couple had any wealth.

There were also discrepancies in relation to her treatment and visits to doctors. Her husband drove her to see the neurosurgeon, who recalled her arriving in an ambulance. Mrs Ali claimed that she required regular injections, and these were carried out by the local pharmacy. She refused to tell me which one, but my enquiries of the local pharmacies suggested she was not telling the truth. She had only visited the neurosurgeon once for 30 minutes. She claimed to have MS but had sought no further treatment.

Mrs Ali did appear to be in good health, but of course, that can occur with MS. The claim was not pursued. I will never know the exact truth. Was it false in that she never had MS? Or was it possible that MS had been diagnosed before she took out the insurance cover? One of these has to be correct.

- - - - - - -

I made another critical illness enquiry in Syria that took me on a lengthy, unusual journey. A young man from Syria lived in a rather expensive property in London and tried to give the impression of wealth. However, the property and contents had nothing to do with his own wealth or financial status. He took out a policy for over £600,000 and a few months later suffered a heart attack in a small town on the border of Iraq and Syria. He produced various medical documents from a hospital there. It is not always possible in such cases for a doctor in the UK to examine such a claimant and confirm whether or not they have suffered a heart attack. Hence over the years, I have dealt with numerous false claims where a heart attack allegedly occurred overseas. UK enquiries threw doubt on the validity of this claim.

So off to Damascus, and my associate there drove me to Deir Ezzor, a large city on the banks of the Euphrates River. A very pleasant place to stay the night. The following morning, we continued toward the Iraq border to Albumakal, a distance of around 530kms from Damascus. I interviewed staff at the small hospital where the man had been treated, and the main records were said to be under lock and key. The keyholder was in Damascus and not due back for several days, very inconvenient. The claimant had gone on a bus from Damascus to the town to visit a friend who was a doctor. The various explanations from doctors and staff did not tally. The sick man was said to have been in ICU for 4 days, seriously ill, yet I was able to show that he spent most of this time on his mobile phone. He had contacted his travel insurer, who sent a car to collect him. However, for some reason, he discharged himself from the hospital and returned to Damascus on the night bus. Further enquiries in Damascus showed that the claim could not be genuine. The man's father had seen his son on that visit but knew nothing about him being ill.

On the way back to Damascus, I stopped at Palmyra and briefly viewed the famous ruins. Quite spectacular, and I cannot fathom why anyone (ISIS) would want to destroy such history!

On the road to Deir Ezzor

- - - - - - -

I will always recall one smallish claim relating to a young Syrian lady who had been a student in Leeds. The claimant was said to be her husb.and in Syria. I went to a small town outside Damascus, and the civil registry office confirmed that the death had been registered there. I tried to locate the home of the family, but it was closed up. So, I went and met the local "mukhtar" (the head of the village come local mayor). Nothing happens locally without the knowledge of the mukhtar. The mukhtar knew the young lady and was certain she was not dead. He spoke to her the previous week, and she was travelling somewhere abroad.

She was not married, and the claimant was not her husband but her brother.

Believe it or not, the doctor who certified the death insisted she had died. When faced with the evidence, he would only say he must have been tricked!

Me with the local Mukhtar (man next to me)

- - - - - - -

Since the invasion of Iraq, I have dealt with 7 death claims from there. I have never travelled there but have obtained evidence to show that 6 of them were false. One claim was investigated by an associate in Baghdad, but evidence obtained in the UK was actually sufficient to show that it was false.

One case was particularly sad because I was certain that the man had died, but not as claimed. The man lived in London and was well known amongst the Iraqi population there. Everyone in that community was aware that he went to Iraq, was kidnapped with his driver, was never seen again and had been killed. It was thought that his body had been buried in the desert. The claimant obtained a death certificate and police report from Iraq. These suggested that he was dropped off by unknown persons outside the emergency room of a hospital and died shortly afterwards of a heart attack. There were numerous discrepancies indicating this was not correct.

I was convinced that he was dead, and the man's wife could not get a death certificate without his body being located. I believe she obtained a false certificate instead. The insurer would not settle the claim, and I was hoping that the claimant would take legal action. Had she done so, I would have stood before the court, stating that it was my belief that he was dead. My task is to obtain the truth and if this means that the insurer has to settle a claim then so be it.

Another case involved a man from Iraq, Mr Halbi, married to a lady from Syria. They lived in London, and he took out several policies totalling £800,000. Shortly afterwards, his wife claimed he had been killed in a hit and run accident in Baghdad, and she produced countless supporting documents. I interviewed the lady and was in no doubt that she was lying. Her husband had been in debt, and his monthly outgoings far exceeded his income. His employer had granted him extended leave to see his mother in Iraq, who was dying. He did not return on time, and his wife asked for his leave to be extended as his mother was about to die. It transpired that at this stage, he had been "dead" for a week!

As Mrs Halbi was from Syria, I travelled there to make enquiries. When I first spoke to her, she gave me the address of her parents in Syria. Later, when I saw her again, by which time it was obvious that I was investigating the claim, she provided a different address. This was totally false and did not exist. The first address did and was a house in an upmarket area outside Damascus. I spoke to a large number of local residents and shopkeepers. All of them knew Mr Halbi. He had been seen in the past few days, and his wife had gone back to London. I sent my local associate to the house to ask for Mr Halbi. A maid answered the door and said she would call him. The father of Mrs Halbi came to the door, followed by the sister of Mrs Halbi, who also lived in London. They insisted that he was dead, but when I questioned him, the father knew nothing about the death, the cause, the date etc. We were asked to go away, so I watched the house from along the road. Eventually, we were threatened with action from the military, so we left the area.

I went to the Iraqi Consulate in Damascus, and the staff were most helpful. They provided evidence that the various Iraqi documents were false. Mrs Halbi never gave up, and her solicitor made various allegations about what I had done in Syria, all completely unfounded. I wonder if Mr Halbi is back in London?

- - - - - - -

A man from northern Iraq submitted a claim for the loss of a hand in a car accident in Iraq. An asylum seeker who managed to return home on holiday. I interviewed him in London, and clearly, he had lost a hand. Enquiries in respect of his employment and finances left me extremely suspicious. No doubt you are thinking, "well, he has lost a hand, so pay up". You would be amazed at the number of claims I have seen where a person has self-mutilated. Almost unbelievable but sadly true.

I asked the man to describe in detail what had happened. In fact, he went and sat in a car and showed me the position his arm was in when hit by an oncoming car. His arm was hanging out of the window, he was in the passenger seat, and a car coming toward him hit it. Amazing that it removed his hand but never damaged his vehicle or other parts of his arm. His explanation of events had changed from what was on the claims form. It also did not make sense why he should have travelled such a distance to the hospital where he was treated. There were suitably equipped places nearer to the alleged scene of the accident.

There was one main discrepancy in his story. He forgot that they drive on the right-hand side of the road in Iraq. He was in the passenger seat, so had such an accident occurred, then it had to have been on the driver's side of the vehicle! This means the other car had to be on the wrong side of the road or on the pavement!

- - - - - - -

I have been fortunate enough to visit Jordan twice to investigate two extremely interesting claims. The first involved a dentist from Greece called Emmanouil Parisis. He worked at a dental practice in Barnstaple in southwest England and had a substantial income. He allegedly died in a traffic accident in Amman, Jordan and was buried there. His Greek wife, Stiliani, claimed that the family had a 4-week holiday in Greece, and she and her children returned to the UK. Her husband had taken his mother from Athens to Amman to see a heart specialist who was Emmanouil's friend. When he died, his brother, Panayotis, flew from

338

Athens to Amman to take his mother home. Panayotis also obtained the relevant documents from Amman relating to the death.

Parisis had a private banking representative in England, and she pursued the claim somewhat vigorously. A large sum of the insurance cover had been arranged by her. My enquiries showed that he was covered for around £1.7m. There was also insurance cover on a large number of loans, about £50,000 and credit card debts of around £90,000. The National Health Service paid out £18,000 death in service benefit. The banking representative told me that such debts were not abnormal for a man in his position. As he was earning around £10,000 a month gross, I found this to be an odd remark to make. Clearly, Parisis was living beyond his means.

I established that he had left the dental practice in Barnstaple and was due to commence work at a practice in Bristol after his holiday. Enquiries in Barnstaple revealed that there had been numerous complaints about his dentistry, and it was discovered that he copied the logo of the Dental Protection, which he used on letterheads to respond to a good deal of complaints against him. No doubt all of the complaints were unfounded! The place where he was going to start work in September would have needed to obtain certain references from the Dental Council, so it was unlikely that he would have been employed, given his history. Plus, he had raised a loan for a car from a finance company falsely stating that it was for the Barnstaple dental practice.

I interviewed his wife, and the bank representative was present. His wife had a death certificate and various documents from Jordan and from Greece, where his death had also been registered as he held a Greek passport. Although Stiliani was quite emotional, what she told me did not stack up.

Later the bank representative rang me several times. She told me she had faxed a copy of the Greek death certificate to the Greek Embassy in London, and they had confirmed it was genuine. She had also rung the Greek Embassy in Amman and was told that they had a record of his death. Why, she asked, was I investigating this claim? I tried to explain that I expected the certificates were all genuine documents, but it did not mean he was dead. I tried to explain that if he died in Jordan, then the Greek authorities could only register the death in Athens on the strength of the certificate from Jordan. She told me she knew he had taken his mother to Jordan because he had sent her a text message 3 days before his death. Plus, Stiliani rang her in tears the day after he died. I was expecting her to tell me that he personally had sent her a text stating that he had just died! I was told that I had no idea what genuine grief was. Oh, lady, you were so naïve and totally wrong!

So first I went to Athens. All of the papers from there were genuine. Parisis's sister, who was also his dental nurse in England, had registered the death using the papers from Jordan. A helpful official showed me the relevant file. It contained a copy of the marriage certificate in which his name was Emmanouil *SARIFIS*. Interesting because if he did originate from Jordan, then Sarifis is a Jordanian name. However, Parisis was a Greek name. The file also showed that his father's name was Sarifis. In 3 different documents, I now had 3 different names for his father!

I had tried to obtain the address and telephone number of Parisis's brother in Athens, Panayotis. You will recall he flew to Amman, obtained all the documents and brought his mother back to Athens. I tried to obtain this information multiple times from the claimant, but she kept giving various excuses and promising that I would get the information. One moment he lived in Athens but later she decided he lived in the USA. She had engaged a solicitor who told me that she only had an email address for Panayotis. She had been told not to ring him as he was deaf! Very convenient!

I did manage to find the home of Stiliani's mother. She appeared to dislike her son-in-law and said she was not aware he had died and had seen him recently (since the date of the death). She appeared to know nothing about his family. Unfortunately, the elderly lady was perhaps unwell, to put it kindly.

Next, I went to Amman. According to Stiliani, her husband had taken his mother there to see a well-known heart specialist called Dr Magdi. Not that well-known, it transpired as no one had heard of him. All of the documents proved to be fake, and there was no record there of his burial at the cemetery.

The most interesting part of this visit was meeting staff at the Greek Embassy in Amman. Yes, they were aware of the death, but how? A lawyer from Athens called Kostas Kalfas rang them, stated he had spoken to someone there on 4th September (the day of the death) about the death and informed them that the man had been buried there. Later he emailed the Embassy with details of the death and indicating that it had been registered in Athens. I was shown the email. I asked the staff if lawyers normally used "yahoo" addresses? I pointed out various facts, and staff there laughed upon realising that the whole scenario was false. Had a Greek national died there in an accident, then the local police always notified the Embassy. Later the Embassy informed me that there was no such lawyer in Greece. So Parisis, alias Panayotis, alias Sarifis, alias the lawyer Kostas Kalfas was clearly not dead!

The matter was reported to Devon & Cornwall Police, who did an excellent job. I believe one of the officers involved had previously had dodgy dental treatment from Parisis and was very keen to talk to him.

As you will see below, he was arrested in Scotland, working as a dentist using the name Neil McClaren. I believe he told the practice owner that his father was Irish. He was registered as a dentist in the UK under both identities. Certificates from Athens University for his dental studies were false. I believe he allegedly "graduated" as Parisis one month and as McClaren a month or so later. Was he ever a qualified dentist? Will the "*tooth*" ever be known? And to think I was accused of "not understanding real grief!"

Dentist faked own death for £1.85m insurance claims

- 28 March 2011

Parisis, aka Neil McClaren

A dentist has been jailed for five years after admitting making £1.85m of life insurance claims after faking his own death.

Emmanouil Parisis, 46, formerly of Barnstaple, Devon, admitted eight charges of false representation.

He faked a car accident in Jordan, moved to Aberdeenshire and changed his name to Neil McClaren.

Parisis received £51,000 in claims, the court heard. His wife was also convicted in connection with the fraud.

Parisis, who was originally from Jordan and had debts of £379,000, forged documents to show he had died in a car crash while on holiday in Amman, Jordan, in 2009, the court heard.

He claimed on 15 different insurance policies, assumed his fresh identity and moved to Peterhead, Aberdeenshire.

The court heard that he liked a champagne lifestyle, but his £135,000 a year salary was not enough to pay off rising debt.

'Complex individual'

- - - - - - -

I investigated another death in Jordan that left me feeling angry and frustrated that justice would probably never prevail. I will call the claimant Dr Ali, who originated from Jordan, and his wife was Rosa, who was Filipino. He was a doctor, and she was a nurse. They met in the Middle East and later married and moved to the Far East to work. He insured her there for the equivalent of £720,000. Seventeen months later, she died in a car accident in Jordan, and various documents were sent to the insurer, including post-mortem and police reports. The insurer was concerned because 2 months before her death, she telephoned the broker who arranged the policy, told him her husband was violent to her, and she feared for her safety.

I travelled to Jordan and went to the rural area outside Amman, where she died. She was buried there in the Muslim cemetery, and there were records indicating that she was definitely dead. It was claimed that's he had been staying there with her husband's family. Late at night, she and her husband decided to go to a nearby town to buy ice cream. On the way back, after midnight, Ali saw his cousins sat on a wall at the top of the hill about 140 metres from his home. He got out of the car to talk to them, and his wife drove toward the home, which was at the bottom of the hill. It was raining. She apparently lost control and crashed into the wall outside the home. She was not wearing a seat belt and died instantly.

Normally I would talk to the local mukhtar (man in charge of the area), except it was the father of Ali. I spoke to local people, and they were all very vague and reluctant to talk to me. The police officer who investigated the accident had moved to a different area, so I could not meet him. However, the body had been taken by ambulance to the mortuary before the police officer arrived on the scene.

I interviewed various members of Ali's family. They tried to give me the impression that Rosa loved visiting Jordan and was always very happy there. Her 4 year old son was born abroad, but Ali's family had been looking after him for some time. Rosa had given birth there, and the child, by then 15-months old, had stayed with the family in Jordan while Ali and Rosa continued working abroad in a hospital. The family explained that she was in a hire car when she crashed and, as her driving licence had expired, the family had to pay for the repair of the car. This latter point was confirmed to me by the hire car company. Ali had shown them Rosa's expired licence when hiring the vehicle, but she was not present. In the event of her driving and having an accident, he was told that he would have to pay for the repair.

It was clear to me that the family were trying to give me the impression that they were all extremely fond of the daughter-in-law. They overdid this to the point that there were obviously lying. The father was a very bombastic character. I asked the family if Rosa had enjoyed good health. The father's response was, "Before or after the accident?" All the family members laughed. I found it very difficult to keep my mouth shut and control my temper. What a horrific comment to make about the mother of his grandchildren! The family also asked why I had been making enquiries in the area the previous day and did not go and see them. I had only met various officials, so clearly, someone contacted the family.

I examined the scene of the accident, took measurements and photographs. I could not understand how the car could have hit the wall front. There was damage, but it just didn't add up. I tried to see the alleged cousins who Ali stopped to speak to, but no one in the area would talk to me. I was asked to believe that Ali went out for ice cream, returned after midnight, saw his cousins sat on a wall at the top of the hill near his home, got out of the car and his wife, whose licence had expired, decided to drive home. It had been raining, and I established that the temperature was 7C. Not many people sit on walls after midnight in such climatic conditions. Was Rosa killed, placed in the driving seat, and the car pushed down the hill?

I established that someone from the Filipino Embassy in Amman had also been making enquiries. I met officials there and was informed that Rosa's sister in the USA had made many serious allegations about the death. The Embassy was making enquiries with Jordanian authorities but were finding it difficult to establish exactly what had happened.

The sister made a large number of allegations. She claimed that Rosa and Ali worked together in Saudi, she became pregnant, and he wanted her to have an abortion back in the Philippines. She refused and returned to the Philippines and gave birth. Eventually, Ali went there and had his name put on the child's birth certificate. Her family disliked Ali as he was beating Rosa, and often she was covered in bruises. Rosa was naïve and told her family that he would change. They lived and worked in a country in the Far East, and her friends there knew that she was being abused. She left Ali, and he begged her to return with a promise that he would attend church with her. He was a Muslim.

Her child was kept by Ali's family in Jordan, and when she became pregnant again, she was sent to Jordan to give birth. There was an occasion there when she was admitted to the hospital after her husband ran her over, but she lied about the cause of her injury. She gave birth, and Ali's family treated her well for 3 months. The father then told her to leave and go back to the Philippines. She went home, and eventually, Ali persuaded her to go with him to Jordan to see the children. She never returned.

According to the sister, Rosa had an expired driving licence but was not allowed to drive in the Far East or in Jordan. When in Jordan, she was only allowed to go out if accompanied by a member of Ali's family. Ali also owned a car in Jordan, so the sister queried why he needed to hire one there. The sister could not contact Rosa in the Far East, and the telephone number there no longer worked. Eventually, she rang Ali at the hospital where he worked. She was told that Rosa was in a car with Ali's sister, and it crashed. She died instantly, whereas his sister hurt her knee (a story not told to me by the family). According to the sister, Ali had told her friends in the Far East that she had remained in Jordan to look after their children. He never mentioned that she was dead.

The sister told me that Ali had been married to a lady from Jordan but left her as she could not have children. After the death of Rosa, it was claimed that he had obtained a visa for his ex-wife and taken her to the Far East. It was suggested that the couple now had a ready-made family. Finally, I informed the sister that Rosa had been buried in a Muslim graveyard, and the family told me she had converted to Islam. The sister was adamant that her sister would never have changed her religion. She used to carry her Bible everywhere.

Once I sent my report to the insurance company, I had finished with the case. I doubt if the Embassy in Amman would have succeeded in having the body exhumed and, if so, then I doubt if there would be proof remaining of potential foul play. I do believe that the insurer refused to pay the claim and that Ali left the Far East, not to be heard from again. What a tragic event for her family to come to terms with!

- - - - - - -

Three times I travelled to Yemen to make enquiries into 5 claims: all were false. I have also managed to obtain evidence in the UK to prove that a claim for over £900,000 relating to a death there was false.

The first visit related to a young man from Yemen living in London. I will refer to him as Almir. He was insured for nearly £1m and allegedly died in a car accident near Sana'a, the capital, in late 2006. Numerous documents were produced from Yemen. I started off at Al Kuwait Hospital in Saana and spoke to several officials to obtain information about the medical death certificate. I did ascertain that had the accident occurred at the place shown on a police report; then, the body would have been taken to another hospital far nearer that location. There was a record at Al Kuwait Hospital of the death, and the man in charge of the registry confirmed that he had signed the document as it was presented to him by a police officer. I could not locate the doctor whose name appeared on the document. There should have been a record of the death at the police office at the hospital. The officer there was most unhelpful, and I suspected he was perhaps involved. Every time I went there, he went for a meal and did not return.

There was a record at the Civil Registry, but the man in charge (it is run by the army) told me in no uncertain terms to leave.

I spoke to the officer whose name appeared on the police report, and he confirmed that it was genuine. He never attended the accident scene but wrote the report when the family told him about the accident. Not the correct procedure, but he would not agree with me.

Next, I went to the cemetery, and staff confirmed that Almir was not dead. They knew his family and gave me directions to the family house. I went there and questioned a neighbour who had seen the "dead" man that afternoon in the street. The family lived in a large, upmarket house and were well known. The father and brother held senior government positions. The most interesting fact to emerge was that the police officer who wrote the accident report was related to the family!

The next morning, I went to the property and eventually met Almir. He explained that he had wanted to obtain a large amount of money in order to show his family that he had been a success in the UK. He asked if we could "come to an agreement?" I told him I would not report the matter to the authorities in Yemen, but I required him to make a full written statement. He reluctantly agreed. I do believe he was attempting to bribe me.

Me with Almir

- - - - - - -

In October 2008, a lady living in north-west England took out life cover of £200,000 on her mother. Two years later, her daughter reported that she had died in Yemen. I interviewed the daughter at her home in England. The family was from Yemen, and the mother had been staying with the daughter to help her with her children. It did not make sense that the daughter had no life cover but insured her mother who was returning to Yemen. The daughter had arrived in the UK claiming asylum. She had never worked in the UK; her husband had left her, and she lived on benefits. Yet, she had just returned from a holiday back in Yemen.

Again, the alleged death was in Sana'a, so off I went. The cemetery where she was buried was the same one I had previously visited. The staff there remembered me; I don't suppose many Europeans visit them there. They did not believe the lady was buried there, but they kept no detailed records of burials.

Once more, the medical death certificate was meant to be from Al Kuwait Hospital. The doctor shown worked in paediatrics, and I was told that it was unlikely he would have handled such a case. He was off duty and did not return to work during the 3 days I was in Sana'a. There was no record there of the death. Again, the death should have been recorded in the records held at the police post, but no records existed there. The death was registered at the Civil Registry, but they would have accepted the medical death certificate as being genuine.

On the death, abroad questionnaire I had completed when visiting the claimant was the telephone number of the claimant's brother. I rang him, he spoke good English and eventually he agreed to meet with me. He refused to say where he lived and would only meet at my hotel. He arrived as promised and spent an hour talking about his mother's death. I précised the findings of my investigation and after a lengthy interview, delayed twice while he went to the prayer-room he admitted that it was a fraud. He told me he had a brother also in England and he had arranged everything. The doctor, who seemed to have disappeared, had arranged the medical documents. The brother promised to bring his mother to the hotel the following morning. He did not arrive and later phoned me to say he was sick.

- - - - - - -

In October 2010, an international insurer had two suspect death claims in Yemen and asked me to travel there. The policies had been taken out in Bahrein, and both persons originated from Yemen and worked in Bahrein. I decided to travel via Bahrein so that I could, if need be, make enquiries in Bahrein on my return. I had to spend the night there on route to Yemen, and the following morning I checked in for my flight, spent a pleasant hour in the lounge and when I showed my boarding pass at the gate, was asked for my Yemen visa. I had recently been there on the above case and did not require a visa. The rule, I was informed, had changed the previous week.

The airline was very helpful and put me in touch with the Yemen Embassy in Bahrein. They told me what documents I needed and said they would issue a visa in 24 hours. I rebooked a flight in 3 days, the next scheduled flight. I needed to get a letter from the British Embassy and managed this that same morning. I rang my associate in Sana'a and later received the relevant invitation letter. As it was a Friday, the Muslim weekend, many places were closed, but I managed to obtain everything and went to the Yemen Embassy the following morning. The next day I collected my visa.

One of the claims in Yemen meant about 3 days driving to the south. The other claim involved travel north to Hodeida, a large seaport in the north. I was not looking forward to the drive south through bandit country. As I had time on my hands in Bahrein, I decided to make enquiries there in respect of Mr Alsair, who had died in the south. It did not take long before I had evidence from his employer in Bahrein that he was alive and well; in fact, he was at work that day. Later I met him at his employer's office. He claimed he did not know that he was insured. A friend had borrowed his passport, which explains perhaps why the insurer had received a copy. My enquiry suggested that certain persons involved in arranging life insurance were setting up a scam in which they insured people and then obtained a death certificate in Yemen. This was probably the first case and put an early end to the scam.

Alsair in the office of his employer – after his "death"

- - - - - - -

The next day I set off for Sana'a, relieved that I only had one long car journey through bandit country. I met my associate, and the following morning we set off to drive to

Hodeidah, a distance of 251kms and this takes around 5½ hours across the mountains on treacherous roads. Leaving Sana'a, we were stopped at the first police checkpoint to be told that I needed a certain pass to travel to Hodeidah. We went back to the main police station, and it took only a short time for a pass to be issued.

The journey was fascinating. Had it not been for the numerous plastic carrier bags littered on trees, one could be travelling back in time. We seemed to only pass through one town and did intend to stop for a cup of tea. However, all the men wore a Janbiya, a dagger with a short, curved blade. These are traditional throughout Yemen, and some antique Janbiyas can cost a fortune. Apart from wearing these around their belts, most of the men carried guns slung across their shoulders. Therefore, the thought of stopping for tea did not seem to be a good idea.

Some of the mountain roads left me on the edge of my seat, and regularly I saw lorries that had left the road and tumbled down the mountain. Once we neared sea level, the road levelled out. Just as well as my associate's car suffered a puncture and the spare was also damaged. A group of young people appeared from what seemed like out of nowhere. They took the wheel away on their motorcycle and returned 30 minutes later with the wheel and repaired the tyre.

I had little information about the man who allegedly died in the main hospital in Hodeidah, but the staff there eventually confirmed that the documents were fake and there was no record there of the death or the doctor shown on the certificate.

My associate had a good friend in the town, and we later met him for a meal. I was invited by my associate to visit his hotel room, where they would both be chewing khat. It is a plant, the leaf of which acts as a stimulant when chewed. Users chew the bitter leaves of this natural stimulant, and it is supposed to make them more alert and increase energy levels. It has been used in the Horn of Africa and Arab Peninsular for centuries, and locals claim that khat is as harmless as coffee or tea. I had to go to my associate's room to ask him something. There were bits of the plant all over the floor, and their eyes and expressions suggested that they were both completely "stoned". At the time, Khat was legal in the UK, but it was later classed as a prohibited drug.

The following day we had another adventurous journey across the mountains. My associate received a telephone call from his wife. I have no idea what she said, but suddenly he drove like a maniac in order to get home. I suggested that if he continued driving as such, neither of us would arrive in Sana'a, and he could forget the *promise*!

I met a friendly policeman on the mountain road

A dangerous road to Hodeidah

Young boy has the Janbiya holder but no knife

Thank goodness we never had the puncture in the mountains!

Lunch in Hodeidah

Stunning scenery in the mountains

I enjoyed my visits to Yemen. I saw some unusual mountain scenery and ancient sites. The people were very friendly and welcoming. Once more, I refer to a country I have visited being destroyed by war and politics—such a shame.

- - - - - - -

I will now mention 2 claims where the persons allegedly died in Palestine. I did not travel there. The problem, I believe, is getting across the border to Palestine. I have met many Palestinians who live in Lebanon and Jordan, and they often find it impossible to travel to Palestine. Such a pity. I have made a multitude of enquiries there in respect of travel claims and have a doctor contact there who has carried out enquiries on my behalf.

In 2012 a man called Alberto Medina, living in South Wales, took out a life policy with a cover of £550,000. On the application, it mentioned that he was of Egyptian origin and had lived in the UK since 2008. In 2014 a man, I will just refer to him as Mike (of Iraqi origin), informed the insurer that Medina had died in a car accident in Palestine. Mike was the trustee and beneficiary.

My background enquiries showed that Medina had been associated with 3 addresses in Wales – I will refer to them as 1, 2 and 3. He had been listed on the voters' registers at two of them, there were credit references in his name, plus he was a director of a limited company.

I interviewed Mike at his home in Wales (1 above). He lived in a run-down dump of a place; I can put it no other way. I had to sit on an old, dirty chair at what he described as a table. While interviewing him, the chair broke, and I ended up lying on the floor in a pile of broken wood. Mike told me that Medina had been his friend and ran a computer business at a shop locally; he did not know where exactly. He had left everything to Mike in his will. Everything consisted of only the insurance policy and possibly the broken chair! If Medina had travelled on holiday, then I expected to be able to view his clothes and personal effects such as TV, radio etc. According to Mike, he had taken everything home on holiday with him apart from a few clothes. Either he had excess luggage or owned very few items! While interviewing Mike, he was providing various answers by reading his notes; he would not allow me to see them, but I did notice the name of an insurance company, not the one with this claim. You will see later the relevance of this. I believed nothing that Mike told me. He had arrived in the UK a few years ago, claimed asylum and did not work. He had 2 sisters living locally (at addresses 2 and 3). I will give no hint of their identities as they are honest, upright citizens who have proved to be worthwhile members of society. I will call them senior and junior. They and other members of their families provided valuable assistance with my enquiries.

One of the sisters, junior, was shown as a director of Medina's company. When I met her, I was told that she had never heard of him, and it was not her signature on the relevant forms. She had allegedly witnessed the signing of Medina's will. Again, it was a forgery. Medina had allegedly used an address which was her flat (2). She denied that anyone of that name had lived there but pointed out that she had rarely been at her flat as she often stayed at her sister's house to take care of her. Her brother Mike had lived at her flat and still had a key. I reasonably assumed that correspondence sent to Medina at that address had been collected by Mike.

Sister senior lived in the same locality (at 3) but was ill and spent most of her time upstairs and bedridden. Her brother Mike had a key to her house and often went there. Senior again had never heard of Medina, and he had definitely not lived at her address. Again, I suspected that correspondence for Medina had been collected by Mike.

My enquiries showed that Medina had instructed a law firm to take action against an insurer in respect of an accident. He allegedly went to an address (the home of senior - 3) on behalf of the owner, a man called Fadil, to fix his satellite dish. There was a flood, he fell down the stairs and injured himself. Fadil did not own the property, it belonged to sister senior, and she had never heard of anyone called Fadil. Senior sister gave me the name of a legitimate business that fitted the satellite dish there. Fadil had taken out an insurance policy on the property, and Medina was claiming damages against this insurer. I spoke to a loss adjuster who had actually interviewed Medina and Fadil at the property. Clearly, while the sister was bedridden, her brother Mike was using the property for what can only be described as fraudulent activities.

There was also another insurance claim involving the loss of property involving a man from address 3 called Yorim. Medina and Yorim reported this to the local police. Later an officer identified Medina as being Yorim! Numerous other suspect claims were also identified. Mostly they involved car accidents. I spoke to the son of senior sister. He told me that in that past, when visiting his mother, he had found correspondence addressed to people he had never heard of. They were mostly from banks, insurance companies, plus parking fines. Suspecting that Uncle Mike was up to no good, he challenged him about this, but Mike denied knowledge of these people.

Mike complained to the insurer about the investigation. One of the ridiculous comments made by Mike was that Medina was a Muslim! Albert Medina is hardly an Islamic name, and Mike's various explanations for this defied logic.

Various documents were produced from Palestine, plus I received telephone calls from a man there claiming to be Medina's brother. My associate in Palestine proved that all of the documents were fake. A Palestinian ID card for Medina was certainly fake. Obviously, the claim was not paid. No action was taken by the police.

When I interviewed Mike, you will recall that he was reading from his notes but would not let me see them. I did see the name of another insurance company at the top of the notes, not the same one dealing with Medina. I rang this insurer. Fadil had recently taken out a life policy with a cover of £500,000. Surely Mike could not be stupid enough to submit another claim! I underestimated the man's stupidity.

In November 2015, that insurer received a claim from a man called Michael Nassir in Wales in respect of the death of Fadil in Palestine in a car accident. Michael was the executor and was living at a different address from Mike, albeit close by. The Palestinian ID card for Fadil bore the same serial number as the one for Medina. He had the same mother and brother as Medina. To complete the "full house," he died in the same hospital, and his death was certified by the same doctor. Could I make this up?

The insurer arranged for my colleague to meet with Mr Nassir and complete a questionnaire. My colleague met with Nassir. One question he asked him was if he had ever been to Fadil's address in Wales or if he knew anyone there (this was the address of the senior sister). He said he had not and knew no one there. He also denied having any relatives in the UK. After my colleague had completed the questionnaire, he rang me. I then knocked on the door and was "greeted" (probably not the correct word) by Mike. His facial expression was incredible. I think he wanted the ground to open up and swallow him.

He had changed his name by deed poll and explained that he had done this as people could not pronounce his surname. His real surname was as simple to pronounce as Nassir; it was his real first name that was difficult, but he had not changed this! I questioned him but decided to leave as every answer was becoming more stupid. Common sense and logic were words not in his vocabulary.

I wonder what Mike is up to now. Surely another death is on the horizon. Medina never existed. As for Fadil, I suspect there might have been a person of that name. His GP's record went back several years, and it is possible that he left the UK and Mike then stole his identity.

- - - - - - -

I have visited Turkey multiple times. One case involved a death at a large government hospital in Ankara. It was very modern and computerised. I explained the reason for my visit to the reception and showed them the death certificate. The lady inserted the man's name into the computer and confirmed that he had died there. I was shown the entry, and it was for the insured. I visited several departments, and everyone assured me that the man was dead.

Eventually, I met the medical director and suggested that I did not believe the man was dead. I asked him if he could call for the medical file. He obliged, and soon the file was on his desk. He examined it in detail and suggested that something was wrong. He called for additional documents that should also exist. They did not! Eventually, the medical director was able to confirm that someone had inserted a false entry into the hospital's computer system.

- - - - - - -

Saudi Arabia has twice featured in fake claims. I had a claim in respect of an accidental death policy for £400k. It related to a person's death in a car accident in Saudi Arabia. The person was actually the driver of the vehicle, a lady. In those days, women were not allowed to drive in Saudi Arabia, so there was a good chance that the claim might be false. Enquiries in Saudi proved it to be false.

Millions of Muslims travel to Mecca each year for Hajj. Several people die, and there are modern facilities in place to record such events and handle the corpse etc. In 1990, 1426 people allegedly died in a stampede. We had a significant claim for a Pakistani lady living in England, but as there appeared to be certain discrepancies, Andy went to Saudi. As he was not a Muslim, he could not enter Mecca, so he arranged for a local contact to make enquiries there.

The computerised system was examined, and it could be proved that an employee, himself of Pakistani origin, had inserted a false entry into the system. With at least 1426 deaths, it was very easy to add one more!

Chapter 23: Nigeria

Time to mention Nigeria again! Some years ago, an insurer was notified of the death of Eric Johnson in a car accident in Nigeria. The claim was made by an accountant in London, Lakani, allegedly on behalf of the widow who was in Nigeria. The policy totalled £200,000, and the man died 11 months after it was taken out.

At the same time, another insurer also received a claim from the same accountant for the death of James Phillips in a car accident in Nigeria. This was 12 months after a policy for £333,000 was taken out. Lakani said he was making a claim on behalf of the widow who was in Nigeria.

In those days, one could not apply for life cover online, so Mr and Mrs Johnson and Mr and Mrs Phillips all met an insurance salesman when applying for the policies.

Both persons appeared to have died in the same accident in Nigeria, and many of the documents produced by the accountant were similar. When I realised that there was a claim for Phillips, I rang the insurer only to be informed that they had paid the claim. The manager always sent us documents for such claims but not in this instance, so I queried why. He explained that he required permission from a director before sending me the papers. He had been suspicious about this claim. However, his director was on holiday, so he had to go via another director who was inexperienced with claims. This director pointed out that the subject lived at an expensive address in Harrow near the famous school, had 2 children attending a private school, was a mechanical engineer and had a substantial income. According to him, such people would not commit fraud, so he was instructed to pay the claim.

I was tempted to take out a policy for a substantial amount, say I was a director of a public company, had a mortgage of £1m on a West End property, owned a Ferrari and had children at Eton. Not a word of truth but something I just made up so that I could put in a false claim. Easy to do on paper!

My enquiries in Nigeria proved everything to be fake, and clearly, these people did not exist. People visiting from Nigeria who were known to the accountant had taken on these identities to get the life cover. The address of Phillips was in Harrow near to the school, an upmarket area perhaps! It was a run-down, filthy building containing about 20 rooms and 30 different tenants, mostly illegal immigrants. The man had no children, was not an engineer and had no substantial income as he never existed!

Police arrested Lakani, and he was charged. Interestingly the bank where the pay-out for Phillips had been deposited had a video of Lakani's wife collecting the money! To my knowledge, some of the money was recovered. This man is still working as an accountant!

- - - - - - -

I had another interesting claim submitted by a UK Customs Officer of Nigerian origin. His wife died in Nigeria, and there was an obituary in a Nigerian national newspaper. Having interviewed the man, I was certain that the claim was false. I passed on the information to Customs and Excise in London. It transpired that the officer was a single man and was on duty in the UK when he claimed to be at his wife's funeral in Lagos. My investigation in Nigeria proved that she was not dead, and she never existed. The officer was charged in London with fraud, granted bail and has never been seen since then.

- - - - - - -

I can recall another claim involving a family that were all killed in a serious accident in northern Nigeria. It was front-page news in a Nigerian national newspaper. It didn't take me long to crack this one. The event was in the newspaper the day before the accident occurred. Oops!

- - - - - - -

A man living in an upmarket house in Regents Park in London had a substantial policy relating to his mortgage. He was said to be involved in import/export. He allegedly died of typhoid in a hospital in Lagos. The claim came at about the same time as there were substantial mortgage arrears in respect of the property in London.

My enquiries in Lagos showed that this was a false claim. Apart from the fact that the man was not a UK residence, so not entitled to take out the policy, he was actually a Brigadier Colonel in the Nigerian army. Luckily when I called at his address in Lagos, he was in northern Nigeria, so I decided against pursuing matters there. I could not fathom how a man earning at that time, in hard currency the equivalent of about £1,300 a year, could afford to pay £3,300 a month in mortgage repayments and keep his two children in a private school in the UK. Maybe I could work it out! Interestingly, I found out that when the policy was taken out, the man had been sent to London for urgent medical treatment. It could not have been him who attended the medical examination. I was informed by a businessman that the insured's import/export business involved him driving army vehicles into the port in Lagos and removing containers with no import duties being paid and no Customs examination.

- - - - - - -

A Nigerian businesswoman in London provided accounts to support her taking out a policy with a cover of £420,000 and died soon afterwards in the city of Benin in Nigeria. I had a lengthy task there at the hospital proving this was a fraud as the doctor was clearly involved. Likewise, the local police had obviously been paid to assist. The claimant in London, allegedly her husband, was here awaiting a decision on his application for political asylum. He was provided with accommodation and various benefits. He was also claiming for another Nigerian lady as a dependant. It turned out that this lady was in London on a shopping trip and was married to a wealthy man in Nigeria! It gets better as the "dead" lady had been removed from the UK as an illegal immigrant on 3 occasions and each time used a different name when returning. I saw her 3 visa applications, all in different names, at the UK High Commission in Lagos. Different hairstyles and glasses were very good, but it was the same person.

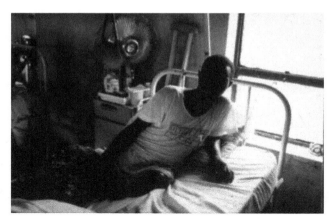

Olu

Olu, a Nigerian living in London, had a policy that paid out in respect of an accident. The insurer received a letter from him. He said that he was in hospital in Benin City in Nigeria after being run over by a lorry. He had lost a leg, and gangrene was setting into the other leg, so he needed to get back to London quickly. He asked the insurer to immediately transfer £25,000 to him for the lost leg so he could get home. If not, he would lose the other leg, so it would cost the insurer £50,000. An unusual claim. Was the claimant trying to pull my leg, I suggested!!

This came at a time when I was travelling 4 or 5 times a year to Nigeria, so I included this claim with the others. I found Olu in bed in the hospital, and obviously, he had lost a leg. I interviewed him, and his English was very poor. He seemed to know little about the UK or London where he allegedly lived. I asked what airline he flew on when returning to Nigeria. He mentioned an airline that only travelled domestically in Nigeria. While I was interviewing him, he appeared to be reading from a notebook. I asked to see it, and he turned away. After a game of cat and mouse, I managed to get hold of it. The first line read, "If someone comes from an insurance company in London you lived at – (UK address)- - - - - - - - . The insurance policy is with - (name of insurer) - - - -. You had an accident on – (date) - - - - - " and so on. The man was not Olu. He was from a very rural village and had lost a leg in an accident. Olu from London somehow heard about this, went to the hospital and managed to have all the medical records changed into his own name. There was even a police report in his name. I felt very sorry for the poor lad and even gave him some money for food. How do I wonder Olu managed to have all the records there changed? Whenever I asked officials, I was just faced with a shrug of the shoulders. Had the claim been paid and had Olu returned to London, I wonder how he would have explained no longer being "legless"!

- - - - - - -

I dealt with a very unusual death in Nigeria in 1992. An Irish couple living in England went on holiday to Nigeria. The lady, I will refer to her as Sheila, worked for British Telecom (BT). Her husband, Maurice, was a nurse. It is claimed that she was taken ill and then travelled across Nigeria to Port Harcourt, where she died. She was insured for around £263,000, plus there was a large death in service benefit with BT.

I interviewed Mr Maurice, and his description of events defied logic. However, I suppose he did not know that I had been to Nigeria many times and must have thought that I would not look at the geography in respect of events. He told me she was taken ill and was taken by Nigerian friends to Port Harcourt to see a doctor. At the time, I calculated that this journey would have taken around 7 hours, travelling through towns with medical facilities. I was told she died as soon as she saw a doctor in Port Harcourt and was buried in a field. Maurice was very small in stature, while his wife was very large. I could think of no reason why they would travel to Nigeria, and when there go separate ways. Well, not exactly true because many Nigerian men prefer ladies of such a build. A strange set-up!

I made enquiries in Port Harcourt, and the doctor involved admitted he had not seen a body. There was no burial, and of course, you cannot just bury someone there in a field. A man working for an oil company there appeared to be involved. I interviewed him, and his attitude was that there was nothing I do against him, so he told me to get lost. How wrong he was.

I met the director of the oil company in Lagos, an elderly, absolute gentleman. What I would call "old school". He told me he had been educated in the UK and regularly travelled to London. Due to the increase in fraud involving Nigeria, he was now being challenged in London in respect of his financial activities. He said that if there was anything he could do to stop fraudsters, then he would. I showed him documents from his employee in Port Harcourt and explained his role in the scam. By the time I left Nigeria, the employee was looking for another job.

In Lagos, I went to the Irish Embassy as both Sheila and Maurice were from the Republic of Ireland. I explained the situation to a diplomat who had a large smile on his face. He told me that a few days earlier, a lady visited the Embassy claiming to be the sister of Sheila and asking if the death could be registered there. The official did not believe her, and I seem to recall that he told me the "sister" was unable to produce her passport. A message was sent by the Embassy to the police in Dublin who visited the family asking about the death. There was no sister. The family immediately rang Maurice in London and naturally he could not admit to the fraud so had to tell them that she was dead. The family demanded that he went to Ireland, so he did. He met the family and the local priest, and a memorial service was held. This eventually proved somewhat embarrassing for Maurice when police in London arrested him and his "dead" wife!

- - - - - - -

I investigated another claim with an Irish connection. I will use the real name of the alleged deceased, and later, you will realise why. Mr and Mrs Okunuga lived near Dublin and in 2004 took out a policy for life cover of €200,000. In 2005 Mrs Okunuga allegedly died in a car accident in Lagos, and piles of medical, police and burial documents were produced. Mr Okunuga said that his wife's UK and Nigerian passports were stolen from the scene of the accident. It was alleged that Mrs Okunuga was born in the UK, went back to Nigeria when young and later returned to the UK and married her husband in Dublin. The claim was not made until around 2 years later, unusual if it was a false claim. There was a newer policy covering around £150,000. You would not believe the number of alleged deaths in road accidents in Nigeria, where a person is carrying his or her passport that is stolen at the scene of the crime, I mean accident!

I arrived on a Wednesday evening in Lagos, allowing me 2 days to investigate this before travelling on to Ghana. One hour before I arrived, the government announced a 2-day public holiday as the elections were going to be held that weekend. This rather hindered my work. Can you imagine a European government suddenly announcing that the next 2 days would be public holidays?

On Thursday, I went to the cemetery. The relevant register was at HQ, but I was told that the signature on the burial permit was of a senior official there who had recently moved away. The man at HQ was telephoned, met me at his office and showed me the register. There was no record of the burial.

I had a medical death certificate from the General Hospital, and there I was informed that the doctor shown on the certificate had just moved abroad. All the records were locked up as the medical records staff were on holiday. The Medical Director was also on holiday so no one there could assist me. I went to the mortuary, which had recently been privatised and worked efficiently. There was no record of the death. Had the person died, then the body would have immediately been moved to the mortuary.

Next, I went to the police and spent time with a very senior officer. He had issued the report, but unfortunately, the register for that period had gone missing, a regular occurrence I came across! The officer did point out that his report never said the lady had died, just that she was hospitalised after the accident. I did not believe a word he said, and his description of police action did not follow the correct procedure. I went back the following day to see the officer only to find a party in full flow. He was celebrating having been promoted to a very senior rank.

On the questionnaire, I had the names and telephone numbers of persons who attended the funeral. I did meet one lady who described in detail the accident and funeral service.

However, this event occurred a year before the death! Other persons I spoke to on the phone were about to travel abroad, be admitted to hospital, travel to the north etc. Anything but meet with me.

I left my associate to meet the medical director of the hospital the following week and obtain a letter stating that there was no record of the death. On the following Monday, he received a call from someone at the cemetery; they had found the grave. My associate Edward went back to the cemetery to be shown a grave that was in the middle of graves that were 10 years older. The cement was still wet; at least the idiots could have waited for it to dry before ringing Edward! Also, the headstone was on the wrong way.

Eventually, the man in charge of cemeteries made a written statement to say that his was an old grave and someone had entered the cemetery at night, re-cemented it and changed the name etc. A few days later, I received a 4-page affidavit by fax stating that there was a record of the burial at the cemetery.

My associate was told at the hospital that he would have to pay a fee equivalent of £40 to obtain a letter from the Medical Director. He did so and returned several times before getting a letter to say that the medical certificate was genuine and Okunuga died there. I wrote an official letter Lagos State Health Commission pointing out the facts that suggested the certificate was false. Within days I received a response plus another letter from the Medical Director stating that the certificate was false. The Medical Director was not being dishonest. She recognised the signature of the doctor on the certificate and never bothered to check all of the records.

This was not the end of the case as I located Mrs Okunuga living in London and went to interview her. She was not the "dead" lady but had the same date of birth, was born in London, schooled in Nigeria and then returned to live in London. When she tried to renew her UK passport, she was informed that she had done so already. There followed a long sequence of events that caused her problems and most involved finance. UK police eventually established that some years earlier, her identity had been stolen. Someone had used it to get a passport, driving licence, bank accounts and so on. If ever the lady experienced a problem, she was given a code to give to the police, and this would show that she was genuine. Mrs Okunuga, who lives in London, is a lovely, Christian lady, and it was a joy to meet her. It seems unfair that she should have to carry the burden of her identity having been being stolen.

- - - - - - -

I had a case where a 16-year-old girl was insured in London. This is not the norm, but there had been a problem with the mother taking a policy, so the insurer allowed the daughter to be covered. It was not long before the girl died in Lagos. I made enquiries there of various family members, all of whom insisted that she was dead. They lived in the roughest part of the City; not a good place for a foreigner to ask questions. As per the norm in such false claims, the family had not rehearsed their stories, and there were numerous differences.

The doctor who certified the death kept avoiding me. Eventually, I went to his hospital, and his receptionist told me he could only give me 10 minutes and I would have to speak to him in the operating theatre. I was determined not to give in, so I had to scrub up and put on the necessary attire. My associate declined the offer to join me. The doctor was cutting open a woman's stomach, and he spoke very quietly, obviously expecting me to come closer. I managed to spend 10 minutes during which time I obtained a story completely different from what the family had told me. I cut the meeting short as I did not want to be held responsible should he make a mistake while operating. I could imagine the headlines – "doctor errs during operation as UK investigator insists on entering operating theatre". I went back to interview the family and their neighbours and found the young lady alive and well. She had no idea how she was being used by her mother.

- - - - - - -

I had a claim for a young man who had been living in London and died in Lagos soon after taking out a large life cover. The claim was being made by his brothers in Lagos, and there was a lack of persons to interview in London. When I arrived in Lagos and explained the case to Ed, my associate, he suggested that we could not possibly make enquiries in the area where the brothers lived. It was a dangerous place, and any white man going there would be unlikely to survive. I told Ed I had an idea, so we went there the next morning. I met 3 brothers and 2 cousins; all were high, having been smoking marijuana. I interviewed them all separately and returned the following day, and repeated the process. They insisted on buying me a beer, but I made an excuse as to why I could not accept their offer.

When I finally departed their enclave, Ed, not having been close by during all the meetings, asked what I was up to. He wanted to know why I had told them that the insurer would be settling the claim. I explained that perhaps a white lie was needed to avoid any aggravation. I had told them all together that the insurer had a problem in that they needed evidence to show which of them should receive the insurance pay-out. It was, therefore, necessary that I spoke to them all individually, take written statements so that the insurer could decide who to pay. I told Ed that I had 5 completely different stories in their written statements. The man died on a Monday, Wednesday, Thursday and so on. I had 4 different causes of death, 3 different hospitals, plus he was buried on different days in different cemeteries. I explained to Ed that there was sufficient evidence to show it was a fraud, and I had not risked our safety by challenging the brothers and cousins. They had even escorted us from the area to safeguard us.

- - - - - - -

I have travelled to the north of Nigeria several times. Most of the residents in the north are Muslims. I have found the north to be safer, less crowded, friendlier, and the weather is much drier. Kano is the second-largest city in Nigeria and has many interesting, historic sites. I recall staying in a small hotel owned by a European and sitting each evening having a cold beer in the rose garden.

Unfortunately, the terrorist organisation known as Boko Haram has ruined that area and endangered the safety of many people there.

Back in 2012, I had a case in which a man was claiming that he had been attacked by armed robbers in northern Nigeria, resulting in the loss of sight in one eye. When I interviewed him in the UK, he informed me that he was no longer able to drive. I rang him later to clarify something, and he was driving his car. The claim for loss of sight was fairly substantial, plus he was claiming nearly £2,000 for hospital charges. I went to Nigeria and flew from Lagos to

Kaduna in the north with Ed. There I hired a car and driver, and we travelled a further 200 miles to Katsina in the north.

Two hospitals were involved, and it did appear that the claimant might have been hit in his eye. Records could not be located, but the treatment had been fairly minor, and the man left Katsina after a day. It seemed he had asked for a receipt showing his treatment to have cost nearly £2,000. It was, in fact, the equivalent of £10.

I returned to Kaduna and had to stay there overnight. The only accommodation was a large, rather run-down, ex-government owned hotel. I complained that there was no seat on my toilet, so I was charged extra to have a room with a toilet seat. My associate Ed and I did not fancy eating at the hotel, and previously I had enjoyed Chinese food in Kaduna. We experienced difficulty getting a taxi as due to Boko Haram, few people go out after dark. Eventually, we obtained the services of a taxi driver and found only one Chinese restaurant open. However, the owner said he was closing, and after agreeing to pay a surcharge, we were given a small amount of time to eat and leave. I had not until then realised the danger of the terrorists in that area. The following morning after a short delay at Kaduna airport, a new, modern place, we returned to Lagos. Later, I heard on the news that the terrorist had stormed buildings in Kaduna, leaving many people dead in the streets.

- - - - - - -

Back in 1991, a man called Yisa took out life insurance with several companies totalling £2.4m. He produced various letters from an accountant in support of his earnings as a self-employed businessman; he allegedly did laundry and ironing! More likely money laundering!! Later he wrote to all the insurers stating that he realised that he had not disclosed on the applications to them the full extent of his cover. Some companies cancelled the policies, but by the time he died in Nigeria, he was still covered for £1.4m. I never understood why when he wrote to the insurers, he never mentioned that he was planning to die!!!

Yisa made a will leaving everything to a man called Folagbade. In the will, he also requested that his body be cremated in whatever country he died.

Later Folagbade claimed that he received a letter from a hospital in Ibadan, Nigeria, and he produced this to insurers. My copy is too unclear to copy here, but it read, "Identification of patient and location of next-of-kin. Please be informed that a man was brought to this hospital unconscious on 12/1/93. Despite all the treatment given to the said man, he eventually died later that day. The documents and national insurance number card found on him refer to that of Sharaffa Pilippe Yisa and the above-named person as the next of kin. (Note: this was addressed to Folagbade at his London address). If you know Mr S. P. Yisa please attend this hospital for identification purposes as soon as possible and have this letter with you on arrival". Signed "Social Welfare Officer".

I interviewed Folagbade, and there was sufficient evidence to prove this to be a fraud. A hospital would not write such a letter, and it would be a police matter. They would notify the British High Commission in Lagos. The evidence also indicated that Yisa never existed. The matter was reported to the police in London, who took action. I never went to Nigeria. In my view, such a trip was not necessary. However, the police wanted further evidence to take the case to court. The officer who went to Nigeria was taken ill and flown home. Happily, he soon recovered, and the case was due to be heard at Southwark Crown Court.

Plenty of witnesses were asked to travel from Nigeria. A day or so before leaving, some were shot by armed gunmen, and later Folagbade's brother in Nigeria was arrested. A very helpful Nigerian police officer was also due to travel to London. His home in Lagos was partly destroyed by robbers connected with the brother, yet he still gave evidence in London. Some of the witnesses arrived in London, and I recall feeling very sorry for them. I believe it was November, and there was thick fog and freezing conditions. The witnesses did not possess clothing for such conditions. The case went well, and Folagbade was jailed. This is the only case in which I have been involved where witnesses were threatened in such a way.

- - - - - - -

The UK insurance industry has received far fewer claims relating to Nigeria since around 2015, and I have only travelled there maybe once a year. In some ways, I miss the adventure of working in Nigeria. There have been a multitude of improvements since around 2016, and the place does feel a little safer. Plenty of international hotels have opened up, and the cost of accommodation has reduced now that there is a competitive market. Some of the roads have improved, and traffic lights now work, at least in some places. Changes to the airport layout have improved arriving and departing.

Chapter 24: Ghana

Ghana was the first country I visited when I started insurance investigations. The system there, in brief, is that a doctor issues a medical death certificate, or a pathologist issues a document relating to the death. A relative takes the certificate to the local registry, registers the death and is given permission to bury the body. Should the family require a death registration certificate (normally for insurance, pension or work-related reasons), then a written request is made at the registry. This is forwarded to the Central Registry in Accra, along with details of the death. Eventually, a certificate is issued there, and this is normally the document used for official purposes, including insurance claims.

In the late '80s and early '90s, I went to the Central Registry on many occasions when the head Registrar at the time had a drinking problem, to say the least. I often met him at the beginning of my visit, requesting an official letter in respect of the authenticity of a certificate (or normally several). I then saw him later in the week for his response, normally on a Friday afternoon. Often, he could not recall who I was or why I was there. I soon realised that this was particularly obvious later in the day after he had consumed a large amount of alcohol. Eventually, when I examined a certificate produced in the UK for a claim, I could tell from his signature the time of day he had signed it. His signature changed along with the consumption of alcohol. I recall him telling me that he checked every certificate he signed and, at the same time, stating that he proceeded to sign numerous certificates looking only at the box requiring his signature. The man was not dishonest, but it became obvious to me that staff members were inserting false certificates into the pile he was given to sign, knowing that he would not be aware of this. In one case, I located the home address shown on a certificate for a dead man (fake). The door was opened by the Registrar's Deputy. Again, he was not corrupt. Surely no one would be stupid enough to use their own address in a fraud. I think someone in his office had a sense of humour.

After the Registrar retired, a man called Sam took over and was a very astute, intelligent person. I met him on many occasions. He used to show me letters in his in-tray from Embassies and High Commissions, often acting on behalf of insurance companies, asking if a death or birth certificate was a genuine document. Rarely were certificates forged, so we both knew the answer to this question which was, "Yes, but - - -". The fact that a death had been registered was not proof that someone was dead. A corrupt doctor or pathologist might have issued a false medical death certificate, and this would be accepted by a registrar at face value. He would register the death, and subsequently, an official registration certificate would be issued. Sam and I agreed that in order to show that someone was really dead, it was necessary to interview the doctor, make enquiries at the cemetery etc. In respect of birth certificates, often these were prepared of production of affidavits sworn by relatives. Were they telling the truth? I was certain that I could have registered my own birth there had my associate Boat sworn an affidavit saying that he was present when I was born, and my late parents called me Mickey Mouse!

Later the Central Registry used a special machine that marked a hologram onto the registration certificate. As most of the certificates I saw in relation to false claims had this on them, the system did not really help my enquiries. Except there was one case where the hologram came unstuck. It had been cut from a genuine document and pasted onto a false one.

A few years ago, I had 6 Ghanaian registration certificates in about 18 months for 6 claims. Every single certificate was a genuine document and had been issued by the Registrar. Five of the claims were false! There appeared to be someone in the Registrar's office inserting false information into the computer there, which subsequently printed the certificates. I have attempted to explain this to insurers and other official bodies, but I suspect that they still try and establish if a certificate is genuine by sending it to Ghana via diplomatic channels.

As a result of this entry (see below) made by a registrar in a rural village, a registration certificate was issued for someone called Bruce, who had died. Clearly, the entry had been changed. The "Fe" in front of "Male" plus the age change is somewhat obvious. The column to the right shows the address of the deceased, so I went there and obtained a written statement about the person who really died then.

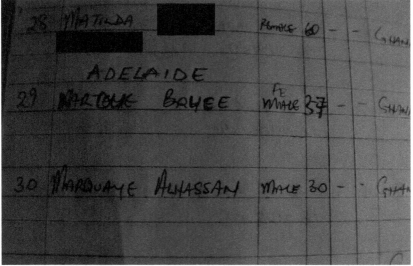

Some years ago, I went to a small clinic in Accra and met the owner; I will call him Dr Tenkora. His clinic was in part of his home in a pleasant suburb. I had a travel claim. The doctor had signed various papers for the claimant stating that he had been hospitalised there and had paid a substantial amount of money for treatment. As I was travelling to Ghana in respect of a large death claim, I took on this work personally.

Dr Tenkora at first tried to support the claim but soon saw the errors of his ways. There were no facilities to treat inpatients. His wife then entered his practice room and shouted at him in their own language. She picked up all the items on his desk and threw them at his head. My associate Boat and I decided to make a quick exit, shielding our heads and waited outside. According to Boat, the wife was complaining that he could not see patients, earn money, pay to educate their children because he was involved in fraud with the "drunks" he met each night. Anyway, eventually Dr Tenkora came outside, and I took a written statement from him admitting that there had been no treatment.

About 2 years later, I had a claim from a lady called Doris in respect of her husband Peter dying in Accra. I had a death registration certificate which indicated that Dr Tenkora had certified the death. According to Doris, her relatives had lost the medical death certificate prepared by the doctor, so they would obtain a further certificate. I interviewed Doris and, although the claim was very suspicious, I did believe that the certificate had been lost because the death registration document appeared to be a genuine document and the doctor's name was on it. As I have mentioned previously, if a doctor issues a medical death certificate, the registrar of deaths will accept it at face value and register the death.

So off to Ghana to continue the investigation. When Boat and I arrived at the doctor's clinic, he was actually writing out a replacement medical death certificate and completing the medical section of a death questionnaire I had left with Doris. He looked up and said words to the effect that he told them that man John would come and interrogate him, but he thought it would not be until he had completed all the papers! It gets better because Doris and her *dead* husband turned up at the clinic to collect the papers. I greeted Doris, and she made a quick departure with Peter. They were driving an old red BMW. That day, I interviewed the many witnesses who had claimed that Peter was dead. All of their stories differed. At each place, I spoke to neighbours of the witnesses who all confirmed that just before my arrival, a man and woman in a red BMW had departed.

Doctor Tenkora completing a questionnaire for the insurer

Doris and Peter arrive for Peter's death certificate

So, would it be the third time lucky for Dr Tenkora? No. Later I had another travel claim in which there was a signed medical certificate stating that someone had been ill and paid a large sum of money for treatment. It came from his clinic but was signed by Dr Afriee. Dr Tenkora told me that Dr Afriee had worked there for him at that time and must have committed fraud. There was no record thereof such treatment. Unfortunately, Dr Tenkora could not give me Dr Afriee's telephone number, address or current place of work. I had located the papers for the previous cases and suggested to Dr Tenkora that Dr Afriee had copied his handwriting! He did not look too pleased. It's about time I heard from Dr Tenkora again.

- - - - - - -

In late 2017 I dealt with a most unusual claim and eventually travelled to Ghana in mid-2018. I will refer to the man as Adu. He lived in London and took out life insurance cover for around £247,000 in 2010. In 2017 a lady in London (Jane), via a solicitor, claimed that he had died from a heart attack in Ghana in October 2015. She produced many documents, including a will showing her young son as the executor and trustee. The lady appeared to know very little about Adu. She told me he was from the north of Ghana, and she met him there when he was young. However, she is from the south, and when I queried this, she told me she studied in the north. She had 2 death registration certificates for him. One showed that he died at home in a village, no doctor certified his death, and he was buried locally. According to the lady, this was incorrect as his death was certified by a doctor at a clinic. The doctor issued a medical death certificate, so the relative in Ghana, Solomon, swore an affidavit and registered his death in the town where the clinic was situated. This could happen in such a rural area, but it was suspicious. Hence, we had two certificates.

The lady appeared to know little about Adu and had not seen him for at least 6 months before his death. She said when she did not hear from him, she rang his mobile and it was answered by a man in Ghana called Solomon, his relation there. Solomon told her he had died at his home and had been buried in the village. The lady said she told Solomon that there was money to claim, so he agreed to send her various documents.

He did have a mortgage on a property in London that was rented out, and the mortgage was in arrears. The will also left a small sum to a lady. Enquiries at her address suggested she was not known, and Jane said she had no idea who this lady was. This claim was shrouded in mysteries! The only way to get to the bottom of things was to travel to Ghana.

The death was allegedly in a village near Techiman in the north on the way to Sunyani. I travelled there with my associate Boat by coach, an 8-hour journey. There I locate Solomon, a cashew nut farmer. He explained that when he was a young boy, his father lived on a farm with a lady who had a son called Adu. When Adu was about 10 the mother left and took Adu to Accra. There was quite a difference in ages between Solomon and Adu, throwing doubt on this story. A couple of years later, Solomon moved about 20 miles to his current home. Anyway, around 2007, about 30 years later, Adu appeared at Solomon's house one day out of the blue. Solomon could not explain how Adu had located him after such a long time. Adu stayed with Solomon, and he knew he had travelled from Accra. He never asked him what he was doing, if he was married, had children, where he had been living.

Adu returned to see him in 2015, and one day Adu said he had a pain in his heart. He went to lay down and died. Solomon buried him in the village's graveyard, having registered his death in the village. He examined Adu's phone and rang one of the numbers on it. The call was answered by a lady in London called Jane, and she told him to send various papers. He did so, and she queried whether a doctor had certified his death. Solomon, for some unexplained reason, recalled that a doctor at a clinic in Techiman had treated him moments before he died. Solomon obtained a certificate from the doctor and then swore an affidavit and reregistered the death. There were numerous discrepancies in what Solomon told me. He did, however, take me to the cemetery and show me a marked grave. It was almost concealed in the bush, remote from the other graves. The metal sign looked quite new, and I suspect it might have been placed there when I commenced enquiries about 8 months earlier.

I went to the clinic, and there was no record of the death. The retired owner pointed out that the doctor who signed the certificate worked at the government hospital across the road and had also worked part-time at the clinic. He suggested that if a man was close to death, he would have been taken to the government hospital and not a private clinic. I met and interviewed the doctor, and after several stories, he eventually admitted that he never treated Adu, did not see his dead body and made out the certificate for a friend; naturally, he could not recall the friend's name.

I initially spoke to various people from the village at the Chief's palace, including a relative of Solomon. No one had heard of Adu or any death in respect of Solomon's family or friends. After having met Solomon, I returned that evening to the Chief's palace and met a man responsible for the cemetery. He explained that he kept no records but that no one could carry out a burial without his permission, plus he would always show them the plot to be used. He recalled a year, or so ago Solomon saying that a friend had died, and he showed Solomon where to bury him. He took me to the cemetery and was adamant that the plot he pointed out was Adu's grave. The adjacent one, he claimed, was the grave of Adu's father, who died there years ago. (His father never died there, according to Solomon and Jane).

Solomon told me this was Adu's grave

The Chief's secretary told me this was Adu's grave

According to Solomon, he had taken Adu's body in the back of his truck to a clinic about 20 miles away from where there was a mortuary. He stated that the mortuary in the main hospital in Techiman had been full, not so according to my enquiries. Solomon showed me several documents from the mortuary, and my enquiries there suggested these were false. There was no record of Adu's body having been kept there. Plus, he could not have taken it there without having a medical death certificate, and one was not available at that time.

Just before I left, Techiman Solomon phoned me and begged me, via my associate translating, not to go to the police. He said Adu was not dead, and he had been asked to get the documents by the lady in England. I tried to establish exactly what had occurred, but he kept changing his story.

One moment Adu was dead, then he was not dead. Solomon promised to come to my hotel and sign a statement. He failed to show up, and his phone was turned off.

A strange case in that I never actually met anyone who knew much about Adu and wondered if it was perhaps a stolen identity. Jane had told me that she met Adu when she was studying in the north of Ghana. Most unlikely because if, as claimed, he left there when aged 10, then she could not have met him there.

- - - - - - -

Some years ago, Mr Owusu claimed that his wife, Elizabeth, had died in Ghana. When I contacted him to arrange an interview, he informed me that he had started work as a pilot with Ghana Airways and would ring me when next in London. He did so, and we met at a hotel near Heathrow. He appeared to be wearing an airline uniform and was carrying the normal type of flight briefcase. I did not believe what he told me. His wife had been a pharmacist with a large UK company, and when I rang, the relevant branch staff were unaware of her death. I was informed that she had left her employment there and returned to Ghana.

In Accra, I proved that all of the documents were fake, and it did not take me long to track down Elizabeth. She had started a pharmacy there and was not aware that she was meant to be dead! She explained that she had decided to move temporarily to Ghana but intended to return soon to her home in London. Her husband had taken her UK passport, so this had delayed her return. She had kept asking him to return it and could now comprehend the reason he was keeping it. Elizabeth was a very intelligent, honest individual from a well-known family in Ghana. When I told her about her husband working for Ghana Airways, she laughed. He did not work for the airline. Elizabeth provided a detailed written statement and said she was willing to return to London and give evidence in court against her husband, who she would be divorcing.

In my mind, this was a case suitable for the UK police to take. It transpired that Mr Owusu was not employed by any airline. He was, in fact, a student at Biggin Hill Airport, south of London, taking flying lessons. He was also claiming on a personal income protection policy for a long-standing illness. At the same time, he was deemed fully fit in order to fly! Apart from trying to steal a large amount from a life insurance company, he was also stealing money to fund his lessons.

The police interviewed Mr Owusu, and I was looking forward to giving evidence in court. But no, it never happened. One day the police officer in the case rang me to say that it was not regarded as cost-effective to bring witnesses from Ghana should Mr Owusu plead not guilty. I pointed out that his wife was probably back in London and would definitely give evidence. I was told, though, that the Crown Prosecution Service required the doctor whose name was on the death certificate to give evidence. Were they suggesting, I asked that they needed a doctor to travel to the court in London to say that Elizabeth was not dead? 'Yes' was the reply. I asked if perhaps the jury might decide for themselves that Elizabeth was alive and well when she walked into the court. No, the CPS needed the doctor. I put down the phone before I said something I might regret. This was simply a stupid method of avoiding the work involved with a court case.

- - - - - - -

I have dealt with numerous interesting claims involving Ghana. One involved a very well-educated lady from Ghana who was a chartered accountant in the UK. Her husband allegedly died in a car accident in Ghana a few months after taking out cover of £300,000. A lawyer from Accra informed the insurance company that he was dealing with the matter, as the lady was too upset to travel back to the UK. So, I interviewed her at her lawyer's office in Accra. This firm of lawyers was one of the best in Accra. The lady provided numerous documents and regularly cried during our meeting. I did query some of her remarks, and the lawyer insisted that what she was telling me was correct. It transpired that he really believed this.

After the meeting, I had time to examine everything in detail and realised that the claim had to be false as there were numerous discrepancies. The accident had been reported to the wrong police station (the report was actually false, though), and the body was taken to the wrong hospital. However, something in favour of the claim was that her husband's UK passport had actually been cancelled at the British High Commission in Accra. Most unusual in false claims because it means that person cannot travel to the UK. That is until their new, fake identity has been arranged! Or perhaps the passport was for a false identity!

Enquiries showed everything to be false, and I tried to meet with the lady. Her address was false, she either rarely answered her phone, but when she did, she had allegedly been taken ill. Eventually, it was agreed that I would meet her at her lawyer's office, but she never arrived. When I showed the lawyer all of the evidence, he was shocked and said that the lady had cried every time he met her. He thought that she was a "con artist extraordinaire", his words. The

British High Commission normally issue a death certificate when a passport is cancelled in this situation. The official I met there was guarded and would not explain why no such document had been issued. I suspect enquiries were being made in London as the passport was suspected to be false.

- - - - - - -

In 2011 a lady in London, Ama, took out a policy for £300,000 and died in Ghana a year later, or so it was claimed. Checks against her London address revealed several credit commitments there in her name. The claim was submitted by a lawyer in London who claimed to be her uncle. He originated from Ghana but was not working as he had been suspended by the law society here. I interviewed him and did not believe anything he told me, even though he had many supporting documents. He claimed that Ama died suddenly from pneumonia while on the way to the hospital but had not been seen by a doctor. Had that been the case, then a post-mortem would have been carried out, but according to the claimant, this would only happen if requested by the family. Wrong.

As I was about to travel to Ghana, I took this case with me. The death had been correctly registered at the main registry in Kumasi. However, this only means that the registrar accepted a medical death certificate as being genuine. The doctor who signed it did not exist, and there was no record of the death at the hospital. The claimant had given me some names and telephone numbers of relatives in Kumasi. One of them turned out to be a bank manager. I met him, and he was clearly involved in the fraud.

I was told that the lady had been buried at the Chief's cemetery in a village near Kumasi. I went there and was informed that only people from that village could be buried there. The man in charge of the cemetery then told me that a man from Kumasi had buried a relative there last year, and she came from London. Several other residents recalled this burial, but no one appeared to know the deceased. I was somewhat shocked when shown the grave.

The date of birth was slightly wrong, but the date of the alleged death was correct. The actual grave looked older than the metal plaque. Someone suggested that Ama might have originated from that village, but I could find no one there who knew anything about her death or her family.

The bank manager gave me the telephone number of Ama's mother, and after a series of calls, she agreed to meet me but only at a garage forecourt. She said she was ill, that mention of her dead daughter had worsened her condition, so she would meet me close to the clinic where she had an appointment with her doctor. I interviewed her in the car with my associate translating, but it was clear that she really spoke good English. She was extremely vague but did give me details of the village where her daughter was buried, a different village!

I went to that village, and no one there had heard of the mother, and there was certainly no grave there. One of the elders said that he thought he recognised the name Ama. I left him my card plus Boat's (my associate) telephone number. A couple of days after my return home, Boat rang me. He had just received a call from Ama. The village elder had given her my card. Boat had, in fact, taken her to see her grave. Not many people get to do this.

I rang Ama, and she informed me that she had studied in London from 1999 until 2003. She left and had not been back since then. She knew none of the people involved with this claim. When she left London, she had not cancelled her bank account. It contained very little and never cancelled her registration with a London GP. This was the account used for the fraud plus the insured had the same GP. The real Ama is a very intelligent lady, and my associate met her and her father, a rather prominent person, in Kumasi. The father knew the lady I had met who said she was the mother. She originated from his village, and the people behind the fraud in London were related to her.

Clearly, this was a case of identity theft. As Ama never cancelled her bank account, it had been used by another person who took on her identity when she left the UK. Ama was a genuine, honest person who never considered what

413

danger lurked when not cancelling such an account or medical registration. And the lawyer who made the claim? Still a free man.

- - - - - - -

A man claimed a considerable amount of money on an accident policy, in respect of fingers and toes lost as a result of a car crash near Kumasi. What he told me lacked credibility. He first said that his hand was out of the passenger window when the car rolled over. He forgot they drove on the other side of the road, so it was the wrong hand. He then recalled that the car rolled over, and his hand ended up underneath the vehicle. A good Samaritan stopped and took him and his injured driver to a private clinic 20 miles away in Kumasi, passing three main hospitals on route!

Enquiries in Kumasi showed that there was no such accident and the medical papers were fake. So, I wonder where he did lose those fingers? Probably sometime before he took out the insurance policy. You have to *hand* it to him for trying

- - - - -

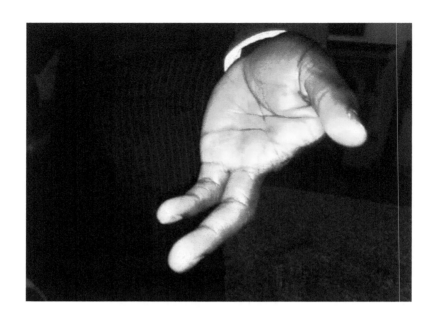

Chapter 25: Far East

I have already dealt with China and Indonesia as they were both worthy of having their own chapters. I have travelled several times to the Philippines working mostly for international offshore insurance companies. Several of these claims have been for amounts in excess of $1m. In each case, on the international policies, the insured has been dead but - - - -. There have been multiple cases where I was able to locate the person's true medical history. Had this been disclosed to the insurer at the outset, then it is unlikely that the policy would have gone on risk. I have had two substantial cases where the insureds *accidentally* shot themselves while cleaning their gun. At least, that is what the police reports stated.

In the first case, the man had been a successful businessman. One day he was talking with his brother while sitting on his bed cleaning his gun as he had just been to the shooting range. Suddenly the gun went off and by the time he arrived at the hospital he was dead. A detailed police report was produced indicating that the gun had been discharged accidentally.

My enquiries in Manila indicated that the man had financial problems. He had borrowed large sums of money, and these were covered by life insurance. Had he lived then, he would have experienced severe financial problems. I could find no evidence that he had been to a shooting range that day. Plus, forensic evidence showed no signs of materials normally used for cleaning a gun. I interviewed the police officer who investigated the case, and he was adamant that his report was accurate. It was, according to him, an accident.

I had a medical report from the hospital, but this only showed death caused by a gunshot wound. However, I was able to meet the doctor who first treated the insured when he arrived in the emergency room. He recalled that the insured's brother told him that the insured had been depressed and said he was going to kill himself. That morning he sat on the bed with his brother, who was holding a gun. He thought he had persuaded him to put the gun away, but suddenly he shot himself. The doctor had recorded this in his notes, and a copy was provided to the insurer. The age of the policies was such that suicide was excluded. I had a further meeting with the police officer, but he denied that it was suicide. Clearly, he had been paid off.

- - - - - - -

I later had another similar claim relating to a very wealthy Filipino businessman. He owned substantial businesses and lived in a luxurious property. It was claimed that he was sat on his bed having a meeting with one of his sons and his servant. He said he had been cleaning his gun, had left it in the ensuite and needed to put it away. He went into the ensuite, closed the door and moments later, a gunshot was heard. The son claimed that his father had accidentally shot himself, and later this was confirmed in a police report. The age of the main, large policy was such that suicide was still an exclusion.

I examined the scene of the shooting and interviewed family members and the police. The officer had recorded the death as being accidental because of what the family told him. It should be added here that in such a Catholic society, suicide is often frowned upon, so rarely is a death classified as suicide. Again, there was nothing in the room that could be used for cleaning a gun, but I was asked to believe that perhaps the father used soap and water. Plus, it is not the norm to clean a gun when it is loaded. There were numerous discrepancies in respect of this claim.

I met the pathologist, and she showed me several photographs. The bullet had entered into the man's chest adjacent to his heart. For it to have penetrated in such a way, then the gun had to be held in both hands close to the chest. It had to be at a certain height and at an angle, suggesting that this could not have been an accident. The pathologist informed me that it could only have been suicide, plus a family member had told her he had killed himself. There was clearly some dispute within this wealthy family, but I could not establish why he would kill himself, but obviously, he did.

- - - - - - -

A Filipino lady, Anna, worked in Ireland for several years, went back on holiday to the Philippines and allegedly drowned there in a creek. This was not a large claim, circa €135,000, but I found various discrepancies in the documents from the Philippines. Had she drowned, it would have been a "medico-legal case", and there would have been a post-mortem. The death appeared to have been certified by a local doctor, not a pathologist. Plus, it appeared that the lady had been buried prior to the death being registered. The correct procedures had not been followed, but in many countries, this can happen in rural areas.

So off on the long flight to Manila. The morning after arriving, I set off by car on the long journey, through the beautiful countryside north to a town near Bayonbong. The next morning, I located the village where the death had allegedly occurred. There was only one creek, and it ran alongside the main road. Very little water was in the creek at that time of the year. The lady allegedly drowned there in

June, and the creek would have then been almost empty. Local people had not heard of such a death there.

I went to the local registry, and the death was in the register. I spoke to the lady who had made the entry. She agreed it should have been a case for a pathologist and could not offer a logical explanation as to why she had registered the death. Clearly, she was lying as she could not stop shaking. Adjacent to the registry, the local doctor had an office. He provided various explanations about why there had been no post-mortem. I spoke to two local police officers, who both gave conflicting accounts of what had happened. Both the doctor, the registrar and one police officer mentioned a man called Ferdinand, a high ranking official in the government office in Bayonbong. They thought he was related to the lady. I went there to see him, but he had left for the day and never answered his phone until I was back in Manila 3 days later!

There were also documents produced by a local undertaker. Again, I received conflicting accounts of events, but eventually, I was told that the undertaker gave a lady some blank documents. He never saw a body.

The place of the alleged burial was a small farming community in Burgos, on the coast. The road meanders around the mountains, and the journey took all day. It was raining up high, and water was pouring down from rocks above the road. Regularly I filled up my water bottle with this fresh water. The scenery was stunning. As we neared the coast, the road straightened, and the temperature rose. We found a place to stay the night, and early the next morning, set off to locate the farming community.

Once there, I spoke to the local chief. Yes, he knew Anna. She was his cousin and had been working in Ireland but was now back home. He took me to see her, and she did not seem too surprised to meet me. Clearly, Ferdinand had been in contact with her.

Anna said that her twin sister had been in Ireland but died last year near Bayonbong. The twin obviously had the same date of birth as her and also the same 3 names. I asked if her sister had a husband and daughter with the same names as her husband and daughter. I suggested she had inherited an Irish sense of humour. She laughed, put her arm around me and apologised. She said that when her cousin, Ferdinand, realised that she had life insurance in Ireland, he took the papers and insisted on claiming against her will. A lovely lady and I departed on the best of terms.

At the same time

The creek where death did not happen!

Vehicle used by the local undertaker

The road to the coast

- - - - - - -

Another unusual claim involved a trip to a small island in the south of the Philippines. A Filipino lady was claiming that her English husband had died. There was nothing particularly suspicious about the claim, but it was similar to a claim in Thailand that proved to be false, plus I had other cases in the Philippines. I flew early morning from Manila to the island. I could not book a return flight and was informed I would have to do this upon arrival. I arrived there Friday morning. I was told that all flights were full, and I might be able to travel Monday evening. I would just have to turn up at the airport and wait. I soon realised that this was a very small place. My enquiry would be completed that morning, so what could I do for the next 3 days?

Anyway, I asked the fare into town on a "Jeepney" and was told it would be $40 for me and Larry, my associate. This was about double the real price, so I queried it. The driver told me to walk, so I jumped on it as it started to move. In the main town, we transferred to a rickshaw and asked to be taken to the best hotel in town. We ended up in a dump, a polite word for the place. There were no window coverings, and the toilet and shower consisted of a hole in the floor. The room was charged by the hour, and I soon realised the true purpose of the place!! The thought of staying there 3 nights left me in despair!

Anyway, we started enquiries and being such a small place. It took about 2 hours to establish that the man had died as claimed. The local priest took me to the home of the mayor. He had the concession to import the main beer sold there and lived in palatial surroundings. We were invited to join him for lunch; a rather delicious fare was laid on. He had a dance troupe from the mainland staying there and apologised that he could not accommodate me. Damn it!

I was taken to see the claimant, a lovely young, educated lady. She explained that her husband had insisted on moving to the island to start a bar, against her wishes. I interviewed her at the bar on a beautiful, deserted beach. If only I had a decent hotel, then perhaps, three nights there would not be so bad. I soon realised that the bar also operated as a brothel. No way could I remain in such a location! The lady explained how her husband had changed the bar, and it was her intention to get rid of it and return to her profession in Manila.

She asked where I was staying. When I told her, she stated I could not stay in such a place. Had she not been taking the night ferry back to Manila, she told me that Larry and I could have been her guest. Another missed opportunity. It then dawned on me; there was a ferry back to Manila.

We rushed to the port and bought 2 tickets – first class – on the night ferry. We returned to the place called a hotel, had a shower (a bucket of cold water over my head) and took a rickshaw to a Chinese restaurant. Later we boarded the boat and saw that first-class meant you could lay down in a dormitory-style, stifling set up socially distancing by about a metre. There was a bar on the open deck, and this seemed a preferable way of passing a few hours. That was until a man claiming to be the mayor of another small island decided to drink the bar dry and threaten to throw people overboard! I arrived back at my hotel in Manila about 9 am Saturday. Luxury at last!

My first-class journey

- - - - - - -

I have travelled several times to Thailand, but there have been few false claims from there. I have travelled to the border of Burma, south to Krabi, plus to the beautiful islands of Phuket and Ko Samui. Several of the claims have involved UK nationals living in Thailand, and it was necessary to look into their medical backgrounds there in order to access a claim. In Ko Samui, I investigated the death of an Australian national. The policy only paid out if he died accidentally, and there was some discrepancy about exactly how he died. It transpired that he drove a motor scooter into the front of an oncoming lorry. Was it an accident or perhaps

427

suicide? Impossible to say. Thai police obviously assumed it was an accident, so no real investigation was carried out.

I was asked by various reinsurance companies in Europe to look into 4 death claims involving Thai nationals in Thailand, all insured with Thai insurers but reinsured with international reinsurers. The claims had all been investigated by local loss adjusters. Perhaps I should say they had been looked at rather than investigated. The loss adjusters appeared to accept what they were told and never challenged people. They had stated that 3 claims were genuine, and the large one, in excess of the equivalent of £500k, was false. I managed to show that the 3 "genuine claims" were very suspect, and the false one was definitely genuine. However, it was difficult obtaining the evidence so long after the various events.

One case involved a young man killed in a car accident in the north and cremated at a temple in Bangkok. I interviewed the Buddhist monk in charge, and he was lying. I had an interpreter, and she refused to challenge the man. She told me she could not query what such a holy man was saying. I could not, therefore, establish how the monk arranged the man's cremation 12 hours before he was in an accident and died. I managed to prove that the man's business and income had been falsely described. Had the truth been told, the sum assured would have been far less. It was difficult to prove that he was not dead; it was more likely he had been murdered. The result was that the payment was far lower than the insured amount.

Another case was in the north, and the man was a drug addict. He had died, but it was clearly drug-related, and the policy was voided. In another one, the person had died but was clearly over-insured.

As for the large claim that was said to be false, it was clearly absolutely genuine. The man's car had caught fire on a journey to the north. By the time the emergency services arrived at the scene, the body had completely burnt, leaving just a few bones. The man was a successful businessman from a well-known and respected family. My investigation showed that without any doubt, he had died as claimed. However, he was grossly over-insured, and several of the policies were new. It transpired he had a close friend who sold insurance. The friend kept asking him to take out insurance in order to increase his commission and realise his annual target. This was the reason he was over-insured.

- - - - - - -

An interesting claim was investigated in Thailand some years ago by Andy Young. A young man from England was married to a Thai lady, and they lived in Pattaya – a den of iniquity! She notified a UK insurer that he had died and sent them the appropriate documents. His elderly mother in England had been told of his death and had sent money to the wife there. Andy found the man alive and well. It was wicked that he had been stealing money from his elderly mother.

The man had been very much involved with a rugby club in England. I went online and found that they were in the process of arranging a large memorial match and hoped to collect money for a charity. How embarrassing had they done that, and then he later turned up to watch a game. We believe that it was his intention to eventually return to that area. I knew this club quite well, and I had met the Chairman so decided to ring him. I was not in a position where I could divulge all the information but provided sufficient information for him to cancel the memorial match. I think that members of that club now know why that happened!

Chapter 26: UK & Ireland

David Swaffer died in Dublin when his hire car swerved off the road, entered a canal, and he drowned. At least, this is what the police assumed. I was asked by several insurers in the UK to look into this death.

David had been born into a well to do family, but later in life, he appeared to have fallen on hard times. He had a home on the south coast of England, but at the time of his death, he was said to be claiming benefits. He had once worked for an insurance company, and it was alleged that he detested insurance companies. So why in the previous 2 years had he taken out life and accident cover for £5.86 million? Plus, there was substantial insurance cover on credit card debts.

He had taken out numerous credit cards, and every single one was absolutely maxed out to the limit at the time of his death, but these debts were covered by insurance. It appeared that he took out one card, used it for purchases plus cash withdrawals and utilised it to the maximum. He would then take out a second card, withdraw cash and use it to pay the minimum monthly payment on the first card. By the time the second card reached the maximum limit, he would take on a third card. And, so it went on until there was not another credit card company left in the UK or Ireland that had not been used. The day prior to his death, he used the last card, bought jewellery in Dublin and shipped it back to his family. That final card had by then been used to the limit!

David had a partner also in Ireland, and she was left with certain insurance proceeds in his will. He had taken out substantial keyman life policies totalling around £3.15m. Keyman insurance is a policy taken out by a business to insure their most valuable employees, but he was unemployed! To obtain this cover, he started two companies in England and showed various relatives as co-directors or company secretaries. The companies never actually traded, and none of the relatives was aware that they were officers of a company. Their signatures had been forged. The payments for the premiums could only have come from cash taken from credit cards.

So why go to such lengths unless the idea is to claim on all of the policies? So, was it an accident? My enquiries showed that the police investigation was probably on par with investigations I had witnessed with the police in Nigeria and India. I do not want to sound disrespectful to the police in Ireland, Nigeria or India. Over the years, I have worked closely with the police in Ireland and have always been impressed. But in this case

- - - - -

Police officers interviewed staff at the hotel where he was staying. His car was noticed in the canal around mid-morning, and a member of staff stated that when she knocked on his bedroom door at around 9 am that morning, someone from that room shouted OK. So, it was assumed the accident had occurred mid-morning on a busy road, and no one noticed it? I went to the hotel, went to a different room but asked the staff member to knock on another door. I heard her knock, shouted OK, and she assumed I was in that room. I was in another room.

The hire car had allegedly mounted the kerb – it was at least 18cm high – crossed various large grass mounds and ended up sideways in the canal. The police notified the hire car company, who took the car away once it was removed from the water. The police only made a cursory examination at the scene. How did the car not suffer damage to the wheels when mounting such a high kerb? How did the underside of the car not damage from hitting the large grass mounds? How did the grass mounds remain intact? How could the car enter the canal sideways on, causing no obvious body damage to the vehicle? Why did the airbags not inflate? I could only come across one conclusion. The vehicle was steered onto the kerb, around the grass mounds and into the canal. It entered a section about 60 metres long. At either end of this section were posts showing the actual depth of the water. This had to be premeditated. Also, information obtained suggested that the car entered the canal during the early hours of that morning. Apart from the actual scene of the event, the financial background only left one conclusion. Suicide. This would not be covered under the accident policies, and the information given to obtain the life policies was false.

There followed what I believe was the longest inquest in Irish history, and much media attention was attracted. Only certain information is allowed to be given at inquests, so the jury was not permitted to examine all the background financial information. However, as the inquest was the main item on the news and on the front page of every newspaper in Ireland, the members of the jury must have realised what was happening. The insurers were represented by a lawyer. After 2 days, the verdict was accidental death. This was based upon the evidence that the court was allowed to hear, so much of the financial evidence was not given.

A lawyer representing the family said that the claims would have to be paid. I pointed out to him and the family that should the case end up in a civil court in England, then most of the evidence that could not be put before an inquest jury could be used in a civil court. The lawyer suggested words to the effect that I was a bad loser. I indicated that the financial evidence I had acquired would destroy any allegation that the death was accidental.

None of the claims was ever pursued. In reality a very sad case. I believe that the evidence suggested that he spent 2 years planning his suicide in order to leave substantial funds to his family and a friend, plus he wanted to make the insurance industry that he detested so much to have to pay out large sums of money. How else could he have continued paying £3545 a month in insurance premiums on around 48 policies? No longer would he have been able to withdraw cash from credit cards.

There was no reason to suspect that his family was aware of what he had planned.

DEATH PLUNGE ROMEO'S 40 LIFE POLICIES

Insurers refuse to pay

By JOHN KIERANS

ROMEO businessman David Swaffer left £6 million in 40 life insurance policies when he died in a mystery drowning accident.

Twenty policies, worth a staggering £300,000 each, were taken out in the last 18 months, the last only two weeks before his car nose-dived into a Dublin canal.

Insurance investigators told an inquest in Dublin yesterday that it all added up to a massive scam.

Their claims were dismissed by the jury, who ruled that his death was accidental. But chief insurance investigator John Saunders said last night: "The coroner's court's verdict is not binding and has no effect on the assessment of any claim under the policies."

Mr Swaffer's two sons, 30-year-old Eric and 21-year-old Hugh, jumped with delight. They are the main beneficiaries of his will along with second wife Jenny.

He also bequeathed £140,000 from one policy to Dublin girlfriend Carmel Reid, with whom he had a 19-year secret affair.

Eric said last night: "It is a very

● Turn to Page 4

ACCIDENTAL DEATH: Mr Swaffer

I had an alleged death in Pakistan in respect of a policy with a cover of around £2m. I travelled to 5 places in and around London to investigate this claim but not Pakistan. Shamshad Billa took out the life policies and indicated that she was self-employed, having a share of an off licence in Islington, north London. She was allegedly getting married and completed a trust form leaving the proceeds to her partner, Mohammed Butt. Her executor was Nosheen Chughtai, also a resident in London. Strangely enough, on the applications, she added a comment that she was a frequent traveller to Lahore, Islamabad, Goa and Mumbai. An odd comment to make as Muslims from Pakistan do not frequently travel to Goa and Mumbai in India! Plus, why tell an insurance company about where you go on holiday if there was no question about this? Unless of course - - - - if you died in one of these countries, the insurer would perhaps think, "yes, she did say she travelled there on holiday, so she must be dead". Do people really think insurance companies are so stupid?????

The policies were taken out in early 2007, and, lo and behold, she allegedly died in Pakistan of 'dehydration' in July that year. The claim was made by Nosheen, and I contacted her to arrange a meeting to clarify the details of the claim. She informed me that I would not be able to visit her home as, being a good Muslim girl, she was not allowed to have a male visitor who was not related. Eventually, we agreed to meet in the bar area of a large hotel in West London near to where she worked. I was surprised when a young lady arrived dressed in a very modern, western fashion and wearing an abundance of make-up.

Suspecting that perhaps she did not live in the address in southwest London shown on the various forms, I arranged to have her followed after our meeting. She actually did live at that address, and it was interesting that when followed, she spent ages on her mobile in a somewhat agitated state. I never believed what she told me, and she did say that I had not been able to visit her at her home as the other girl living there would not allow male visitors, somewhat contradicting her earlier explanation.

Her story was that she had met Shamshad Billa 5 years previously at a wedding, and they became friendly. Nosheen knew that she lived in a flat above an off licence in Islington. In July, she received a call from a man in Pakistan saying that Shamshad had died. She went to her flat above the off licence where she found a life insurance policy plus a will making her the executor. She then rang the man in Pakistan and asked him to send her a death certificate. She failed to mention that she found 3 insurance policies; there were also claims with other life offices, and I never told her that I also represented them! I found it difficult to obtain a logical response as to how she had managed to enter the flat and why, when there, she should start examining paperwork belonging to a person she hardly knew!

I carried out numerous database searches, and Mohammed Butt, the alleged fiancé, was shown at the off-licence along with Rozeena Butt. There was also a record of an address in east London for them. I went there, and the house was empty. An elderly neighbour told me that the Butt family had moved to Hornchurch. I asked her whether she knew a person called Shamshad Billa. She seemed to think that this was also a name used by Rozeena Butt.

Nosheen had told me that a death certificate had been faxed to her from Pakistan, and she agreed to fax it to me. She did so, and the fax number shown at the top of the death certificate was not Pakistan. It was a telephone number from the area where the Butts had lived in east London!

Various forms had allegedly been signed by a lady living just outside London. I met her and established that she had a sister called Rozeena Billa, who became Butt when she married. However, when she was born, she was called Shamshad Billa and later changed her first name to Rozeena! They had another sister who had a daughter living in London called Nosheen Chughtai.

The sisters were born in Leicestershire, and I obtained a copy of the birth certificate of Rozeena Butt and could prove that she was also Shamshad Billa and was the aunt of Nosheen Chughtai. So, the "dead" lady, Shamshad Billa, was in fact, Rozeena Butt, the wife of Mohammed Butt, not the fiancée, and they owned the off-licence. I did establish, though, that the off-licence was not actually in Mohammed's name as he was a Special Constable in the Met (London) Police. Special Constables are not allowed to own licenced premises. The claimant, Nosheen, was the niece of Rozeena/Shamshad, so they had not met at a wedding and become friends.

I did get to speak to Mohammed at the off-licence, and he answered very few questions, saying that I needed to speak to his solicitor. I also spoke to his wife on the telephone, and she denied she was Shamshad Billa. There were so many discrepancies in what both persons told me that there was sufficient evidence to report the matter to the police.

Mohammed and Rozeena Butt, plus Nosheen, were arrested and charged with fraud. They pleaded not guilty, and I attended Crown Court as a witness. When I started to give evidence, it became obvious to me that my interview of Nosheen was not to be included. For some reason, it must have been ruled inadmissible. Normally in such proceedings, a representative of the Crown Prosecution Service (CPS) will inform a witness that part of the evidence had been ruled inadmissible and therefore should not be mentioned in front of the jury. Nothing was said to me, so when I had finished giving evidence, I asked the CPS why the interview had been ignored. I was informed that under The Regulation of Investigatory Powers Act 2000 (RIPA), I should have obtained the permission of a senior police officer for permission to conduct surveillance on Nosheen. It will be recalled that I had arranged for her to be followed after I interviewed her. As I had not obtained permission from a senior police officer, my interview of her had been ruled as being inadmissible.

Total rubbish! How did they know I had not obtained permission? No one asked me. However, I had not asked permission; legally, it was not required. RIPA relates to public bodies such as the Police, Customs, Revenue, DSS etc. Insurance companies are not public bodies and do not need permission to conduct surveillance on claimants. I could not believe that a court could make such an error, one that could have resulted in a miscarriage of justice. Anyway, all 3 defendants were found guilty, and Mr and Mrs Butt were sentenced to prison, while Nosheen received a suspended sentence. Interestingly when Mohammed Butt was arrested, he had moved on from being a special constable and was on a police training course at Hendon in London.

نکومت بنجاب پاکستان
THE GOVT OF PUNJAB PAKISTAN

ولادت سر ٹیفیکیٹ

DEATH CERTIFICATE

CRMS No. **D3S3103-07-0010**
NATURE OF DEATH **NORMAL**

FORM No. **P000702616**

رست ورثہ	وجہ موت	تاریخ دفن	جائے وفات اور تاریخ	جنس	مذہب	جائے پیدائش اندراج	تاریخ پیدائش	وجہ	ولدیت کا نام	شناختی کارڈ نمبر	تندہ کا نام
طبعی		13-7-2007	رورل	12-7-2007	مورت	اسلام		7-12-1971		محمد صادق	شمشاد بی بی

APPLICANT NAME **MUHAMMAD AJMAL**
APPLICANT CNIC 3530172825721   RELATION WITH DECEASED ETC
ADDRESS NEIGHBOURHOOD ZIA UL DIN COLONY.
CITY DEPALPUR TEHSIL DEPALPUR DISTRICT OKARA

DECEASED NAME/ CNIC	FATHER NAME/ CNIC	DATE OF BIRTH	SEX	RELIGION	PLACE/DATE OF DEATH	DATE OF BURIAL	REASON OF DEATH	SICKNESS PERIOD
SHAMSHAD BILLA	MUHAMMAD SADIQ	7-12-1971	FE MALE	ISLAM	RURAL HEALTH CENTER SHABOON 12-7-2007	13-7-2007	NATURAL	D

BLOOD RELATION PERSON CAUSING DISPOSAL OF BODY
NAME MUHAMMAD AJMAL
CNIC 3530172825721   3530172825721
GRAVEYARD NAME BABA QOHREY SHAH
ENTRY DATE 28-7-2007   28-7-2007
ISSUE DATE 9-8-2007   9-8-2007
ADDITIONAL INFORMATION REASON DEHYDRATION

```
P 0 0 0 7 0 2 6 1 6
```

Her death certificate

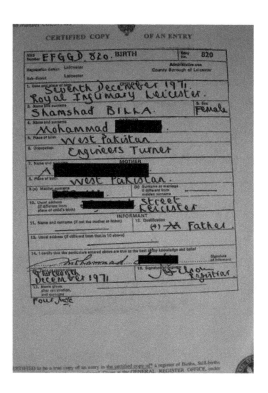

Her real birth certificate before name change

Press reports

Essex Road off licence boss jailed for faking her own death

AN off-licence boss who teamed up with her police officer husband to fake her own death in a £2m "Reggie Perrin" style scam was jailed for 25 months today.

Hornchurch woman fakes death to claim £2m insurance

A depressed English housewife who faked her own death after getting the idea from a clairvoyant has been jailed for 25 months.

Rozeena Butt, 39, her trainee police officer husband Mohammed, 45, and her niece Nosheen Chughtai took out more than £2.2 million ($3.5 million) in life insurance using a birth certificate she had in another name.

Butt had been encouraged to carry out the fraud by a clairvoyant she had become close to in early 2007, as well as a Sri Lankan mystic she had been introduced to.

Her husband received an 18-month sentence, while her niece was given a 51-week suspended term.

Chapter 27: Other Types Of Claims

Over the years, different insurers have asked for assistance in relation to new products introduced onto the market that have resulted in large numbers of claims. Some years ago, an insurer dealing with pension products was approached by a broker who wanted to try and sell a new insurance product. He was hoping that he could do this via the insurer utilising their licence. Basically, the product covered illnesses and accidents. Different amounts could be insured; for example, paying a monthly premium of say £40 meant that if the insured became ill and was off work for 4 weeks, then they would be paid around £800 a month for a period up to 12 months. If they were incapacitated due to an accident, then they would receive this amount immediately. Depending on the chosen premium, the monthly amounts payable could be £1500.

Within about 8 weeks, around 120 policies were sold. Out of 120 insured persons, there were 110 claims received within that time! Over 100 of these were persons resident in Northern Ireland, many of whom lived close to the land boundary with Ireland. The insurance company had very few experienced staff, they employed mostly young ladies and could not cope. They had little, if any, experience dealing with claims. Regularly they received calls threatening to bomb their office if their claim was not paid immediately. Realising that such claimants lived in what was once an IRA-controlled area frightened staff members.

I was asked to investigate these claims and spent over two weeks travelling around Ireland. There was not one single claim that I thought was genuine. It was difficult to assess if this had been set up as a fraud or if certain people had taken advantage of the system. One lady in Belfast had an accident and claimed she could hardly walk. To be paid out, insured persons needed to prove that they had been in employment and produce proof of income. This lady was a shop window designer and extremely well paid, at least according to all the documents she produced. When I called her home, her flatmate told me she would not be home until after 4 pm as she was at university. She was a full-time student!

Numerous claimants produced self-employed accounts prepared by a man. Let's call him Morgan. He was actually a bookkeeper, and I established that he spent most of his life in the local pub. If you bought him 2 pints of Guinness, he would prepare a set of accounts that you could send to the insurer when claiming. I regularly interviewed claimants who could not recall their income or occupation; they had forgotten what an inebriated Morgan had prepared.

Many of the claimants lived in what was then regarded as IRA strongholds, and the authorities took a keen interest in what was happening. In such a scenario, word soon spreads about an investigation and the claims are reduced in no time to 2 and then zero. The most blatant claim was from an agent selling the policies in Ireland. While he was introducing new business to the insurer and being paid a commission, he had personally taken out a policy and was claiming disability!

- - - - - - -

A broker in London came up with a similar insurance product and persuaded an insurer to front the business. It was a product for drivers of the black cabs in London. If a driver was incapacitated, he did not need to claim for 2 weeks or more. This meant that by the time the insurer became aware of a claim, the driver might be back at work, so it was too late to mount surveillance or call at his home to find out if he was out working. The number of claims increased so much that I was surprised that there were no black cabs left on the streets of London. One driver's claim continued for some time, and when interviewed, he said he could only drive a few miles due to his incapacity. I returned to his home 4 days later, and the mileage on the cab had increased by 700 miles. Only he was insured to drive it.

I interviewed one driver, and he was insistent that his Rottweiler remained in the room. It laid across my feet. It soon became apparent that when I asked an awkward question, the man raised his voice. The animal then looked at me and snarled. I decided this would be a very short interview!

When drivers realised that they would always be interviewed when claiming the claims reduced to zero and the insurer stopped selling the policy. I do not wish to sound too critical of black cab drivers. I have taken taxis in over 90 countries and, in my view, London black cab drivers are the best in the world!

- - - - - - -

A finance company specialising in home loans and re-mortgages asked an insurer to provide an insurance policy that would cover repayments in respect of sickness and redundancies. This was some years ago, and the loans ranged between £4000 and £8000. Within a short period, out of around 130 policies, there were about 115 claims. Nearly all of these claims came from low paid workers in the Asian communities in northwest England. One agent had sold all of these policies and earned a considerable commission.

I spent several weeks in the northwest and realised that the agent was telling people that they could borrow money against the value of their property. They could then get a medical certificate from their doctor or a letter to say they had been made redundant. The agent told them that they would not have to repay much of the loan as the insurance company would be repaying it.

I interviewed numerous claimants who were unaware of what they were meant to do for a living. One man, who was a builder, could not work due to a severe back problem, and his doctor supported his claim. I went to see his doctor, and the claimant was on the roof of his surgery, building an extension!

I interviewed an Asian lady who had allegedly been made redundant from working in a sweatshop (a garment factory). Documents indicated that she had a large income for such work. Her loan was actually used to buy a Porsche car. She never had a driving licence! The owner of the sweatshop had made her "redundant", drove the Porsche, and when I visited his office, the claimant was busy working there on a sewing machine.

I realised that several claimants had been made redundant from a textile factory. I called there, someone spoke to me through a grill and asked me to wait. I nipped outside to see several workers exit via the fire escape to the rear and disappear quickly. When I eventually met the owner, he explained that the business was so bad that he only had 3 employees, and I could see them sitting at their machines. He could not explain why all the other machines were turned on!

The person who sold the policies disappeared, and I believe he returned to live in Pakistan. Very soon after I started my investigation, claims were reduced to just one.

- - - - - - -

Over the years, there have been problems with identity thefts used to steal people's investments and pension funds from insurers. With most of these, the countries involved were Ghana, Benin, and yes, you guessed it, Nigeria. There was a period when I believe that staff at the international post sorting office in Nigeria were stealing envelopes that contained details of a financial institution on the outside. I spent ages trying to suggest to financial institutions that they sent correspondence to West Africa in plain envelopes.

The fraudsters, if realising that the correspondence referred to a person in Nigeria having any overseas investment, would then get to work. They would identify that person, establish details of their residence and office and then try and bribe staff to steal personal information. They would obtain a false passport containing a photograph of the target. They would then contact the financial institution and withdraw funds. There were 3 occasions where they could not withdraw money as it was in a pension fund that had not matured. However, if the fundholder died, then the funds could be paid. Yes, I had 3 claims where the fundholder died and supporting death certificates obtained in Nigeria and Benin. These were easy to investigate if I was asked about such documents before claims were settled. It was easy to contact the real person by telephone.

One case involved a well know businessman from Lagos. He needed money from his investment fund, so he contacted the company in London but was told they could not speak to him unless he knew the relevant password to his account. When he said there had never been a password, they refused to talk to him. Eventually, he flew to London, engaged the services of a lawyer who contacted the insurer. I then became involved.

Someone with an African accent had regularly contacted the insurer from Ghana and withdrawn funds after sending confirmation via fax. This person always asked to speak to the same lady stating that she understood his business commitments etc. He was extremely friendly and told her all about the hotel he was building in Ghana. Hence he needed his funds. After several transactions involving in excess of £100k, he suggested to the lady that he could be a fraudster. How, he asked did she know she was talking to the real owner of the funds? He suggested setting up a password, and thereafter whenever he rang, he gave the password. Hence when the real owner of the fund rang, he did not know about any password, so the call was ended. I proved that money had been stolen by this fraudster, so the real owner had to be reimbursed.

I went to Ghana a few days later on another claim. While there, the insurer rang me to say that the fraudster had again rung and wanted further money. On my advice, the insurer said that he should leave his number and they would ring back later at an agreed time. I checked the number, and it belonged to an office that did typing, photocopying, fax service etc. When the insurer rang the number, Boat, my associate in Accra, and I were in the office with Ghana police and the man was arrested. His home was searched, and two other men arrested. One escaped, but two were held in custody. They were Nigerians using false identities. They had run up colossal phone bills with Ghana Telecom, and I saw a list of the numerous calls made. They had spent hours each day ringing all around the world. No doubt they were involved in many scams.

One of them was granted bail by a judge, and the police were convinced that a large payment had been made for this to happen. This man was never seen again. I interviewed the other one in prison. He told me that if he gave me any information, he would be killed within days. Being a man of ill health, he died in prison but not even his real name was ever known. It goes to show that these fraudsters, known in Nigeria as 419ers (the penal code for fraud), comprise large groups of organised fraudsters.

- - - - - - -

While life claims have been my major work, I have also dealt with numerous claims relating to ill health. These fall mainly into the categories of Income Protection Insurance (IPI) and Critical Illness (CI). IPI normally covers around 80% of a person's income if they are off work for a period of time, normally after a period of 3 or 6 months. CI is payable if one has a critical illness such as heart attack, stroke, MS and so on. You will probably ask how a person can pretend to suffer from a stroke or MS if it is not genuine. Correct, but perhaps the person only took out the insurance after the event occurred! In respect of a heart attack, I have dealt with a large number of false claims. A person can return from abroad with documents from a doctor indicating that they suffered a heart attack. It is not always possible to examine that person in the UK and obtain evidence that there was no heart attack.

One interesting claim came from Dr Korshid, an Iraqi national who worked as a locum at several UK hospitals. He took out critical illness policies totalling £203k and just over a year later claimed he had suffered a heart attack while on holiday in Turkey. He produced a significant number of supporting medical records from a hospital in Ankara. The insurer wrote to the hospital and received a response from a Dr Hursitoglu. He confirmed details of the heart attack and sent additional medical records. An independent ECG was carried out in the UK, and the doctor expressed doubts that the ECG from the UK and the one from Turkey related to the same patient.

We were instructed to make enquiries and first examined the claimant's passport that indicated he had made several visits to Turkey. Plus, his income hardly covered his monthly financial commitments. We extended enquiries to Turkey and made enquiries at the relevant Ministry about Dr Hursitoglu. He was from Iraq, and when we saw his photograph, we realised that Dr Korshid and Dr Hursitoglu was the same person. Dr Korshid had taken Turkish nationality, changed his name to Hursitoglu and was employed at the hospital in Ankara. He had obviously written his own medical report!

The doctor is wanted in the UK and Turkey and is believed to be somewhere in the Middle East.

- - - - - - -

Some years ago, I was asked by an Australian insurer to make enquiries about a claimant who had moved back to Egypt from Australia. The man worked in Australia for years as an engineer and had problems with unions and fellow workers. He claimed he was too ill to work, and doctors supported his claim, albeit one or two specialists appeared somewhat reluctant to do so.

I had an address for him in Alexandria in northern Egypt. Enquiries revealed that he had registered in Egypt as an engineer soon after returning from Australia. But why if he was meant to be so incapacitated and unable to work? What an ideal scenario for him. To return to his own country, live among friends and relatives, receive a large income from an insurer in Australia and continue working.

The address in Egypt that he had given to the insurer was unlikely to be where he was really living. It was a block of flats, and I went there and spoke to a lady. She would only say that she would arrange for the claimant's wife to ring me. Later she did and told me that when I called, she had been with her husband visiting a doctor. She asked me to return to the flat at 6 pm.

I did so and met the wife, an educated lady who had worked as a dentist in Australia. She informed me that when I met her husband, I might find it distressing, so she wanted to forewarn me. She then took me into a bedroom, and he was in bed. She spoke to him in English as one would speak to a 2year old. "Come on, E-----, this is nice, Mr Saunders, who has come a long way to see you. Now look up and say hello". He grunted and disappeared under the bed cover. This ridiculous scenario continued for a few minutes until he uttered several words such as "wee-wee". His wife said he needed to go to the toilet. She asked me to help her get him out of bed. I agreed reluctantly. He then did a brilliant impersonation of a chimpanzee. He leant forward, bent his knees and dragged his arms along the ground while making animal noises. He then returned to get into bed, and his wife wanted me to talk to him in "baby talk". I left the room and said I could no longer watch this ridiculous charade.

His wife followed me. I informed her that she was insulting my intelligence with such a stupid charade. I pointed out that before meeting her, I had checked with the

457

concierge of the block of flats. He had confirmed that the claimant had arrived 30 minutes earlier driving his wife and children in the family car, something he did most days when visiting family at the apartment. I had also ascertained that he had registered a business in Egypt. End of the claim. But how could two educated people act so ridiculously and expect me to fall for it?

- - - - - - -

A young lady in west London took out a critical illness policy with a cover of £500,000 and within months claimed that she had MS. Medical reports from a hospital in west London confirmed that she did have MS. She had only been registered with her doctor for about a year and had only sought treatment for minor problems. According to the lady, she had previously lived in east Africa and been in good health.

We made countless enquiries and realised that the lady was married and had also used her married name. The policy and medical records were in her maiden name. Enquiries suggested that she had previously lived in north London, where she had mainly used her married name. Enquiries of the various health bodies in north London indicated that the lady had been registered there under her married name. Not only did she have a doctor in north London but, when she actually took out the policy, she had already been receiving treatment for MS for several months. The report from the specialist treating her in west London stated that when he broke the news to her that she had MS, he was surprised that such a young, attractive lady took the news with no obvious surprise. That is because she was already being treated for MS on the other side of London! Her claim was obviously not paid.

- - - - - - -

I had another similar case. An Asian male in London claimed on his £220,000 critical illness policy that he had liver failure and he did have a successful transplant. I interviewed him, and he was the most polite person I had ever interviewed. However, although he clearly had a medical problem, something did not add up. The man had recently bought an expensive car and had extensive work carried out on his house and garden. He appeared to have been living above his means. Many large, recently obtained loans were also covered by insurance.

Without actually naming the man, I will try and use false names to explain what happened. Let's say the man's name was "Shevingenaniva". Checks showed that he had operated businesses in the past using an abbreviation of his name, "Sheving". I rang the various medical authorities around

London and found that a man called "Sheving" with the same date of birth as "Shevingenaniva" was registered with a doctor in another area of London. Without a signed authority form, it was not possible to obtain information about that person's medical history.

I was convinced that the claimant had been ill for some time, registered with a different doctor using his abbreviated name, took out insurance cover, and then sought treatment from his new doctor for a liver problem. By moving to a different location, he would be treated at a different hospital so doctors would not recognise him. I visited him again and explained what I had found out and what I believed to be the truth. I handed him an "Access to Medical Records" form made out in his abbreviated name. I added that if I was wrong, then such a signed form would be of no use. He was again extremely polite, made me a cup of tea and asked for time to consider my request. His claim was then withdrawn, so my theory was correct.

- - - - - - -

A lady from Lithuania was working in east London. She took out a policy covering serious illness and within a year claimed for an incapacitating back problem. I interviewed her, and she insisted that she needed a relative to translate as she could not speak English. According to the staff at the bank where she took out the policy, she spoke good English, and no translator was required.

So off to Kaunas in Lithuania. She had produced extensive medical records from the main hospital there. My enquiries showed that they were all genuine, and there was no record of any previous treatment there. I had an address where she had once lived. There was no one at home, but a neighbour knew the lady and told me where she had worked years ago before travelling to London. She had been a tram driver. I went to the officers of the tram company, and they had never heard of the lady. Again, I will change the name but let's call her Lausken. I showed the manager a copy of her passport photo, and he told me she was called Verskin. Lausken had been her maiden name, but she was married and called Verskin. She had been sacked some years ago due to an alcohol problem.

I went to a clinic near her home and found a medical record in her married name. It mentioned that she had a back problem and needed tests. There was no record of any tests. I suspected that she had moved to London and been treated there under the name of Verskin. It was likely that she had then registered with a doctor using her maiden name, taken out the policy and submitted the claim. Her doctor would have no record of any previous treatment.

Again, I completed a medical record's access form in her married name and interviewed her again. She refused to sign the form, and the claim went away! It was obvious that she had been in London for several years, spoke reasonable English, had a severe back problem and then changed to using her maiden name, thereby concealing any record of a previous medical problem.

- - - - - - -

Over the years, I have also been involved in looking at pension claims. Immigrants who arrived to work in the UK in the '60s and '70s have retired and often gone back to their country of origin. Many people who worked for London Transport or the Royal Mail, for example, went back to live in Nigeria, Ghana, India, Pakistan, Jamaica etc. They are in receipt of a pension from their previous employment. I was asked, some years ago, to make enquiries in various countries to ensure that the pensioners were, in fact, still alive. Most of this work was conducted by my overseas associates. Companies paying pensions were suspicious that some retired persons were over 100 years old. My enquiries revealed that about 5% of people still in receipt of a pension had, in fact, died.

I personally made such enquiries in Jamaica as I had to travel there on another enquiry. I think that out of 50 pensioners, 5 were either dead or untraceable, probably because they were deceased. I travelled to some beautiful places in Jamaica. It was a joy to meet some pensioners who had worked hard for years, lived in council flats in poorer parts of London but were now living in beautiful properties along the coast of Jamaica. They all seemed to have inherited the British tradition of taking care of their gardens and offering me a cup of tea (or glass of rum).

- - - - - - -

Over the years, we dealt with several claims involving self-mutilation. The thought of this sends a shiver down my spine. I recall one claim that Andy Young investigated in northern India. A man claimed that his young son swung on a revolving washing line in the backyard. It hit his eye, which was badly damaged, resulting in a specialist removing his eyeball. This was worth £50,000 on his accident policy.

Andy located the clinic and realised that there were several eye clinics in the same street. He went to the first one, recounted the alleged scenario, and the doctor said he remembered it. He had told the man that there was no way he would remove his eye to support an insurance claim. His job was to heal people. Andy went to the next clinic. Guess what, exactly the same response from the doctor. The next clinic, the same again. And then he went to the clinic where the eye was allegedly removed. I remember it well, said the doctor, a tragic case, and I had to remove the poor man's eyeball!!

Chapter 28: Other Countries

As mentioned at the beginning of the book, I have made enquiries in 83 overseas countries. They are not all mentioned here because perhaps the claims investigated in some of them were fairly mundane. There are, however, a few I would like to mention here.

Some years ago, a lady in East Anglia claimed that her husband, Swaley Mohamed, had died in Mauritius. He owned two nursing homes. Until then, I never realised how many persons from Mauritius ran nursing homes in the UK. The man was insured for nearly £700,000, and several of the policies had been taken out years earlier to cover business loans. I interviewed the lady and her young daughter, who had been in Mauritius with her father when he had a sudden heart attack and died.

I was not convinced that they were being truthful, and my enquiries suggested that a successful insurance claim would perhaps prevent financial ruin. I was informed that the local police had an interest in the man.

So off to Mauritius, a long flight, but sometimes I had to take the rough with the smooth! My first enquiry was at the cemetery. There was no record there of Swaley. I went to the registry, and again there was no record. I located the doctor who had signed the death certificate. He worked from a one-room practice and insisted that he had examined Swaley's body when he died from a sudden heart attack. I explained that the procedure in Mauritius did not allow him to issue a death certificate in such circumstances. It took a while, but eventually, the doctor saw the errors of his ways and decided to tell the truth. There was no death.

Mauritius is around 3 hours ahead of London. As soon as I arrived back at my hotel, I rang the police in East Anglia and updated them. It transpired that before I even had a chance of a swim or cold beer, they had arrested Mrs Swaley and her daughter. I did later establish that Mr Swaley had travelled back to London sat next to his daughter, who was in possession of his death certificate. Swaley was soon located in London, and the family members were charged with fraud.

Interestingly after I visited the registry, I was asked to attend a meeting at the Ministry. Officials had never before come across such a fraud there and wanted to take action. I was asked to stay there for several days to assist. One of the best invitations ever but I had to get back to London.

- - - - - - -

In 2017 I went to Kosovo on behalf of an Australian insurer. An Australian resident who originated from Kosovo had died there in a car accident. Various documents were false, and his mother there had tried to register his death at the local registry. When I spoke to her, I was able to prove that the man was already back in Australia.

- - - - - - -

I had a similar claim for a South African company. A man living there who originated from Bosnia had died while back there on holiday. An easy claim to prove as false, and it seems that these people do not think that anyone will visit these countries and make enquiries.

- - - - - - -

Greece featured some years ago when a heavily insured Greek restaurant owner from London died in Athens. His family claimed nearly £1m. This was a case where the man's businesses appeared to be in financial distress. Enquiries in Athens showed that the documents were for another person and had been altered. The Greek symbols had been changed. This would probably have been obvious had the certificate been in English, but you can see below that changes to words using the Greek alphabet would not be so obvious to a person not speaking or reading Greek.

Α α, Β β, Γ γ, Δ δ, Ε ε, Ζ ζ, Η η, Θ θ, Ι ι, Κ κ, Λ λ, Μ μ, Ν ν, Ξ ξ, Ο ο, Π π,

The man was arrested by Greek police. It transpired that he had earlier claimed from a UK insurer for his brother's "death" and the claim had been paid. The brother had moved to Athens and was apparently unaware that he was meant to be dead.

Some years later, the main man featured on a British television programme. It was alleged that years ago he was in Cairo and proposed to an Egyptian lady. He took her money, flew back to Athens, and she was found dead in her flat the following morning. Police there wanted to speak to the man who had since then changed his name and moved to London before 'dying".

- - - - - - -

I investigated a case on behalf of an international insurer that provided accidental insurance cover for various companies. A man from Hungary was working for an oil company operating in Senegal. He was staying in the company's house in Dakar and was allegedly murdered by armed robbers. If true, then the insurer would need to settle the claim. The claimant was his wife in Hungary. In Dakar, I met the public prosecutor who was handling the matter. He had provided a letter for the claimant confirming that her husband had been murdered by intruders. The public prosecutor would only say that he was still actively investigating the matter. He took out the file from his cupboard, and it was covered in thick dust. A very active investigation.

I met company personnel and discovered what had happened. The man had returned to Senegal from Hungary, and along with two other staff, they bought supplies to travel upcountry with. The other two persons left the man at the company's house and agreed to meet him there early the following morning to travel. They arrived the next morning, and the house was locked, and there was no response from the man. He did not answer his phone, so they called the police. An officer borrowed a ladder and managed to enter the property via the upstairs balcony. The man was dead, lying on his bed in his underwear. A plastic bag was tied around his neck, and there were empty vodka bottles on the bed. There was a note on the bed written in Hungarian, and a translation showed it to be a suicide note. Staff explained that all doors were locked inside, nothing was missing, and clearly, the man had committed suicide. It was not an accidental death.

The next day I returned to see the public prosecutor. Again, he insisted that it was a murder case, and he denied the existence of any suicide note. I suggested he was looking for a murderer who was perhaps 2 cm tall, as only such a person could have entered the premises through the small gap under the main door!! The public prosecutor had obviously been bribed!

- - - - - - -

I travelled to Guyana to make enquiries about a man who had accidentally fallen out of a window at a hospital where he was being treated. Correspondence from the hospital supported this claim. It transpired that the man had mental problems. He got out of bed, ran along the ward and threw himself through the window. Not exactly an accident.

- - - - - - -

I have investigated several claims in respect of alleged deaths in Sudan, and two of them were for a man who died twice! The first claim was for a small accidental death policy. I interviewed the man's wife in England, and the claim was not pursued. Three years later, the lady again claimed that he had died in Sudan. This time about £400,000 was at stake. My colleague at the time interviewed the lady, and I knocked on the door after about an hour and spoke to her. She denied having ever met me or having put in a claim previously. In order to prove that I had been to her house previously, I was able to describe the kitchen there, but she remained adamant that I was wrong.

Later her friend rang and said she had been mistaken and now recalled the previous interview. She had told him that she was concerned that her husband might have tricked her. Therefore, she rang her mother in Sudan, who visited the family home and found that her husband was still alive! She added that she was withdrawing her claim as "she did not want the money". I wonder when he will next die!!

- - - - - - -

Chapter 29: Anecdotes And Other Stories

I thought I would conclude by mentioning a host of interesting events not covered elsewhere.

I have visited Malawi several times, a beautiful country that should attract more tourism. I have been there in the cool season when it is perhaps 17C in Lilongwe and drizzling. An hour later, I have been sunbathing and swimming in Lake Malawi, work having been completed, of course. One evening I was returning from Blantyre to Lilongwe, a journey of nearly 4 hours. Our car had a puncture in the middle of nowhere. My driver fitted the spare tyre, but this lasted only a short distance – another puncture. There was no way of getting a repair until the following morning, and we were in the middle of nowhere. I gave the driver some money and said I would try and hitch a lift back to my hotel in Lilongwe. A lorry stopped, and I sat, very uncomfortably behind the driver and his mate on the cargo. When back at my hotel, I waited at reception to get my key and noticed that a multitude of guests walked away from me, muttering various comments. Someone asked why there was such a dreadful smell in reception. I then realised it was me. I had been sat on a load of dry fish, and what a stink!

- - - - - - -

I was dealing with a claim where a man allegedly died in an accident in Pakistan. I asked his brother if a post-mortem had been carried out. He said it had not because his brother was already dead! The claimant later withdrew the claim suggesting that it was too much bother! £600k – no, not worth the effort!

- - - - - - -

I recall flying from Accra to Tamale in the north of Ghana. At Tamale airport, my friend Boat and I were waiting for a car when I noticed a most unusual sign. It showed how to use a condom and was on the outside of the toilet door, facing the waiting area. I wonder if the person responsible put the sign on the wrong side of the door!

From Tamale, we drove north to a small town and made enquiries in a village. You will recall that I mentioned earlier that often when visiting villages, it was necessary to speak to the local chief's "stool-keeper" (secretary) and drink Schnapps etc. This is a photo of me with the chief in his "palace". The Chief told me, via the "stool-keeper", that he was 103 years old, had 40 children and 6 wives. This made sense when it was explained that whenever one of his many brothers had died, then he took on the responsibility of their wives. I refrained from enquiring about what he meant by responsibility. Therefore, some of the children were not actually his. I asked the ages of his own children, and he told me the youngest was 6 months old, plus he had a son of 3. Without wishing to appear rude, I did ascertain that what I heard the first time was correct. My good friend Boat found it difficult to keep a straight face. I tried in vain to find out how he managed to conceive so late in life, hoping that I would come across something that could rival Viagra on the market, but I failed.

We had a problem finding accommodation locally but slept in a room belonging to a small company whose workers were away. I found the shower most unusual.

- - - - - - -

This is a scene from an African mortuary. The facility did not work, and the pathologist informed me that this was the best method for storing a corpse before carrying out an autopsy upside down in a barrel of water. I suspected that the pathologist liked a drink, and the cause of death on many medical certificates was probably shown as "death by drowning".

- - - - - - -

In Accra, I often use to stay at a hotel near the airport. It was comfortable, and the rooms were all on the ground floor, surrounded by lush vegetation and a large pool. Later they built a large shopping mall nearby, and it was possible to buy decent food and drink there. Unfortunately, the hotel closed and was sold for redevelopment. Maybe not so unfortunate as it did deteriorate. One Sunday evening, Boat dropped me off close by as the road was flooded after a torrential storm. Luckily, I was wearing shorts and Croks, so I was able to wade through the water. Upon reaching the hotel, I realised that floodwater had poured through the place. It seems that when they had recently built the main by-pass adjacent to the hotel, they made an error with the drainage. It could not take such excessive rain, so everything went back along the main drainage pipe toward the hotel. Floodwater poured over the wall into the pool and ground of the hotel. Rooms at a lower level nearer the pool were under 3 feet of water. Guess where my room was? I walked through the water but could not open the door of my room due to the pressure of water inside. Eventually, I opened the door a couple of inches, and it stayed that way as the curtain jammed in the door. Water gradually rescinded, and I entered when it was only 2 feet deep. What a mess! Luckily my suitcase was floating near to the bed, which was also afloat. I was given a room nearer the main building that was not affected, but it took about an hour to transfer my property. Thank goodness that my laptop and electrical equipment were in my suitcase, plus my passport and money were in a locked safe at a high level in the room. My shoes were floating, and I only had Croks to wear. I rang Boat and asked him if he could arrange to bring me a pair of shoes the following morning as we had several meetings. He brought me a pair of winklepicker type shoes made of alligator skin. Not good for my image, though!

My bathroom

Drying my shoes etc. the next day

- - - - - - -

One Monday morning, on one of my first visits to Nigeria, I visited the mortuary in Lagos Island, a mistake I only made once. I was with my associate, Erasmus and asked for the pathologist. A man gave me instructions on how to find his office, or so I thought. We went through a door into a rather dark, smelly room and in the distance, I could see a ray of light from the exit door. Suddenly I walked into an object and then Erasmus fell over. Corpses were stacked 2 deep on the floor! Erasmus fainted, so I placed him across my shoulder and headed for the exit. When I arrived outside, a man shouted, "Stop, thief!" He was serious. Stealing dead bodies for voodoo is a regular occurrence in West Africa. Luckily Erasmus came to and was able to explain why I was carrying him. To think that toward the end of the Biafran war, Erasmus cycled halfway across Nigeria to return to Lagos. I learnt that the mortuary there was full on a Monday morning after numerous bodies were removed from the local streets.

- - - - - - -

I once visited Maputo as the war had just ended, and it was not very safe. I seem to recall there was only one safe hotel to stay in. That hotel is now, I believe, the Polana Serena on a boulevard close to the sea. A beautiful hotel, but after a couple of nights there, I wanted to get out and visit a local Portuguese restaurant. I was fed up paying exorbitant prices for a beer and food in a rather unfriendly environment. The hotel manager assured me that this boulevard was the only safe place to walk in Maputo. It was lined with exotic shrubs, many embassies, and there were several restaurants at the end. A few metres along the road, I was aware of a man closing toward my rear. I looked around and, on seeing a young man dressed immaculately in designer clothes, thought I was ok. Suddenly he grabbed my arms, pushed me headfirst into a fence and demanded money. I always told myself that if such a situation arose in Africa, then do not fight back as Aids was prevalent at the time. However, being mugged by a man in designer clothes and speaking good English - - - - - - I decided not to give in and fought back. Three elderly people walked up to us and asked what was happening. The man let go of me and told them that I was mugging him. They spoke English, and I suggested that it was unlikely I had travelled all the way from London in order to mug local people. As they left, he again tried to attack me, but I struck him back and ran to the hotel. I then took a taxi to a restaurant recommended by the hotel manager. The following day I informed the manager that I was undecided about what was the worse advice he had given me. Walking along that street and getting mugged or going to the restaurant he recommended and being up all night with food poisoning!

- - - - - - -

I have previously referred to the traumas involved in arriving at Lagos Airport. In the past few years, it has improved significantly, but once you get through Customs, there are still numerous individuals attempting to find someone to fall for their latest con. There was a time when a robber would engage in conversation with a person holding a sign awaiting the arrival of a passenger. In conversation, the robber would try and ascertain as much information as possible about the person being met. The person would then be tricked into moving away from the waiting crowd and imprisoned in a vehicle. The robber would take on his identity, meet that person, who would then be driven to a rural area and held captive. His family overseas would then be asked to pay a large ransom. However, they seemed to pick on the wrong person, as rarely did the person's family have substantial funds.

For a while, one particular scam was carried out by health officials at the airport. They examined your health card and indicated that you had not been injected for yellow fever. I am not sure if anyone from the UK has introduced yellow fever to Nigeria. The health official would ask you to accompany him to his office. There, on the desk, was a filthy medical container containing a syringe. He would inform you that it will cost $25 to have the injection. "How much not to have it?" was the obvious response. "That will be $50, sir". I heard about this scam, and on my next visit, sure enough, I was asked to accompany the health official to his office, even though I had the required certificate. I spoke loudly on my mobile to the secretary of the British High Commissioner in Lagos. Yes, he was on his way to meet me and should be at the airport. I ensured that the health official heard this conversation. I spoke in very loud, "posh" English and then asked him if I could go and inform the High Commissioner that I was being delayed at the health office. The official decided I did not require an injection and wished me a good day. I then turned on my mobile! This ploy has worked on several occasions in Nigeria.

- - - - - - -

While writing this section, numerous events that occurred in Nigeria keep coming back to me. In Benin City, a police officer jumped in front of our car and then accused the driver of running over his foot. The driver, my associate and me were then arrested and taken to the police station. There I made a complaint to the senior officer about being harassed by a very drunk police officer. The drunk officer experienced a problem stating his case. He became incoherent and then fell over. Not guilty was the verdict!

- - - - - - -

My friend in Lagos, John, supplied me with a car and driver belonging to his company when he was working for an insurance company there. I paid the going rate for hire but had a safe vehicle and driver. Regularly I would work long hours, and at the end of my visit, the driver would be well rewarded by me. Soon after John left Nigeria, the company there had a problem with cars, so I arranged a hire car and driver through a large company. Every time I hired a car from them, I had a different driver. It was often the norm that the driver would ask for cash in order to fill up with fuel each evening. I expected them to give me a receipt and often suspected that the true amount paid was lower. At the beginning of my enquiries there, I would explain to the driver that if he was honest with me, he would be well rewarded. However, - - - -.

On one occasion, I was being driven to the airport to leave Lagos. In the front of the car, I noticed a large number of medical receipts. Just before we arrived at the airport, minutes prior to "tipping time", the driver explained in detail how his wife had been ill in hospital for 2 weeks, he could not afford the bills (the equivalent of about £90), so he had to take her home, and she was expected to die. Very sad, you would think. I did ascertain from him that he only had one wife. I reminded him that 5 days earlier, when he realised that we were travelling north for 3 nights, we stopped at his home so that he could pack some clothes. While he was in the house, I met his wife, and she appeared to be in very good health. Also, I was aware that his employer arranged for free health care for him and his family. I did still give him a tip.

Later with another driver and the end result was completely different. At the time of my visit, there were fuel shortages, and it meant having to queue to buy fuel. The evening before leaving Lagos to travel north, I gave the driver money to fill the tank. I informed him that he would be well rewarded if he was efficient and, above all, honest with me. He told me that because of regular fuel shortages, his company had fitted an extra fuel tank on the vehicle. My suspicious nature immediately kicked into overdrive. Especially when the next day he told me the amount he had paid plus he had left the receipt and change at his home.

We were away from Lagos for 5 nights. The hire company gave drivers a cash allowance for overnight accommodation and food that was subsequently added to my bill. It was very meagre, and every evening I gave the driver additional cash. I also gave him cash to refill the vehicle. The man was really insulting my intelligence when each day he provided me with a receipt for the total amount of cash I had given him. It appeared that our car was as economical as a Jumbo jet! No problem because I was keeping a tally of the real expenditure, and he would suffer when it came to "tipping time".

The last evening away, I went to check into a hotel in Ibadan with my associate. The hotel required cash upfront, as per the norm. I suddenly realised that around the equivalent of £60 in Naira was missing from my briefcase. It then dawned on me that when we stopped earlier at the house of Ed's sister (Ed was my associate), I sat in the back seat counting my money. I wanted to ensure that I had sufficient Naira for the hotel and did not need to change money prior to arriving there. The money was in my briefcase, which was on the floor of the car and left unattended for less than a minute when I spoke to Ed's sister. Only the driver could have taken the money.

My associate, Ed, and I immediately went to the car and accused the driver of theft. We asked him to empty his pockets. He started to do so and then ran behind the car. Ed saw him lift up his shirt and put something up his backside. I refrained from removing it.

The next day when we returned to the hire car company in Lagos, I went and saw the director. Subsequently, the driver was called into the office. The car did not have an extra tank, and a calculation indicated that the driver was obtaining false fuel receipts. He had stolen around £40 allegedly when buying fuel, a figure I had already calculated. It had been my intention to give him a tip. It would have been words to the effect, "stop stealing". I was very annoyed upon being told by the company that 2 weeks earlier the driver had driven 3 Japanese businessmen and they had accused him of stealing money. I did receive a discount on the hire charge. The driver was immediately sacked. Had he been honest, he would have been far better off financially after my visit

- - - - - - -

I once had to travel to Monrovia in Liberia, West Africa. This was just after the war there, and it was only possible to fly there via Freetown in Sierra Leone. I arrived early evening in Freetown and checked into a place impersonating a hotel near the airport. There I paid for a ticket to Monrovia. I already had a ticket to fly a few days later from Monrovia to Abidjan (Ivory Coast) and on to Ghana.

The following morning, I boarded the aircraft for Monrovia. It was a very old Russian jalopy flown by a Russian crew. It had 20 seats, and one steward stood at the back of the aircraft on take-off and landing. Upon arriving in Monrovia, I was seized upon by Customs and Immigration officials. I realised that I was easy prey as every other passenger seemed to have a United Nations or other official badge. I had to change money in order to pay a tax. A small amount, but I never realised that there was an import tax to walk through the gate. Tongue in cheek, I asked for a receipt and was told to return the next day.

My departure flight was 3 pm on Friday. I checked in at the airport, but there was nowhere to sit in the tiny space referred to as a lounge. I managed to find an area in the shade outside and had to stand. It was rumoured that the football team from the Ivory Coast, they were due to play Liberia that weekend, was due to arrive on the Air Ivoire plane for which I was waiting. A large crowd gathered, awaiting their arrival. Regularly we were told that the aircraft would land any minute. This continued until about 5 pm, when we were told that the flight was cancelled. Passengers transiting Abidjan would be put on a small aircraft (that Russian one again) and flown there. As for other passengers, just go home; we don't really care! When I told the airline rep that I was transiting to Accra, he said it didn't count as they only meant passengers transiting Abidjan for Europe. $30 later, he agreed that Accra could now be in Europe, and he put my suitcase on board. I later established that the flight we were due to take could never be classified as "arriving any minute" as it had broken down somewhere in the northern Ivory Coast earlier that day.

My flight to Accra was on Air Ivoire and due to leave Abidjan at about 7 pm. I arrived there after 7 pm, went to the transit lounge and was informed that the flight was delayed. There were around 12 passengers waiting in the transit lounge for that flight. At around 10 pm, a young lady announced that the flight was cancelled, and she went to leave the lounge. I rushed to the door to prevent her exit and asked what we should do, plus when could we fly. I pointed out that none of us probably had visas to enter the country and could not stay overnight in this tiny, ill-equipped lounge with no facilities. She made multiple calls and eventually she confirmed that accommodation was being arranged in a city hotel. It was quite a smart hotel, and I seem to recall that it was perhaps one of the French-owned establishments. We were taken there by an airline coach and told to be ready at 7 am the following morning. We all walked out of the airport with no official checks as everyone had gone home.

We arrived at the hotel after midnight and, after breakfast, the following morning, waited for the return transport, but nothing arrived. The hotel staff said that, as the airline owed them so much money, we would all have to pay for our rooms and breakfast. It was not cheap. I devised a plan and took the other passengers into my confidence. We placed our luggage near the exit. Several people went outside and arranged 4 taxis to take us to the airport. When I saw them arrive, I would set off the fire alarm, and we would all run out of the hotel, collecting our luggage on the route. It worked a treat, and we all arrived at the airport not knowing when or if our flight would leave. We all had a problem with immigration as we had no arrival stamps or visas, but we were allowed to proceed. Eventually, we arrived in Accra at lunchtime. I was so delighted to meet my good friend Boat and have a beer!

- - - - - - -

Over the years, travel facilities around Africa have all improved significantly. The worst experience was Lagos domestic airport; sorry, Nigeria, but nowhere in the world have I found anywhere to match that domestic shambles. When I last flew from there, it had at last improved significantly. I recall the first time I travelled upcountry from there. I always travelled by car as even Nigerian roads were safer; that shows how bad aviation was there. Ed and I were going to Enugu and decided to fly there. The flight was delayed, and then we were told to board. We did so only to be told the flight was now going to Kaduna, not Enugu. We left the aircraft, stood on the tarmac, and it was decided that the plane was going to Kaduna and Enugu. Previously when boarding, I was harassed by a man wearing a Nigerian Airforce uniform. He demanded money. Before boarding the second time, he became very angry because I refused to pay him. As I was walking up the rear steps of the aircraft, he grabbed my leg. I kicked out, and he went flying! When we returned to Lagos before getting off the plane, I saw the same man waiting by the steps. He appeared to have a very swollen eye. I put on my sunglasses, borrowed Ed's hat, walked as if I was an old man and luckily escaped his clutches.

- - - - - - -

A story about my early travels to Ghana when there were few decent hotels available. I stayed at a large, government-owned establishment in central Accra. I cannot recall the name, but it was later rebuilt and became the Novotel. Meal facilities were inadequate as a large crane had crashed through the roof, destroying the kitchen. I had finished work and had a few hours to spare before flying home. The brochure in the room had a photo of a large swimming pool surrounded by lush vegetation. It was a beautiful day, so the thought of a swim and sitting in the sun appealed to me. The man at reception gave me directions to the pool; it was a fair distance away. When I located it, I saw a large hole containing a few inches of green slime, frogs and weeds. I could not remain there, so I returned to reception and asked the receptionist why he had not told me about the state of the pool. His response was, "with respect, sir never told me he wanted to swim". I couldn't argue with that.

- - - - - - -

I visited Zimbabwe several times and sadly watched the place deteriorate under Mugabe's despotic rule. Food shortages worsened every time I went there, and fuel became scarce. But Mugabe's wife still shopped for numerous luxury goods in Singapore and built a "palace" using funds meant for the poor. Mugabe's family and henchmen used huge farms as weekend retreats, and the land produced nothing. The Zimbabwean dollar became worthless: they kept just adding a few noughts on the end. I went into supermarkets where every shelf was totally empty. I suspected they were only open so that people could see that food was not being stockpiled. A good friend of mine took me to a decent restaurant. You could not pay by cheque because by the time it reached the restaurant's account, it was almost worthless. People used a barter system. My friend would have a meal and repay the restaurant owner by providing services available from his own business.

Having 20 billion dollars in my wallet somehow never enthused me. I did not feel rich as it was probably worth around 4 cents, then 2 cents a day later! The photo below was perhaps the last time you could pay in cash for a meal!

Open but nothing to sell!

And please keep the change waiter

- - - - - - -

Once when in Ghana, friends of Boat had tickets for a soccer international; Ghana was playing Niger. At the end of the game, there was an almighty scramble to leave the stadium. A Police band had played before the game and at halftime, and they decided to leave the stadium in their coach moments before the final whistle. Unfortunately, the coach took the wrong exit. It was somewhat wider than the exit and the gates and posts came tumbling down.

Chapter 30: Genuine Claims

One might form the impression from my book that my job has always been to void all claims. Wrong. My task has always been to ascertain the truth. It is down then to the insurer to make the final decision. I have had a couple of cases when I have disagreed with the insurer's decision and have told them as such. I mentioned in a previous chapter about a death certificate from Iraq. It had to be a false document, yet I was certain the man was really dead but, as his body had never been found, his poor wife in the UK could not claim so obtained a certificate. I argued that irrespective of this, the claim was genuine.

Some years ago, a new claim's manager took over at a certain company. He asked to see me to discuss a problem claim. The company specialised in providing accidental death policies and had an agreement with various local authorities in England that provided this cover free to employees. A lady of Nigerian origin had claimed that her husband died in a car accident in Lagos, and she provided various documents, albeit sometime after the death. The company had paid someone to investigate the claim, and he had what was described as evidence that it was fraudulent. The company refused to pay, and the lady had issued court proceedings. The claim's manager asked if I could again investigate the claim as the court case was only 4 weeks away, and he was not satisfied with the evidence. On reading the file, I shared his view.

This company had regularly used me in the past. For some reason, the claims team was told by a director to use another investigator. I will call him Tom. It appears he had approached the company through a contact, and the director wanted to try this new man. You will recall that I mentioned Tom in chapter 15. He was the man who claimed he had evidence that a person had not died in Sri Lanka in the tsunami. His "evidence" was complete nonsense and all hearsay. We had to reinvestigate that claim. It was false, and we obtained what would be described legally as evidence.

I could not believe the rubbish he had reported once more, this time with the Nigerian claim. If you want to prove if a claim is false, then travel to Nigeria. A dangerous place best avoided was, no doubt, his opinion. He asked an investigator in Lagos to make enquiries on his behalf. This man reported that there was no record at the hospital or mortuary (to be fair certain mortuary records were missing). They had never heard of the doctor there, plus the police had no record of such an accident, and the two police officers named in the report did not exist. None of this so-called evidence appeared in the form of a written statement. I knew the investigator he used in Lagos, and, having met this person, I would never rely upon the veracity and accuracy of his reports. In my view, he was an "armchair investigator" who made most enquiries on the phone.

The dead man did appear to have 2 names and had travelled regularly around west Africa. One place he had visited was the Gambia. Many UK nationals go there on holiday and sit on the beautiful beaches. The man had been to several other West African countries, but for some strange reason, Tom decided to go to the Gambia. He spent several days with immigration trying to prove that the dead man had flown there after his death. Rubbish! Had a person of the same name travelled to the Gambia, there would be no proof that it was the deceased. It would only mean that someone travelled using that passport. The main investigation should have been in London and Nigeria, but perhaps their beaches were not so enticing!

I travelled to Lagos and again investigated the claim. It was true that the main mortuary register was missing from that time, but the doctor who allegedly certified the death had existed. There was another register in the mortuary. This was for property taken from deceased persons. The dead man's name appeared on the correct date. His body had been taken to the mortuary along with a lady killed in the same accident. Two officers accompanied them to the mortuary: the "non-existent" officers shown on the police report.

At the police station, they could not locate the accident book for that date. Again, however, they kept a record of the property, and our deceased's name appeared. There was also a record of his brother collecting his effects. The police officers did exist and had been transferred to other stations nearby. I spoke to them, and they both recalled the crash.

I went to the Lagos home of the "deceased", and on the gate was a large poster relating to his funeral. All the neighbours were aware of his death. Next, I interviewed his brother, who had sent further evidence to the wife in London in support of her claim. I did not need to go to the Gambia but did fancy a few days sunbathing.

I reported the matter to the insurer, and the claim was paid immediately. From the brother in Lagos, I learnt about the occupations of the sons and daughters of the deceased. They were professional people in London who would no doubt have been believed in a court, particularly after showing the video of their late father's funeral.

- - - - - - -

There was one other significant case, also involving Nigeria. A man who originated from Nigeria took out an accident policy for £200,000. Within one month, his wife in London claimed that he died in a road accident in Nigeria. Number one on the Richter scale of suspect claims. But - - -

An experienced, retired police officer had just joined me, and we went together to interview the wife in London. Whenever I asked for a certain Nigerian document in respect of the claim, she left the room to sort through papers and mostly found the correct document. In my experience, whenever a person submits a false claim, they hand you all of the false documents to start with. My colleague and I were both convinced that this was a genuine claim. The lady had a young baby and could not travel to the funeral as she was then expecting. She had recently travelled to Nigeria for a week with the baby for the funeral that had been delayed. The lady and her husband were members of a local church. I went there and met the English pastor. He told me that he and all the parishioners were aware of the death, and one lady accompanied the wife to the funeral to assist her with her baby.

I informed the insurer that the claim was genuine. I was informed that they did not believe this, so they wanted enquiries made in Nigeria. I had other travel plans, plus there were problems at the time travelling to Nigeria due to strikes and unrest. I told the insurer that I would get my man in Lagos to make enquiries as I was certain that it was genuine and it would save money if I did not travel.

Ed's (my associate in Lagos) report confirmed it was genuine. There were certain discrepancies, mainly due to the body not going to the main hospital because of industrial unrest at the time. The insured was driving a vehicle that overturned. He was killed outright while his passenger, a pastor, only received a minor injury. Again, I told the insurer it was genuine. I also pointed out that the insurer employed agents who often sold such policies to earn a considerable commission, and I suggested that the policy might have been mis-sold.

Some months later, the insurer sent me a lengthy report that contained numerous pages of irrelevant photos. Their head office in the USA had arranged for a company there to investigate the claim using their agent in Lagos (my old friend). The report suggested the claim was false, and they wanted my opinion. I said the report was absolute rubbish, and it was obvious that the agent wanted to continue the investigation and earn more fees. Most of the points made were totally irrelevant. The agent appeared to have walked along the street near the deceased's house in Nigeria. He asked numerous people if they knew that the man was dead. Many said he was dead, and they were ignored. Numerous people said they were unaware of his death, so they were asked to put this in writing. Selective evidence! This was almost a fraud in itself. Again, I told the insurer they were wasting their money, and the claim was genuine.

A few months later, they sent me another lengthy report from the same agency. Total rubbish, full of innuendos and no evidence whatsoever to suggest the man was not dead. Their main point seemed to be that his name still appeared on the electricity bill at the house in Nigeria. I refused to comment further other than state it was a genuine claim. The company ceased trading in the UK and their client base, plus this claim was taken over by another company.

Some months later, on behalf of that company, I arranged to go back to the church in London where I met some people who had attended the funeral in Nigeria. Everyone knew about the death. The claim was paid, and I had sympathy for the aggravation caused to the poor widow.

Due to the insurance industry having received so many false claims relating to Nigeria, they tend to suspect every claim from there. I think it only fair to point out that I have seen a large number of claims relating to Nigeria that were very genuine.

Chapter 31: My Thanks Plus My Most Memorable Meeting

I would like to thank my wife and two daughters for putting up with my many absences abroad. Also, for the long hours sometimes away from home in order to finalise enquiries. At least when my daughters were young, I did often bring back small presents for them. Perhaps I overdid the small, wooden elephants, though! Plus, the Hardrock Café t-shirts from places that did not have a Hard Rock Café!

A special thanks to Pat and Andy Young for making the decision years ago to employ me and present me with a tremendous opportunity to travel, plus many challenges that I enjoyed. Unfortunately, Andy is no longer with us.

I have already mentioned Boat in Ghana and Edward in Nigeria. There are too many people who have assisted me in many countries to name here. Plus, if I did so, then there is a chance that I might miss someone out from the past.

In England, Peter and Mike worked with me at various times, and I would like to thank them for their endeavours. Barbara was probably the most efficient secretary one could hope for.

Over the years, I have dealt with some exceptional people in insurance companies involved with claims. Many have now retired, but I trust that you have left a lasting legacy behind.

People often ask me if there is one event that is paramount in my recollection. I think it was around February 1997. After the end of apartheid in South Africa, the African continent opened up to South African products. One could enjoy a South African beer or bottle of wine in most African countries. South African Airways (SAA) were flying to West Africa. After an enquiry in Ghana, I flew to Johannesburg on the airline. It stopped in Luanda in Angola. I was in business class with just one other person. She was an extremely intelligent, smart African lady. The steward explained to us that Angola was trying to support its national airline by delaying all SAA flights there. This lady and I stood for ages looking over the tarmac awaiting the arrival of passengers. She had been to an international conference in Ghana.

When we arrived in Johannesburg, we were the first two people to leave the aircraft and walked along the gangway in conversation. We rounded the corner, and a hand came out welcoming me to South Africa. It was Nelson Mandela. He was meeting the lady I was talking to, and I then realised she was Graca Machel, who later became his wife. She has been honoured by many international organisations for her charity work. She was honoured with the Dame Commander of the Order of the British Empire by Queen Elizabeth II for her work involving human rights. What an amazing lady! At the time, I was reading Nelson Mandela's wonderful book, Long Walk to Freedom, and it was in my briefcase. I hesitated for a moment - - no, I could not really ask him to sign it. This was an experience that I could never forget.

I took a taxi to my hotel and told the driver who I had just met. His words were, "I think the white man was drinking too much on the flight".

- - - - - - -

In November 2018, I sold my business to the Brownsword Group in Manchester. Although I have semi-retired, I still act as a consultant for them and see all life and health claims.

No more visas needed! I have retired, well nearly!

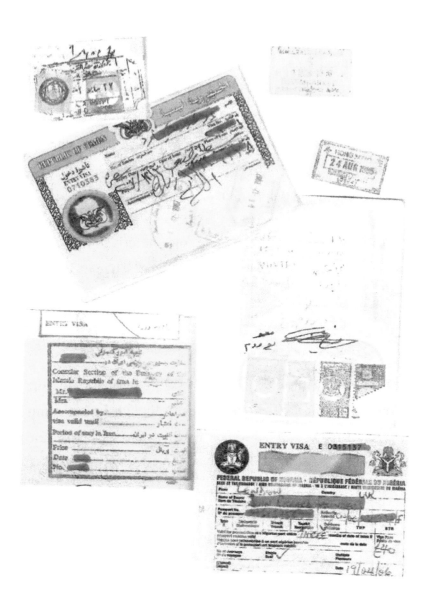